# The Daily ℭ

# SECOND BOOK OF OBITUARIES

HUGH MASSINGBERD edited Burke's Peerage publications for 12 years (initiating a wide range of new titles such as the *Guide to Country Houses*, *Royal Families of the World*, *Presidential Families of the USA* and *Irish Family Records*) and has written more than a dozen books, including *Great British Families*, *Great Houses of England and Wales*, *Royal Palaces of Europe*, *Blenheim Revisited*, *Family Seats of the British Isles*, *The London Ritz* and *The Monarchy*.

He joined the staff of *The Daily Telegraph* in 1986 as obituaries editor, a post he held until retiring from the chair in 1994, after being on the point of appearing in the column himself.

*Also in this series*

# The Daily Telegraph

## BOOK OF OBITUARIES

*A Celebration of Eccentric Lives*

# The Daily Telegraph
# SECOND BOOK OF
# OBITUARIES

*Heroes and Adventurers*

*Edited by*
# HUGH MASSINGBERD

PAN BOOKS

*For the Three Musketeers –*
*Philip, Ted and John*

First published 1996 by Macmillan Publishers Limited

This edition published 1997 by Pan Books
an imprint of Macmillan Publishers Ltd
25 Eccleston Place, London SW1W 9NF
and Basingstoke

Associated companies throughout the world

ISBN 0 330 35298 9

A CIP catalogue record for this book is available from
the British Library

Typeset by CentraCet Limited, Cambridge
Printed and bound in Great Britain by
Mackays of Chatham plc, Chatham, Kent

# INTRODUCTION

AFTER the first volume in this series of biographical short stories, *The Daily Telegraph Book of Obituaries: A Celebration of Eccentric Lives*, appeared in 1995, several kindly readers buttonholed me concerning the entry for the late Lt-Col Hugh Rose. They recalled his service with the Gurkhas on the North-West Frontier and in Tibet, Persia, Aden, Egypt, Malaya and Borneo; how he was the first European to climb the Kuh-i-Taftan, an active volcano in Baluchistan; his rescue of an English peer's son from the Hadramaut and his sharing the cockpit of his aircraft with a wild Arabian oryx destined for London Zoo; his appointment to be Chevalier of the Ethiopian Order of Menelik II. Back home, Rose floated a property company in South Kensington, published a book of poems and skied into his ninth decade. The consensus seemed to be that "They really don't make 'em like Colonel Rose any more".

Back in the late 1960s, when I first began dreaming of a John Aubrey *Brief Lives*-style approach to obituaries, such splendid all-rounders certainly appeared to belong in the world of forgotten fable. Along with the rest of the West End audience I sniggered unrestrainedly at the Buchanesque sketch in Alan Bennett's witty and nostalgic *tour de force*, *Forty Years On* (1968) about "The Breed":

Whatsoever things are true, whatsoever things are pure, whatsoever is best in England I take to be the Breed. That exclusive club, whose members are the very pith and sinew of this island. You may run across them in the Long Room at Lord's, or dining alone at White's. Once met you will always know them, for their hand is firm and their eye is clear and on those rare occasions when they speak it is well to listen for they choose their words dangerously well. They hold themselves on trust for God and for the Nation and they will never fail her for the Breed never dies . . .

The underlying assumption, of course, was that "The Breed" had now not only died but was utterly extinct. Yet, even as I cackled away in the stalls of the Apollo Theatre, I found myself musing on whether the mould had indeed been broken. After all, there were still plenty of men and women around of an older generation who had done extraordinary things in the two World Wars and in the service of the Empire. Their youthful lives were almost beyond the imagination of those of us born into an era of peace. We who have never known war tend to regard half-century, or more, old deeds of courage in wondering disbelief, and ask ourselves whether we could ever have been capable of the feats of our parents and grandparents.

In any event, when I eventually became Obituaries Editor of *The Daily Telegraph* some 40 years on from the end of the Second World War I was determined that any departing member of "The Breed" should be given a decent send-off laced with affection, respect, humour – and only the faintest hint, in true *Telegraph* style, of self-parody. To my intense pleasure I discovered that there was absolutely no shortage of material. On they rolled, a veritable pantheon of paladins, knights errant, exotic adventurers; heroes of the Western Front, the Battles of

Britain and the Atlantic; bristling Brigadiers and bastions of the Raj who had fought on the North-West Frontier; burnt-up "Guinea Pigs" whose spirit had not been extinguished; salty sea dogs, wizard prangers and undercover agents for Special Operations Executive in occupied Europe. Their tales of dash and derring-do cried out for the rattling good yarn treatment of the *Boys' Own Paper*.

Fortunately I was able to recruit the ideal team which could bring a sympathetic zest to the narrative accounts. My first deputy editor, David Twiston Davies, had an infectious passion for defending the reputation of the British Empire (exemplified in his stirring collection of Canadian obits, *Canadians From Afar*). For our stalwart Service specialists we were blessed with the outstanding talents of three acclaimed authors in their fields, Philip Warner (Army), John Winton (Navy) and Edward Bishop (RAF) – the "Three Musketeers" and dedicatees of this book. In addition, Ted Bishop took a particular interest in the SOE obits, an area in which Simon Courtauld, a keen student of the Great Game, also made a significant contribution. Margot Lawrence gave us the benefit of her singular knowledge on women medical workers, and such luminaries as Patrick Leigh Fermor, Julian Amery, Tim Heald, Nicholas Bagnall, David Bowman, Gillian Bence-Jones and Xan Smiley added piquant flavour to the pot.

Day after day the Three Musketeers would deliver, invariably on time and in immaculate order, crisp and cracking adventure stories redolent with atmosphere, and phrased with an exquisite precision in military lore and vocabulary. It was indeed a privilege to sit at the desk and to be responsible for publishing such thrilling "copy". Although we may have joked about "The Moustaches" (a sobriquet for the never-ending military candidates in the queue for the column, based on Lady Rumpers's observation in Alan Bennett's farce *Habeas Corpus* that her husband "Tiger" only went into the Army "in order to put his moustache to good purpose"), it was an affectionate mockery, born of a bemused respect. I was struck by how a generation considerably younger than my own within the obits department shared a sense of awe in being connected with this treasure-house of military history. Our admiration for the Three Musketeers knew no bounds. All of us on the desk knew that "The Moustaches" were the pride and joy of the column.

To encourage *esprit de corps* we organised various "obits outings" to battlefields and war cemeteries. As *Private Eye* reported, not entirely inaccurately, of one such jaunt:

The idea was that Montgomery-Massivesnob [*sic*] and his troops would take the ferry to Boulogne, where Sir Gawain Stamp [*sic*] would show them round a war cemetery, to put them in the mood for writing more obituaries. Alas! The ferry was stuck in Folkestone harbour for several hours, during which time the assembled ex-Colonels and hacks made an in-depth study of the vodka supply in the boat's *Orient Express* lounge. By the time they finally reached Boulogne all enthusiasm for visiting Sir Gawain's beloved war graves had disappeared. Instead the party took themselves off to the Restaurant de L'Haute Ville for a five-course lunch (*avec vin*), which continued until they were due back at the ferry.

Happy days!

Here I must pay tribute to my dear colleagues on the desk during my eight-year stint – the brilliant David (Lewis) Jones, who took over from David Twiston Davies as deputy editor in 1987 and eventually succeeded me in 1994 after I had to give up the chair due to ill health; my three consecutive assistant editors, Claudia Fitz-Herbert, Aurea Carpenter and Kate Summerscale (who, in turn, succeeded David Jones as obits editor for a much underrated and all-too-brief reign); as well as Robert Gray, Will Cohu, Diana Heffer, Martine Onoh and, of course, my revered editorial assistant, Teresa Moore, who has rendered most valuable practical help in putting this collection together. I am grateful to the present incumbent of the obits chair at the *Telegraph*, Christopher Howse, for generously giving permission for such extra-mural activity and for allowing me to continue to snuffle about in his archives. It is good to know that he too appreciates the importance of the military obits. Thanks, also, to Cynthia Lewis and Sam Clement.

During my time on the desk it was very encouraging to have the protection and support of the then Editor, Max Hastings, himself a distinguished military historian – especially as some of the would-be "politically correct" apparatchiks on the paper (no names, no pack drill) appeared to find the profusion of Moustaches in the column embarrassing and supposedly "unhelpful" for marketing. Occasionally I would be taken to one side and solemnly asked whether we had to have "*quite* so many old colonels" – as if I had some control over the death rate among World War veterans or could somehow arrange for a more appropriate supply of fresh young corpses (such as, say, bright businesswomen cut off in their prime) to fill the column. I was even urged to tone down the use of nicknames) – there seemed to be a suspicion that I was making up these robust sobriquets, though they were, naturally, part and parcel of the characters concerned. It was particularly dispiriting to be accosted by alleged obit-fanciers observing: "Of course I love all your Wodehousian Barts and dotty Dowagers but don't you think all those Air Marshals and Rear-Admirals are really rather a *bore?*"

If only people would cast prejudice about military rank aside they might realise what they are missing – and even conclude, as *The Economist*'s Christmas 1994 analysis of "The Obituarist's Art" put it: "All regular readers of obituaries will have their favourites but for a large number the art must seem to reach its zenith in the *Telegraph*'s obituaries of long-lived military figures." But enough of this special pleading: the life stories that follow, evoking a vanishing breed of Englishmen, can surely speak for themselves.

I merely wish to record how enjoyable it has been to sift through the Moustaches again for the purpose of this book, even allowing for the thankless task of whittling them down to a mere 100 examples from the thousands published between 1986 and 1994. The result does not pretend to be remotely representative or comprehensive, but is no more than a highly personal and subjective selection of some of the brief lives that I have most relished re-reading for the umpteenth time.

There is plenty of gallantry and heroism to astound one but the book is not simply a catalogue of citations for medals and decorations. Nor is the selection based on seniority ("other ranks" feature as well as the half-colonels) and fame – on the whole I have left out obvious celebrities and concentrated on unsung characters whose vital achievements deserve to be better known. Group Captain Fred Winterbotham of the Ultra decoding system and Colonel Maurice Buckmaster of SOE are cases in point, as well as such figures as the possible models for James Bond (Commander "Biffy" Dunderdale) and "Q" (Charles Fraser-Smith).

It would be quite wrong if the sub-title of the book, *Heroes and Adventurers*, gave the impression that there are not "Heroines and Adventuresses" within its pages. In fact, nearly a fifth of the entries are for women – whether indomitable agents of the Resistance, doughty aviatrices, inspirational survivors of "Tenko" treatment by the Japanese or suffragettes.

Above all, though, it is the rich vein of human eccentricity, of wit and grace under pressure and of glorious absurdity that make these larger-than-life character studies so irresistible – to me, at any rate. Among my favourite anecdotes in the pages that follow (I will leave you to find them) are the accounts of the Siege of Spin Baldak, the last occasion when a British Army unit used scaling ladders, when it was observed that the enemy should have been chloroformed before the operation took place; and of the subaltern in Srinigar who was bitten in the buttocks by a bear – he survived but the bear expired. The sporting exploits range from riding an ostrich to organising a foxhunt at the Front. We hear of the well-dined major-general trying to light his cigar with a geranium – and succeeding after a tactful ADC had inserted a lighter from the other side. Monocles become wedged in eye-sockets or are ejected upwards, and caught again, to keep sleepy or restive audiences alert. Toasts and mottoes embrace *"Floreat Boris Excreta"* and "Balls to the Commissar". A German prisoner-of-war camp commandant exclaims to escapers: "You think I know nothing. You are wrong. I know *damn all*!"

The Abominable Snowman, naked, head-hunting Nagas, white bullocks painted green, odorous lion cubs doused in *eau de cologne*, leopard-skin flying helmets and the wily Fakir of Ipi flit in and out of the action. A Gurkha commander steps briskly into his crisp shorts which are standing erect in the corner of his office, having been starched by the faithful *dhobi wallah*. An Australian sea dog, in response to a request from one of his sailors for compassionate leave on the grounds that his home town was under flood water 6ft deep, and his wife was only 5ft 3ins high, silently hands over an orange box and stamps to post it. And then there is the enduring image of an English officer strolling nonchalantly about the "Bridge Too Far" at Arnhem sporting an old bowler hat and a tattered umbrella. "That thing won't do you much good," comments a comrade-in-arms, to which our hero replies: "But what if it rains?" Surely this Breed is immortal?

HUGH MASSINGBERD
*London, May 1996*

# Lt-Col "Billy" McLean

Lieutenant-Colonel "Billy" McLean, who has died aged 67, spent 40 years playing his own version of the Great Game. Like some latter-day knight errant, he travelled tirelessly in the Muslim world, working always against the encroaching influence of the Soviet Union, while at the same time seeking adventure among tribal peoples.

McLean's unusual life often had elements of intrigue that no one else could unravel. "What is Billy really up to?" was a question that would be asked at the bar of White's Club as he set off on another trip to Jordan or Iran, to Morocco or the Yemen.

In McLean's character there were shades of Buchan and Lawrence and Thesiger. All seemed to coalesce in the Yemen, where for five years from 1962, McLean helped the royalists under Imam al-Badr to resist President Nasser's attempts to take over the country. He made numerous reconnaissances in the Yemen desert and many arduous journeys, by camel and on foot, to the royalist forces in their remote mountain strongholds.

It was entirely due to McLean that Britain never followed America in recognising Nasser's, and the Soviet Union's, puppet republican government in the Yemen; and it was he who persuaded the Saudis to increase their aid to the Imam's forces. Thanks also to McLean, the royalists received Western mercenary support and arms from the .RAF. Largely as a result of McLean's efforts, North Yemen did not become one of Nasser's fiefdoms and did not join its neighbour South Yemen in the Communist camp.

Neil Loudon Desmond McLean was born on November 28 1918, a direct descendant of "Gillean of the Battle-Axe", known in Argyll in the 13th century.

After Eton and Sandhurst (where he rode several winners at point-to-points), McLean was commissioned into the Royal Scots Greys and sent to Palestine in 1939.

At the end of the following year he went to occupied Abyssinia, where he proved himself an outstanding guerrilla leader, as part of Orde Wingate's Gideon Force. He led a force of Eritrean and Abyssinian irregulars — known as "McLean's Foot" — against the Italians near Gondar.

His burgeoning career as an irregular soldier continued in Special Operations Executive; in 1943 he led a five-man military mission to Albania, to co-ordinate resistance to the Axis powers. Peter Kemp (*qv*) described his first meeting with McLean when he parachuted into Albania to join the mission: "Approaching up the hill with long, easy strides came a tall figure in jodhpurs and a wide crimson cummerbund, a young man with long, fair hair brushed back from a broad forehead and wearing a major's crown on the shoulder-straps of his open-necked army shirt."

With one break, McLean remained in Albania until the German retreat from that country and inspired those under him with his military skill and courage. He was promoted to lieutenant-colonel at the age of 24.

His contacts with the Albanian communist leader Enver Hoxha turned sour when left-wing elements of SOE favoured the partisans at the expense of the Zogist faction led by Abas Kupi, which McLean supported against charges of collaboration with the Germans.

In 1945 he volunteered for SOE duties in the Far East, where he became military adviser in Kashgar, Chinese Turkestan. Here he learnt the ways of the Turkis, Uzbeks, Kazaks, Tajiks and Tartars, who were under threat of domination by the Soviet Union, and travelled extensively in Asia. McLean's fascination and sympathy with Muslim minorities and tribal peoples would continue for the rest of his life. He devoted much of his time to the cause of the Pathans and the Kurds, as well as the royalist Yemenis.

After the war he sought election to Parliament, twice unsuccessfully for the Preston South constituency, in 1950 and 1951. He became Conservative MP for Inverness in 1954, and held the seat until the 1964 general election.

As a Highlander himself, McLean was able to identify with the Celtic character of his constituents. But they could not be expected to appreciate the reasons for his long absences in the Middle East.

While he was an MP, and afterwards, McLean was, as described by a colleague, "a sort of unpaid under-secretary for the Foreign Office". His political contacts in the Muslim world were probably unique among Westerners, in particular his relationship with King Saud during the Yemen war and his personal friendship with King Hussein over many years. In the mid-1960s he was involved in an unsuccessful attempt to "spring" a revolutionary leader from jail in Algeria.

McLean was always passionate in defence of British interests, as he saw them, which did not always accord with the Government's view. In his later years, still pursuing those interests, he visited Somalia, Iran, Western Sahara, the Pakistan-Afghanistan border, China, Israel, Turkey and Jordan.

In 1979 Harold Macmillan wrote to McLean: "You are one of those people whose services to our dear country are known only to a few."

By his many friends and admirers he will be remembered as possibly the last of the paladins. While his role may not always have been fully appreciated in Britain, his independence and total integrity were recognised in all the countries where his influence was felt.

Alongside his flair for guerrilla fighting, he had a passion for secret enterprises, deep-laid schemes and political complexities. He combined acute political understanding with military gifts ideally suited to irregular warfare.

His comrade-in-arms in Albania and the Yemen, David Smiley, has written of McLean: "His charming character seemed languid and nonchalant to the point of idleness, but underneath this facade he was unusually brave, physically tough and extremely intelligent, with a quick, active and unconventional mind."

His wisdom, sense of humour, human curiosity and kindness endeared him to a wide circle of contemporary friends and younger people, who saw his values as ones they could respect without sentimentality or danger of being considered old-fashioned. He revelled in argument and banter, and was always interested in the opinions of the younger generation.

McLean was both a keen shot and underwater-fisherman; one of his great pleasures was to spear moray eels off the north coast of Majorca. He was very partial to Middle Eastern and Chinese cooking.

He married, in 1949, Daska Kennedy (*née* Ivanovic), who supported, sustained and understood him during his unconventional life.

November 20 1986

# MARY LINDELL

MARY LINDELL, the Comtesse de Milleville, who has died in Germany aged 91, was a British-born heroine of the French Resistance in the Second World War.

Codenamed "Marie-Claire", she headed the Resistance organisation at Lyons where she ran an escape route out of occupied France for Allied airmen, soldiers and refugees.

In 1942 she smuggled the only two survivors of the celebrated "Cockleshell Heroes", Major "Blondie" Hasler and Marine Bill Sparks, out of France to Spain following their successful raid on German Blockade-running ships at Bordeaux. This Commando mission was described by Mountbatten as "one of the most courageous and imaginative operations of the Second World War".

Recalling the event 40 years on, the Comtesse said: "Because of a mix-up in instructions from London I waited for Major Hasler at the wrong place and it was an anxious time, with the Germans knowing some Commandos had escaped before I was able to contact him and Sparks. It was vital to get them back to England for British Intelligence and I delegated my son to take them through southern France into Spain using one of our escape routes through the mountains. The whole area was swarming with Gestapo men, informers and troops. But they got through safely."

She herself was frequently imprisoned and interrogated by the Gestapo. Finally, in 1944 she was shot through the head and thrown into the notorious Nazi concentration camp for women at Ravensbruck near Berlin, where, as she later put it, "conditions were pretty dim for the general public".

In 1983, after Klaus Barbie, the "Butcher of Lyons", had been returned to the city following his extradition from Bolivia, the Comtesse revealed that she had paid 45,000 francs to Barbie during the war for the release of her elder son from Fort Montluc prison.

She told how she had asked an SS officer how much he wanted for her son Maurice de Milleville's release. He had replied: "30,000 or 40,000 francs".

Then she produced the banknotes, torn in half, and said he could have the rest when her son was brought to her alive at the home of some friends in Lyons. M. de Milleville was duly released, having been badly beaten and looking "like strawberry jam".

The Comtesse's younger son, Octavius, was deported by the Germans and died in Mauthausen concentration camp. Her daughter also worked for the Resistance.

"My mother had a very narrow channel of interest," Maurice de Milleville said, "her heart was in getting people out of France. There was no other thing."

Although married to a French Count, Miss Lindell remained invincibly, and somewhat imperiously, British. "We were sick to death of the French", she recalled in a television programme, *Women of Courage* (1980), "and knew that someone would have to stay behind and stand up to the Jerries and see things through."

She steadfastly retained her British passport during her encounters with the Gestapo, although, as she said, "I always made out I hated England as part of my cover".

The Comtesse was not, by all accounts, easy to work with. Some of her Resistance colleagues complained that she would not obey instructions. She herself admitted to arrogance and attributed this to having been well-to-do all her life. She claimed never to have known fear and because of this refused to take credit for the bravery that brought her a fistful of medals.

She won the Croix de Guerre twice, once for her bravery as a Red Cross nurse at the Western Front in the First World War and again for her services to the Resistance in the Second World War. She was also eventually appointed OBE.

After the war her tiny autocratic figure was a familiar sight at meetings of the RAF Association in Paris where she lived with her dachshund, Tommy.

January 10 1987

# LADY BERRY

LADY BERRY, who has died aged 99, was one of the indomitable heroines of the medical unit in Serbia run by her subsequent husband, Sir James Berry, during the First World War.

When war broke out in 1914, Mabel Marion ("Jane") Ingram from Wimbledon, then studying medicine at the Royal Free Hospital, hoped to offer her services for work in Army hospitals, but at that time women doctors were expected to work only among women and children.

However, following the defeat of Austria-Hungary by Britain's gallant ally Serbia at the end of 1914, a Serbian Relief Fund was set up to deal with the flood of Serbian casualties.

Jane Ingram was one of the young women to volunteer as a medical assistant and dresser for a Royal Free Hospital Unit, staffed mainly by women, to go out to Serbia under the leadership of the surgeon James Berry and his wife Frances, also a doctor.

Arriving in Serbia (where conditions were still similar to those of Florence Nightingale's day), the Berry unit had not only to deal with the wounded but also found a typhus epidemic raging. Thus they also had to care for the civil population. In some areas the mortality rate was 50 per cent, with corpses lying about in heaps of 200 or so; one-third of Serbia's doctors died. The Berry unit made an important contribution to bringing the epidemic under control by the late spring of 1915.

That autumn Serbia was again invaded by the Central Powers and the Berry unit accompanied the Serbian Army's fighting retreat to the Adriatic coast, treating casualties while trekking through the snowy passes of Albania in the depths of winter. "The bearing of these British women was beyond all praise," a Serbian medical liaison officer wrote later. "Equalling the soldiers in endurance, they outdid them in morale, giving to others most of the little they had, putting their last wraps on exhausted soldiers."

Eventually Jane Ingram was among those taken prisoner by the Austrians and repatriated to England. But in 1916 she again joined the Berrys in a Red Cross hospital unit bound for Russia where two Serbian divisions were fighting on the Eastern Front. After a dangerous voyage, they finally reached Odessa where there were over 1,000 wounded Serbians with only minimal medical attention.

Miss Ingram and her colleagues had to work heroically round the clock until the situation was under control. "It is no wonder England is a great nation, if the women are like that," a local official told the author Arthur Ransome, then a war correspondent.

A fearfully hard winter followed, during which the virtual breakdown of the Russian railways led to shortages of supplies, and then came the Russian Revolution. The position of the unit became daily more difficult but ultimately Miss Ingram, the Berrys and the others were repatriated once more.

After the war Dr Ingram, having completed her training, settled into general practice at Roehampton. She served as a school doctor and became – most unusually for that time – a police surgeon.

Following the death of the first Lady Berry in 1934 Sir James (knighted in 1925) and Dr Ingram were married in 1935. She continued her medical practice after their marriage, only retiring some time after the National Health Service was set up. Sir James died in 1946.

In 1935 the work of British medical women in Serbia was recognised by Yugoslavia by the erection of a commemorative fountain at Vrnjatchka Banja (the "Hot Spring") where much of the work of the brave Berrys was based.

March 2 1987

# TOM BOYD

TOM BOYD, who has died aged 72, was one of the heroes of the daring raid on St Nazaire in March 1942, an early success of Mountbatten's Combined Operations unit during the Second World War.

The object of "Operation Chariot", as it was code-named, was to destroy the *Normandie* liner dock, the only dry dock on the Atlantic seaboard capable of taking the German battleship *Tirpitz*.

Boyd, then a 27-year-old Lieutenant in the RNVR, commanded a motor launch, *ML60*, in the flotilla of launches, torpedo-boats and gun boats escorting the former United States destroyer *Campbeltown* up the River Loire. Rather in the manner of an Elizabethan "fireship", the *Campbeltown* was packed with several tons of explosives.

On the way up the Loire towards the dock, Boyd, a Yorkshireman once described as a "big, happy fellow", remarked to his coxswain: "This is a queer do." His shipmate replied: "It'll soon be a bloody sight queerer, sir!"

In the event, although the attacking force was detected, and came under fierce fire from the shore, the *Campbeltown* successfully crashed the dock gates. Boyd took *ML60* very close inshore and – under intense fire from enemy guns and brightly illuminated by searchlights – managed to knock out one enemy battery from a range of only 200 yards. Later he took *ML60* alongside, under withering fire, to rescue the survivors of another ML before retiring downriver on one damaged engine.

Although many of the Chariot force were killed or captured, delayed action fuses detonated the charges inside the *Campbeltown* the day after the raid, doing enormous damage to the dock and thereby denying the *Tirpitz* its possible shelter.

Five VCs were awarded for the raid and Boyd was one of only four to receive the DSO. The citation spoke of his "great gallantry and skill in bombarding enemy positions on shore at point-blank range."

When, after three days and three nights at sea, Boyd eventually sighted the Lizard on the way home, he said that he knew the landmark well, having once, as a navigating officer, run another motor-launch ashore there, thus earning the sobriquet "T. Lizard Boyd".

Thomas William Boyd, the son of a Hull trawler owner, was born in 1914 and educated at St Bees. He played rugby football for Yorkshire.

At the age of 12 he came home from school for the Christmas holidays to be told by his father that he was to sail to Spitzbergen as a "hand", because some of the crews were grumbling. Boyd recalled of this nautical baptism that the spray froze on the decks, ropes cut sores in his hands and that he cried in his bunk at night.

Another boy in the crew stole his belt so young Tom held the thief's head over the side till he had half filled him up with salt water. But the ship's master (a "Wallace Beery type" in Boyd's description) caught hold of young Tom and announced: "You may be Tom Boyd, junior, but I'm going to give thee a proper hiding."

Such trawling yarns delighted American audiences when Boyd and some other war heroes toured America to stimulate the sale of War Bonds in the summer of 1942. They were given a "ticker-tape" welcome in New

York where Boyd said over the public address system: "I can't believe there are so many people in the world or that so many could have turned out to see some very ordinary Englishmen."

Besides his exploits at St Nazaire, Boyd also took part in the evacuation of Dunkirk and served in the Far East, ending up as a Commander.

After the war, he became chairman and managing director of the Boyd Line. He was president of the Hull Fishing Vessel Owners' Association and of the British Trawlers Federation, and an honorary Brother of Trinity House. He was appointed OBE in 1963 and was a Deputy Lieutenant for Humberside.

He married, in 1937, Barbara Gresham; they had a son and two daughters.

March 24 1987

# BRIG TED HUGHES

BRIGADIER TED HUGHES, who has died aged 89, took part in the Siege of Spin Baldak in 1919 – the last occasion when a British Army unit used scaling ladders.

Then a subaltern of 22 in the 1st Gurkhas, Hughes was serving in the third Afghan War. The Amir Abdullah had declared war and begun to invade India which he imagined was too war-weary and denuded of troops to resist the Afghan attack. But the Indian Army had 10,000 men encamped on the Afghan border in May 1919 and it was decided that the first retaliatory action must be to capture the key fort of Spin Baldak.

In his subsequent account of his experiences – a

richly sarcastic memoir that was enjoyed more by his contemporaries then by his senior officers – Hughes wrote: "The Higher Command – acting doubtless on the excellent principle that if you can't surprise the enemy it is better to surprise your own side than no one at all – supplied little or no information about the fort and its garrison."

It was, however, known that the fort was enclosed in a 200-yard-long, 15ft high outer wall and within this was an even higher wall. Hughes's regiment was ordered to take the south side with scaling ladders.

The plan was first to place the scaling ladders in the ditch, so that the regiment could climb down one side and then up the other. Then the men were meant to climb the wall, haul up the ladders, climb down, go through the ditch, and then climb the next wall.

Hughes observed that the Gurkhas were "greatly diverted by this simple plan and declared that nothing like it had been seen since the siege of Jerusalem". The observation was made, though, that the enemy should have been chloroformed before the operation took place.

Hughes continued: "03.00 hours saw that mighty army move forward to the storming of the fortress. Everything was to be done in deathly silence – not a whisper was to rouse the unsuspecting Afghans. Indeed, the only sounds were the crashing of ammunition boxes and entrenching tools as the mules threw their loads – and the thudding of hooves as they bolted into the night: every few seconds the air was split by the yells of some officer urging the men to greater silence or the despairing call of some NCO who had lost his section.

"A sound as of corrugated iron being dropped from a great height denoted that the scaling ladders were being loaded on the carts: with these two exceptions, no one would have had an inkling that several thousand armed men were pressing forward to the fray."

In the event the scaling ladders were too short even for descending into the ditches but fortunately the Afghan garrison commander had no stomach for a fight in the fort and retreated with his army to the hills. The British occupied the fort for a month, strengthened the defences, and improved the water supply; then they handed it back to the Afghans.

Hughes's story of the siege of Spin Baldak, which differed considerably from the official version, made him an obvious choice for a posting to Iraq whence he proceeded in 1920 with a draft from his own battalion to join the 3/5th Gurkhas who were engaged in suppressing an Arab rebellion.

Francis Edmund Charles Hughes was born in 1897 and commissioned from Sandhurst, into the 1st Battalion of the 1st Gurkhas in 1916. He served in Waziristan the following year and again in the 1920s.

In 1924 Hughes was awarded the silver medal of the Royal Humane Society for a brave attempt to save a life on the Beas river.

In the 1930s he attended the Staff College and served on the general staff of Meerut District. During the Second World War he served in the Western Desert and Burma.

April 17 1987

# CAPT PETER DICKENS

CAPTAIN PETER DICKENS, who has died aged 69, was a brilliant and daring leader in the Light Coastal Forces in the North Sea during the Second World War.

Operating in what was known as "E-boat alley" Dickens, a great-grandson of the famous novelist, carried out a remarkable series of attacks on German shipping and motor torpedo-boats. He won the DSO and DSC, was appointed MBE, as well as being mentioned numerous times in despatches and Admiralty communiqués.

From the moment he joined Coastal Forces in 1942, Dickens – handicapped though he was with a flotilla of motor torpedo-boats that were, in the words of his brother-officer Peter Scott, "none too reliable" – turned in one success after another. He was to the fore in six successful coastal engagements in his first year with the "little ships", including sinking several German armed trawlers and such heroic actions as taking off the crew of a damaged British gunboat near Terschelling and setting fire to the vessel while all the time under heavy enemy attack.

Dickens was the master of the deliberate, unhurried approach. Peter Scott described his method as being that of "a highly-developed and scientific study of the technique of attack, combined with all the perceptions of a stalker."

Dickens believed that an unobserved attack should always be the prime method. This involved firing torpedoes before the enemy knew that MTBs were in the vicinity; the torpedoes could be aimed without the distraction of starshells and when the enemy would be unlikely to alter his course or speed.

Scott regarded Peter Dickens as "the greatest MTB exponent of his time". Dickens later wrote a realistic and thoughtful account of his experiences leading the 21st Motor Torpedo Flotilla in *Night Action: MTB Flotilla at War* (1975). Although he was far too modest to tell his readers that he was a legend during his spell in Light Coastal Forces, the fighting quality of a courageous man not afraid to admit his fears and failings comes triumphantly across.

Peter Gerald Charles Dickens, son of Adml Sir Gerald Dickens, was born in 1917 and educated at Dartmouth.

When he was first lieutenant of the *Cotswold*, a Hunt Class destroyer countering mine-laying "E"-boats, Dickens had to be rescued when the destroyer was itself mined. Among the officers to receive the *Cotswold* casualties was the scion of another literary family, Lt-Cdr Robert Hichens (later killed in action off the Dutch coast). This was the first meeting between two of the great heroes of the "little ships" who were to work extensively together at Beehive, the Coastal Forces base at Felixstowe.

After the war Dickens was captain of the destroyer *Daring* and of the Chatham Dockyard before retiring from the Navy in 1964 when he became an honorary ADC to the Queen.

In retirement Dickens distinguished himself as an able naval and military historian, writing books on the SAS, the battle of Narvik and the Hesperus. While researching his book on Narvik, Dickens was so struck by the courage, integrity and sense of humour of the German Adml Wolff and the British Adml Micklethwait, who had last encountered each other in a Norwegian fjord in 1940, that he invited the two former enemies and their wives down to Sussex for the weekend. "We had a wonderful dinner party," Dickens said, "where they fought their old battle again with spoons over a chocolate and cream mousse depicting the fjord and the two destroyers."

Dickens was the seventh member of his family to become president of the worldwide Dickens Fellowship. He was also president of the Coastal Forces Veterans Association which delighted in the nickname "Costly Farces" bestowed on them by the regular Navy.

He married, in 1950, Mary Alice, widow of Sir Anthony Twysden, 11th Bt, and daughter of Rear-Adml Evelyn Blagrove. They had a son and two daughters.

May 26 1987

# PHILIP WAREING

PHILIP WAREING, a Battle of Britain fighter pilot who has died aged 71, made one of the most remarkable escapes from a German prison of war camp in Poland during the Second World War.

In the late afternoon of December 16 1942, Sgt Wareing was detailed with other inmates at Schubin camp, a converted girls' school 150 miles west of Warsaw, to collect bread from a railway siding. When one of the working party dropped a loaf on the line, Wareing, on the pretext of picking it up, made his getaway in the gathering darkness. Well prepared, he had food, maps, a compass and was wearing grubby army trousers, a cloth cap and an RAF tunic which he had altered to pass as a civilian jacket. On reaching Bromberg, some 20 miles north of Schubin, he found a rickety bicycle which he pedalled and walked to Gradenz.

At the railway station there, he swapped this bicycle for a new one which a German had just left propped against a wall, and set out for Danzig. There was a terrifying moment as he crossed a heavily-guarded bridge over the Vistula. While guards were questioning two Germans in uniform, Wareing bicycled past them.

On arriving in Danzig, he was dismayed to find he had forgotten to bring the money he had ready for an escape. But it was not long before he saw some Swedish ships whose Blue Peter pennants indicated imminent departure.

After hiding among timber piles, he walked up the gangway of one of the ships which was loading coal. Later that day he was spotted by a party of Russians working in the coal hole but after he had said quietly "Angliski pilot" the Russians left him alone. Late that night when they had gone, he concealed himself amid the coal.

The ship sailed the next morning. Two days later a member of the crew saw Wareing, but the ship was close to Halmstad where the Swedish police collected him. Shortly afterwards the British Legation in Stockholm arranged his repatriation.

Philip Thomas Wareing was born in 1915 and educated at Bishops Vesey's Grammar School, Sutton Coldfield. He joined the RAF Volunteer Reserve in 1939.

He ended up in Schubin after baling out of his flaming Spitfire over Calais on August 25 1940. As a member of No 616 (South Yorkshire) Squadron which was stationed at Kenley – a smoking ruin at the time, where pilots sometimes slept under the wings of their Spitfires – Wareing found himself one of seven Spitfires engaging 30 Me109s.

He shot down at least one enemy fighter, but soon, as he described it, "my lovely Spitfire was riddled like a sieve, on fire and the propeller was not turning." Despite the radiator being hit, and enemy bullets rattling on the armour plate protecting his back, Wareing continued to fire at four 109s in line ahead.

Then, as another enemy fighter poured fire into his Spitfire, the petrol tank over his legs went up and the blast helped him escape from the cockpit. Fearing that he might be shot at as he descended, Wareing delayed opening his parachute until enemy aircraft had moved away, and landed in a ploughed field.

Before an enemy motor-cyclist with sidecar arrived to take him prisoner, he remembered to wipe the recognition signal letters of the day from one of his hands, using his blood. At a nearby Luftwaffe base he was treated as a comrade, the German pilots apologising that all the captured Naafi whisky and beer was finished and they could offer only cognac.

His membership of the German Alpine Club before the war added to the camaraderie, and he was presented with cigarettes and chocolate. Before leaving the enemy base, Wareing gave his name and address to a Luftwaffe pilot who was shot down over south-east England shortly afterwards. So, after finding Wareing's name in the pilot's pocket, an intelligence officer was able to tell his mother that her son was alive. At that stage all she knew was that he was missing – though his Squadron's commanding officer had written to her, "We all hope that he will turn up yet."

By the end of the war, Wareing had been promoted to flight lieutenant and served in Australia. He worked in Air Traffic Control for a while after leaving the RAF and was also involved in delivering cars.

He was twice widowed and is survived by a daughter in Australia.

*May 28 1987*

# Wing Cdr "Dizzy" Allen

Wing Commander H. R. "Dizzy" Allen, who has died aged 68, was a Battle of Britain pilot with an official score of 6½ aircraft destroyed who later wrote several acerbic books on the air war.

"A hard-arsed pilot" by his own admission, he ascribed his buccaneering approach to flying and life in general to his claimed descent from Capt Sir Henry Morgan, the 17th-century terror of the Spanish Main. Like Morgan, he strenuously objected to being "buggered about by bureaucrats".

Commissioned the day before war was declared, on September 2 1939, Hubert Raymond Allen was still "as green as an unripened strawberry", when he put his Spitfire into a flat spin, but was lucky enough to be able to recover. His nickname "Dizzy" was the result.

Allen joined No 66 Spitfire Squadron at RAF Dux-
ford, and took over leadership a year later, when only he
and a sergeant pilot were left of those present when he
arrived.

Allen made his first "kill" on August 30 1940, when
with two others, he shot down a Dornier 17. He always
contended that the official dates of the Battle of Britain
– July 10 to October 31 1940 – were restrictive, quoting
his own experience on February 14 1941, when No 66
Squadron was intercepted by a wing formation of 50 Me
109s.

His Spitfire was badly hit, a bullet penetrated his
arm and grazed a rib. With his right arm hanging limply
as it spurted blood, he got on his attacker's tail, closed
to 250 yards only to find his guns failing to fire.

When he managed to crash land at Biggin Hill, the
Spitfire had 43 holes and a great gash from an explosive
cannon shell. He was awarded the DFC, although he
contended he would have received the VC had his guns
responded.

Allen went on to command Nos 1 and 43 Squadrons
and later became air adviser to the First Airborne
Division and Tactics and Gunnery Officer in No 12
Group.

After the war, he held various staff appointments,
among them personal staff officer to the Chief of Staff,
Allied Air Forces Central Europe, Air Defence Adviser to
the Dutch Government, and membership of the Joint
Planning Staff specialising in the Far East.

During his career he clocked up more than 3,000
flying hours and flew 45 aircraft types, excluding var-
iants, among them the English Electric Lightning.

Determined to make the most of his last flying appointment he made himself deputy to the official test pilot, thus adding six types to his score.

As a staff officer Allen planned the Buckingham Palace flypast for the 1953 Coronation Review, and the subsequent Queen's Coronation Review.

On retiring from the RAF Allen decided to become a Queen's Messenger, partly influenced by the opportunity to remain airborne, though a professional passenger on international air routes. But after 18 months enjoying the cosseted existence of ceaseless first-class air travel, he left the Corps, feeling the "spirit of adventure" beginning to pall.

As an author Allen was particularly critical of RAF Bomber Command – "I do not believe I could ever have obeyed orders as a bomber pilot" – suggesting that RAF targeting policies were not correctly thought through. He argued against the creed of Sir Arthur "Bomber" Harris "that desolation was the only worthwhile policy", which he attributed largely to the legacy of Lord Trenchard, and regretted that the RAF's failure to pinpoint small targets in the early part of the war led to the conclusion that burning 70 of Germany's largest cities would win the war.

Noting that Allen referred to gremlins in Rolls-Royce Merlin engines in his *Who Won the Battle of Britain?* (1974) Richard Hough said in *The Daily Telegraph*: "I fear that one escaped and found its way into the author's typewriter."

Dizzy Allen was as ready to criticise in the press as in his books. When, under the Firearms Act, police seized broken and rusty RAF and Luftwaffe guns from a Battle of Britain museum in Kent, he protested: "It's absolute bloody nonsense and I have told Reggie Maudling" (referring to the then Home Secretary).

He is survived by his wife, Anne, two sons and two daughters.

June 6 1987

# MAJ-GEN BILLY STAWELL

MAJOR-GENERAL BILLY STAWELL, who died aged 92, was in overall charge of the Special Operations Executive branch in the Middle East which was the only area in the SOE network not to be breached by enemy agents during the Second World War.

As a Special Forces Commander Stawell was also closely involved in developments in Yugoslavia, where his deductions were often at variance with the official view of the British Government which transferred its support from the followers of Gen Mihailovich to Tito's partisans in November 1943.

A modest, kind, gentle man, tall, fair and good looking, Stawell was the epitome of the best type of soldier of his generation. His contemporary, Field-Marshal Lord Harding of Petherton, who served with him in places varying from Aldershot in the 1930s to the Mediterranean theatre of war in the 1940s, said of him: "He was an excellent soldier, a fine comrade and a firm friend."

The son of a member of the Indian Civil Service, William Arthur Macdonald Stawell was born in 1895 and educated at Clifton and Woolwich. He was commissioned into the Royal Engineers in August 1914.

During the First World War he commanded a signal troop of the "Sappers" in France and Belgium. He won the Military Cross in 1917, but was severely wounded. Indeed he was exceptionally lucky to survive as his femoral artery was cut – a wound which normally causes death within a couple of minutes.

His convalescence took a year, at the end of which he met a sportsman by the name of Wingfield who convinced him that any animal, even a bird, was ridable if it was large enough. Stawell, always a keen horseman and polo player, was duly persuaded to try getting astride a bull and an ostrich – both of which mounts he managed successfully, albeit briefly.

Subsequently he was posted to the Middle East where he served in Greek Macedonia, Serbia, Bulgaria, the Aegean Islands and Turkey. While in Constantinople he organised a pack of hounds of mixed breed which supposedly eliminated the last jackals from Europe.

Between the wars Stawell served in India with the Madras Sappers and Miners, a mounted regiment, and also held various Staff appointments which included brigade major at Aldershot, deputy assistant adjutant-general in India and commander, Royal Engineers.

In 1940 he was assistant adjutant and quartermaster-general and then went to the War Office as deputy director of Military Intelligence from 1941 to 1942. Before going out to the Middle East in 1943 he was a Brigadier (General Staff) Home Forces. At the end of the hostilities Stawell was seconded, as deputy chief of operations, to the United Nations Relief and Rehabilitation Administration (UNRRA) which assisted millions of people from North Africa to Europe.

In 1947 he became deputy chief of the Intelligence Division in the Control Commission, Germany, before retiring in 1948.

Stawell continued to be active in retirement in Suffolk, playing a dedicated part in local affairs and remaining an enthusiastic yachtsman. He was appointed CBE in 1944 and CB in 1945.

He married, in 1926, Amy Bowring, from New York, who died in 1986. They had a son.

June 17 1987

# Lt-Cdr Hugh Darbyshire

Lieutenant-Commander Hugh Darbyshire, of the Royal Indian Naval Volunteer Reserve, who has died aged 73, had a hectic naval career in Coastal Forces and was mentioned in despatches for his part in an arduous and dangerous, but now almost totally forgotten, naval campaign of the Second World War – the war in the jungle creeks or "chaungs" along the Arakan coast of Burma in 1943–1944.

As senior officer of the 55th Motor Launch flotilla, Darbyshire led many sorties along the coast by night, to harass Japanese positions or to land secret agents. In February 1944 his flotilla bombarded the island of Akyab, held by the Japanese, who replied with machine-guns and shell fire.

Darbyshire was unscathed, but was not so fortunate in another bombardment of the island of Ramree. While retiring, he and three of the 10 launches in company were bombed and strafed by Japanese aircraft.

He was blown off his bridge, and signalled frantically in plain language to his base at Chittagong: "For Christ's sake do something". RAF fighter support arrived. So too did a signal from the C-in-C, Adml Somerville, directing Darbyshire's attention to the Biblical warning. "Thou shalt not blaspheme even in times of distress".

Darbyshire himself had an appropriate sense of humour. In one clandestine operation with the Army his landing craft was hit by a Japanese cannon shell. Darbyshire, who was a big man, sealed the shell hole by sitting on it.

Hugh McDonald Darbyshire was born in 1914 and educated at Pangbourne. In 1933 he went out to Calcutta to join a firm of tea merchants.

He was a member of the Calcutta Light Horse and was on the Indian Army reserve of officers. But in 1939 he volunteered for the RINVR and was commissioned as temporary sub-lieutenant in February 1940.

His first ship was the RIN sloop *Lawrence* serving in the Persian Gulf. In 1941, after the outbreak of Rashid Ali's revolt in Iraq, it was the *Lawrence* which took the boy King of Iraq and the Regent Amir Abdul Illah from Basra to Kuwait.

The following August, when he was serving in the Australian sloop *Yarra*, Darbyshire took part in the invasion of Persia and the seizure of eight Axis merchant ships sheltering in the port of Bandar Shahpur.

Darbyshire was in the party which stormed the

10,000-ton German Hansa Line ship *Hohenfels*, whose crew detonated scuttling charges, so that a ventilator fell upon Darbyshire from a great height and flattened him. But once again he escaped serious injury. He awoke later in the sick bay.

In April 1942 Darbyshire joined the cruiser *Dorsetshire* but on his first trip to sea in her she and her sister ship *Cornwall* were both sunk in the Indian Ocean by Japanese aircraft. Darbyshire was having a bath at the time. When he was eventually picked up, stark naked and black with oil after 36 hours in the sea, the sailors who hauled him out were heard, or so Darbyshire always said, to speculate on whether or not they had rescued the Loch Ness Monster.

He was a good leader in battle but a reluctant staff officer. Representing coastal forces on the staff of the flag officer commanding RIN in Delhi he said he only met the admiral once "in the heads – the only act we seemed to have in common!"

Darbyshire was known to his RIN colleagues as "a bit of a rebel" with an irreverent attitude to senior officers. One naval stores officer who crossed his path was surprised to receive a signalled demand for an admiral pattern Oxo-meter and a can of Pissolene. Darbyshire later explained that an Oxo-meter was an instrument for measuring bullshit and Pissolene was needed to oil it.

He returned to England in 1955 and ran residential courses for Overseas Service of Farnham. In 1960 he returned to India as comptroller of the household to the British High Commissioner.

Back home he became county secretary and treasurer of the British Legion in Surrey. He served in the RNR for many years and was awarded the Volunteer Reserve Decoration and Bar.

He leaves a widow, Hester, and many friends in the Royal Indian Navy (1612–1947) Association.

August 25 1987

# LT-GEN WILMOT VICKERS

LIEUTENANT-GENERAL WILMOT VICKERS, who has died aged 97, was the last surviving Indian Cavalry officer from the days of hard-riding irregulars – originally opportunist adventurers, who provided their own horses, uniform and equipment or, latterly, cash to the Raj in lieu.

Known as the "*Silledar* system", it nourished a distinctive breed of leader in the era of Skinner and Probyn whose names live on through the titles of their regiments. Vickers personified the type of officer who gave his life to the Army and his regiment and to the welfare of his soldiers, setting the highest standards for his successors in the armies of India and Pakistan. His sporting example has also been long available to young polo players through his book *Practical Polo*.

Wilmot Gordon Hilton Vickers was born in 1890. Like so many of the Indian Army (which succeeded the East India Company's forces after the Mutiny of 1857), he was the son of an Indian Army officer. Also in keeping with tradition he attended United Services College,

Westward Ho!, and the Imperial Service College, Windsor. From Sandhurst he was commissioned in the 31st Lancers of the Indian Cavalry, later the 13th Duke of Connaught's Own Lancers.

The outbreak of the First World War coincided with the ending of the *Silledar* system and Vickers saw service on the North-West Frontier. In time his exceptional horsemanship (he was a high-handicap polo player) was acknowledged through his appointment as Commandant and Chief Instructor of the Equitation School in Saugor in the mid-1930s. But Vickers was also destined for higher command which he achieved after attending the Imperial Defence College and holding staff regimental appointments.

By the outbreak of the Second World War he was commanding an infantry brigade, being rapidly promoted to the post of Major-General responsible for administration in Iraq. In 1942 he returned to India as Quartermaster-General, remaining in this post until retiring in 1944 after 34 years' service.

Thereafter Vickers devoted himself to public service at home. That quiet, unruffled approach and kindness which had characterised his relationship with young officers, invested his duties as Chief Warden of Civil Defence in Gloucestershire, Commandant of the Army Cadet Force and Deputy Lieutenant.

Retaining his sharpness of intellect until the end, Vickers, in reminiscent mood, would keep his listeners enthralled as he talked of soldiering in India before 1914.

He was appointed CB in 1942 and OBE in 1949.

He is survived by two sons, one of whom is Lt-Gen

Sir Richard Vickers, director-general of the Winston Churchill Memorial Trust.

*September 18 1987*

# "BLACKIE" BLACKSELL

"BLACKIE" BLACKSELL, who has died aged 75, was the teacher and RAF physical training instructor selected by the plastic surgeon Sir Archibald McIndoe to boost the morale of his Second World War burns cases – the "Guinea Pigs" – at the Queen Victoria Hospital, East Grinstead.

At the outbreak of the war Blackie, a secondary school teacher at Barnstaple, was rejected by naval doctors, but accepted by the RAF where he became a physical training instructor. Posted to Plymouth, his skilful taming of the high-spirited Australians of No 10 RAAF Flying Boat Squadron so impressed McIndoe that Sgt Blacksell, to his astonishment, was ordered to report to the Queen Victoria Hospital, East Grinstead, known as "the Sty".

"Good God," exclaimed a legless and horrified Guinea Pig when Blackie laid out his gym shoes, shorts and vest on a bed in Ward 3. "You're not bloody well doing PT with us." But very soon Blackie, a large, lovable man, was the life and soul of the spirit of Guinea Piggery – especially the "grogging parties". He became the "Pigs'" leader and supporter in the hostilities which developed with the service authorities over pay, pensions and indeed an official reluctance to recognise such desperately injured people as individuals.

It was Blackie who over the years orchestrated McIndoe's insistent theme: "A Guinea Pig should be a useful member of the community and not playing a cornet in Piccadilly". But Blackie was never a soft touch, as evidenced by his classic reprimand: "Pull your socks up even if they are on tin legs."

James Edward Blacksell was born in 1912 at Sheffield where his father was a cabinetmaker. The family later moved to Devon where he was educated at Torquay Grammar School before reading geography at Reading University.

After the war Blackie returned to the secondary modern school at Barnstaple (later a comprehensive school and community college) which thrived under his headmastership as a flagship in the state system. In the early 1950s he was one of the founders of the Taw and Torridge Festival of the Arts and also of the English Stage Company, serving on its management council.

Blackie persuaded Neville Blond of the Marks & Spencer dynasty, an old friend and neighbour of the Guinea Pigs, to chair the ESC and, for his own part, was an enthusiastic reader of scripts, among them the young John Osborne's *Look Back in Anger*.

Besides running the school, Blackie was also an education consultant to Macmillan, the publishers. On retiring from the headship in 1974, Blackie finally responded to repeated offers from Marks & Spencer, and took a part-time post advising on the company's sponsorship. He also provided a simliar service for Sotheby's.

Despite such widespread activity Blackie continued to give priority in his spare time to the Guinea Pig Club, counselling members on jobs, money and domestic problems for more than 40 years. Sadly Blackie was absent from last month's annual reunion, when more than 200 Pigs sang, to the tune of *The Church's One Foundation*, the anthem he had written for them: "We are McIndoe's Army. We are his Guinea Pigs."

Blacksell, who was appointed MBE, is survived by his wife Joan, their three sons and a daughter.

*October 20 1987*

# LT-COL GEOFFREY KNOWLES

LIEUTENANT-COLONEL GEOFFREY KNOWLES, who has died aged 87, survived a mauling by a black bear in Kashmir in 1922, and soldiered on to command Prince Albert Victor's Own Cavalry, 11th Frontier Force, against Rommel's Afrika Korps in North Africa and the Japanese in Burma.

One of the last British officers to join the old Indian Army from Cheltenham College through the Officer Cadet Battalion, Newmarket, in the final weeks of the First World War, Knowles completed his training at Madras before joining Prince Albert Victor's Own Cavalry on the North-West Frontier in 1920 in the aftermath of the third Afghan war.

Obtaining privilege leave in the summer of 1922, Knowles decided to try his luck with black bear and set off from Srinigar with a friend and two shikaris who were reputed to know the best areas for finding this species. Living up to their reputation the shikaris produced a large black bear, walking towards Knowles and his companion. When the bear was eight yards away

Knowles fired and hit the bear in the shoulder, sending it rolling down the hillside.

Restraining his shikari from rushing down after it, Knowles cautiously followed the bloodstains. Then, as he described it in *The Piffer*, journal of the Punjab Frontier Force: "With a loud 'Woof Woof' the bear came out of some undergrowth ahead of us and walked towards us on all fours."

At this point the edge of the narrow path gave way causing Knowles to fall head first and knock himself out on a rock. The last he could remember was the bear coming through the bushes, about to land on his backside.

After biting Knowles through the thigh and implanting his pawmarks on his posterior, the bear made off and the next Knowles knew was a shikari nursing his head in his lap with tears falling on his brow. Back at camp his friend doused the wounds with iodine, and later that day Knowles heard that the bear had died. Returning to the regiment he was advised to stick to duck shooting.

The early part of the Second World War found Knowles serving as second-in-command of the regiment in the Middle East before returning to India to command the 3rd Gwalior Lancers. But following the loss, as a prisoner, of Col "Bolshie" Tatham, Knowles was posted back to the desert to command Prince Albert Victor's Own.

Knowles took the regiment back to India to retrain in armoured cars before participating in a number of vital actions in Burma. Assisting the relief of Kohima in March 1944, his squadrons kept the Dimapur-Kohima road open until June when they headed a breakthrough to the south, meeting Col Cyril Morrison's tanks of the 7th Cavalry, coming up from Imphal.

Although Knowles handed over command to Morrison at the Chindwin river at Christmas, 1944, his part in the later successes of the Prince Albert Victor's Own was reflected in his appointment as OBE.

After staff appointments in Burma and India, serving as Military Secretary from 1948 to 1952 to Governors-General of Pakistan, and further staff appointments at the War Office and in Jamaica, Knowles retired in 1957 to Suffolk where he served as a county councillor.

He is survived by his wife, Sally.

December 3 1987

# MAJ-GEN ERIC HARRISON

MAJOR-GENERAL ERIC HARRISON, who has died aged 94, enjoyed a life which would have graced the pages of the *Boys' Own Paper*.

Besides giving distinguished service in both World Wars, he was a remarkable all-round sportsman – a representative rugby player, an Olympic athlete, a legendary rider to hounds, pig-sticker and big game hunter – as well as an artist, author and gardener.

Eric George William Warde Harrison, son of an Indian Army major, was born in 1893 and educated at Cheltenham and Woolwich, where he played rugby for the Army and Kent and was chosen for a tour with the Barbarians.

Commissioned into the Royal Artillery, he was posted to Shoeburyness where he was invited to play soccer for Southend United, then in the Second Division. Taking up hurdling, he was soon selected to run for England against Scotland and Ireland in the 120 yards hurdles.

At the outbreak of the First World War he was posted to the anti-aircraft defences of Harwich and nearly shot down Britain's only airship when it came unmarked over that area. Soon afterwards he was sent to France where he was involved in the murderous battles around Hooge, the Menin Road and Polygon Wood, and in 1915 was awarded the Military Cross at Givenchy. By the end of the Battle of Loos, he claimed, "I had shot my guns from every observation post of importance along the whole Corps front."

In 1918 he was made a Brevet Major, the youngest in the British Army at the time, and was surprised to be put in charge of the Corps Infantry School until a genial Irish colleague assured him: "My dear old boy, remember the worst you can do is make a complete balls of the whole show."

Harrison spent the final stages of the war with 58th London Division, and by the Armistice had been mentioned in despatches four times.

On returning to England he was selected to train for the "Mother Country" XV, the forerunner of the British Lions, and scored seven tries when playing wing-three-quarter for the Army against Oxford University. After injury ended his football career Harrison concentrated on fishing, riding and hurdling. He was selected for the 1920 Olympics but at the preliminary medical inspection a doctor said he had moved his heart and forbade him to compete. Harrison received the decision with some scepticism, for two days earlier he had won six events for his unit in an Army championship. A week later he won the 120 yards hurdles for England against Scotland and Ireland.

He was then offered the mastership of the Royal Artillery Harriers. Although a normal day consisted of hunting in the early morning, partridge-shooting in the afternoon and fishing in the evening, Harrison managed to scrape into the Staff College. Despite asthma when training for the 1924 Paris Olympics, which were featured in the film *Chariots of Fire*, he managed to reach a semi-final.

His next posting was to India where he took up big game shooting and became Master of the Lahore Hounds which hunted jackal. Although he only took up racquets after arriving in the country, he won the doubles title in the All India Championship, and also proved himself a fearless pig-sticker.

In 1932 Harrison was posted back to England to command a battery in Aldershot, but managed to transfer to Catterick where the hunting was better. At this time he took up painting after reading Churchill on oils and eventually had two pictures accepted but not hung by the Royal Academy and three hung by the Paris Salon.

In 1934, to his astonishment, Harrison was appointed to command the OTC at Oxford University where he lectured on military history and also became Master of the South Oxfordshire Foxhounds. At the outbreak of the Second World War he was given command of the Royal Artillery's 12th Territorial Division at Sevenoaks where Home Guard units were full of retired generals acting as platoon commanders.

He was relieved to be posted to Northern Ireland

which provided some salmon and trout fishing, as well as snipe shooting, and in 1942 was sent to North Africa with 9th Armoured Corps which became involved almost immediately in the forcing of the Fondouk Gap. After working closely with Lt-Gen Horrocks in the tail end of the North African campaign he was appointed Commander, Royal Artillery, at Eisenhower's Allied Forces HQ. He continued in the post during the Sicily and Italian campaigns, being mentioned in despatches, but returned home in 1943 to become GOC, Sussex and Surrey District.

Harrison retired from the Army in 1946 to resume his Mastership of the North Cornwall Hounds and become a noted rhododendron grower. He served as a Deputy Lieutenant, JP and High Sheriff and was a reforming chairman of St Lawrence's Mental Hospital, Bodmin.

Breeding labradors, trout fishing, and travel helped to fill the rest of the General's time, but he also wrote three books including a delightful autobiography, *Gunners, Games and Gardens* (1979). He was appointed CBE in 1943 and CB in 1945 and was ADC to King George VI from 1945 to 1946.

His first marriage, to Audrey Coller, was dissolved and in 1961 he married Mrs Roza Stevenson, who died in 1967. He used to say, "Everyone should be put down at 70", but he belied the words himself. In his nineties he was still fishing, shooting, gardening and painting, and his memory remained unimpaired.

December 22 1987

# AIR VICE-MARSHAL JOHN "THE BARON" WORRALL

AIR VICE-MARSHAL JOHN "THE BARON" WOR-
RALL, who has died aged 76, led a Hurricane fighter
squadron throughout the fall of France and in some of
the fiercest fighting of the Battle of Britain.

The desperate predicament of Worrall – at 29
somewhat older than most of his pilots in No 32
Squadron – as they fought to protect their Biggin Hill
base and other No 11 Group airfields in the summer of
1940, can be gauged from a typical exchange:

Controller: "24 bombers with 20 plus more behind
them."

Worrall: "Got it."

Controller: "20 plus more bombers and 20 fighters
behind and above."

Worrall: "All right."

Controller: "Now 30 more bombers and further 100-
plus fighters following."

Worrall: "Stop. No more information please. You are
frightening me terribly."

It was hardly surprising that Worrall became known
as "the Baron", a sobriquet recalling the First World
War ace "the Red Baron" von Richthofen; his other
nickname "the Mandarin" alluded to his mastery of the
Chinese language which he had studied at the School of
Oriental Studies and in Peking before the war.

John Worrall was born in 1911 and educated at Cranleigh and Cranwell. After a year with No 1 Squadron flying Hawker Fury biplane fighters at Tangmere he was posted to No 208, an Army Co-operation Squadron equipped with two-seater Hawker Demons.

After his return from China there was an interlude as an intelligence officer at the Air Ministry before he joined 32 Squadron in May 1940 as Hitler launched the *blitzkrieg* drive to the Channel ports. It was a hectic period, with Worrall leading daily patrols from Manston to Abbeville or Merville from which he operated during the day before flying a return patrol home in the evening.

By mid-August when Worrall handed over the squadron, his "splendid leadership", to quote the citation for his DFC, had been "reflected in the work of his squadron" which had already destroyed 43 enemy aircraft and possibly a further 22.

A softly spoken, modest character according to brother pilots – though at least one Biggin WAAF recalled him as fun and gregarious – Worrall displayed great skill and courage. On July 19 he led 32 Squadron through the Dover anti-aircraft barrage to tackle Ju-87 Stuka dive-bombers attacking the harbour. Next day, diving out of the sun, he led his Hurricanes through a heavy Me-109 fighter escort to engage a mass of Stukas over a convoy 10 miles out at sea – Worrall claiming a 109 of the four aircraft destroyed and two damaged.

For the remainder of the Second World War Worrall held several staff appointments in the Middle East and later commanded West Malling and Kai Tak, Hong Kong, where he was able to use his Chinese.

In 1954 he returned to Fighter Command as Commander, Eastern Sector. Other staff appointments followed before he retired in 1963 when he was appointed CB.

In civilian life Worrall was managing director of the Advertising Poster Bureau. An enthusiastic skier, he was chairman of the RAF Ski and Winter Sports Association.,

He was twice married and had two sons and a daughter.

January 15 1988

# CAPT J. W. GRANT

CAPTAIN J. W. GRANT, who has died aged 86, was the senior surviving officer of the celebrated Second World War light cruiser *Penelope* – sometimes known as "HMS Pepperpot".

Grant was her executive officer and second in command when *Penelope* arrived in Malta in October 1941 to join Force K in the Mediterranean, disrupting enemy convoys taking supplies for Rommel's Afrika Korps from Italy across to Libya.

Grant was mentioned in despatches for his part in one night action in the early hours of Nov 9, when Force K – forewarned by Ultra special intelligence – sank all seven merchant ships in a convoy and one of its escorting warships. Force K was back in harbour unscathed an hour later; *Penelope*'s only casualties being six canaries who died of heart failure when the guns fired.

In March 1942, Penelope took part in one of the most famous of all cruiser actions, known as the Second Battle of Sirte, when Rear-Adml Philip Vian with four cruisers and seven destroyers successfully defended a

Malta convoy against a vastly superior Italian fleet which included heavy cruisers and the battleship *Littorio*. At the height of the excitement, Grant – whose action station was aft – rang the bridge to find out what was happening and was told there "seemed to be a battleship about." Grant asked where. "If you put your head out of the scuttle, sir, you will see it trailing us."

Indeed it was, but by masterly use of destroyer smokescreens and skilful handling of his greatly out-gunned and outranged cruisers, Vian held the enemy battleship off until dusk and the convoy escaped. Even *Penelope*'s surviving canaries, now battle-hardened, sang on deck throughout the battle.

The part played in this action by *Penelope*, her captain, officers and ship's company later formed the basis of C. S. Forrester's novel, *The Ship*. *Penelope* was showered with well-deserved honours, Grant himself receiving a DSO.

Alongside in Malta, *Penelope* became the special target of Luftwaffe bombers who eventually hit and damaged her. When she finally sailed for Gibraltar, having fired some 5,000 4in shells and 75,000 rounds of smaller calibre in her own defence against attacking aircraft, she had more than a thousand wooden plugs sealing the shrapnel holes in her hull – hence her sobriquet of "Pepperpot."

Penelope was always one of the happiest of ships, for which Grant can take much credit. She had her own songs, verse and radio scripts, many of them printed in *Our Penelope* (1943), to which Grant contributed.

*Penelope*'s sense of humour was famous. When the Italian Gen "Electric Whiskers" Berganzoli was captured, *Penelope*'s comment was: "Electrico B of Benghazi tried hard to look though like a Nazi / at his foes he would glare through a jungle of hair / but they only guffawed and looked blasé."

On leaving *Penelope*, Grant became an equerry to King George VI and, in 1944, was mentioned in despatches a second time as Chief of Staff to the Flag Officer British Assault Area for the D-Day landings in Normandy. Later, he commanded the escort carrier, *Searcher*, in the East Indies Fleet.

John William Grant was born in India in 1902 and joined the Navy in 1915, going to Osborne and Dartmouth. He never specialised, but served in all kinds of ships from battleships to Yangtze river gunboats.

Grant had a lifelong interest in training young people. Before the war he served in the training cruiser, *Frobisher*, and was also involved in the organisation of a new training scheme for "upper yardmen" (officer candidates from the lower deck).

After the war, he commanded the training carrier, *Indefatigable*. In 1953, he was ADC to the Queen. On retiring from the Navy, he was director of activities at Gordonstoun under Kurt Hahn and then headmaster of the Gloucestershire County Council school at Cowley Manor until his retirement in 1967.

He leaves a widow, a son and a daughter.

January 30 1988

# COL CHARLES CLARK

COLONEL CHARLES CLARK, who has died aged 99, had a remarkable record in the First World War, winning the DSO and MC, and on one memorable occasion setting about the organisation of a foxhunt at the Front.

Encouraged by the presence of a former Master of the Wexford Hounds, Clark and some companions in the South Irish Horse acquired a somewhat scruffy fox, whose stamina they built up with a liberal diet of fowl. Unfortunately before the chase could begin the fox was claimed by a member of another regiment, who proved that he had brought the beast to France as a pet and that it had escaped.

When war broke out in 1914, Clark, already a member of the Warwickshire Yeomanry, was quickly commissioned into the Machine-Gun Corps. He served in the trenches for two years, during which time he was awarded the MC on the Somme and also developed a special mounting for heavy machine guns which enabled them to blanket the target with plunging fire.

In 1916 Clark became a convert to tank warfare and by 1917 was the first commander of the central repair works, which concentrated on keeping tanks mobile and battle-worthy in the appalling conditions of the Western Front. He soon extended his activities into maintenance and recovery in the forward areas. By 1918 he had added a DSO to his MC and had been twice mentioned in despatches.

Charles Willoughby Clark was born in 1888 and educated at Atherstone Grammar School, which he left at the age of 14 to begin his apprenticeship with Alfred Herbert, the Coventry machine tool company, working for a penny-halfpenny an hour in a 54-hour week and clocking on at 6 am. By the end of his apprenticeship he was earning 3d an hour.

After two years working for Daimler's he returned to Alfred Herbert's where he specialised in developing the export market and subsequently built up a worldwide market for its products. At the outbreak of the Second World War he recruited and commanded a Balloon Barrage Unit for Coventry, for which he became the Squadron Leader in the Auxiliary Air Force.

Herbert's was frequently bombed but maintained a high output of essential war equipment and opened an additional factory at Lutterworth. Clark's first attempt to acquire a building in the area brought him into conflict with Frank Whittle, who was secretly developing jet engines in it.

In 1958, when he was already 66, Clark became chairman of Alfred Herbert, an appointment he held until he was 77. By the time of his final retirement the firm was in severe trouble from foreign competitors, and although heavily subsidised by the government it eventually ceased to trade. Clark was unfairly blamed for the company's troubles, which derived from complacency, failure to modernise and restrictive practices. During his chairmanship it had always been profitable.

Clark had always been a keen sportsman and rode to hounds with the Atherstone Hunt. He was also an eminently enthusiastic fisherman, expert with the fly and on the chalk streams, but also able to land a 260lb swordfish in New Zealand.

He was a Deputy Lieutenant for Warwickshire and Master of the Playing Card Makers. His wife, Dickie, whom he married in 1916, and his son and daughter all died before him.

March 11 1988

# GP CAPT BARRY SUTTON

GROUP CAPTAIN BARRY SUTTON, who has died aged 69, was a Battle of Britain Fighter pilot who – like Richard Hillary, author of *The Last Enemy* – was badly burned and wrote a classic account of the air war in the summer of 1940.

But, in contrast to Hillary's prose, Sutton poured out his heart in a long poem, *The Summer of the Firebird*, which was broadcast by Martin Jarvis on BBC Radio 4 to mark the battle's 40th anniversary.

An authorised "ace", with at least 6½ kills over France, Britain and Burma, the quiet and modest Sutton was sensitive about his success. Reflecting in his poem on a bomber and its crew he had shot down while flying with No 56 Hurricane Squadron, in August 1940, he wrote:

> *They found the wreck near Colchester*
> *And offered me a prize I would have wished not to see:*
> *A thin wallet in which there were two green banknotes,*
> *   two tickets for a theatre in Paris and a snapshot of a*
> *   young woman whose eyes condemned.*

Fraser Barton Sutton was born at Witney, Oxford, in 1919 and educated at Northampton School. In 1936 he joined the *Northampton Chronicle and Echo* as a reporter, later switching to the *Nottingham Journal and Evening News*, while training at weekends in the RAFVR.

Granted a short service commission in April 1939, he joined No 56 Squadron and was wounded in one foot during the fall of France. He was in the thick of the July and August fighting over the Channel and southern England, evocatively describing the inside of his Hurricane cockpit:

> *Breathe its heady mist of hot oil, hot glycol,*
> *The musky tang of those snarling pipes*
> *Ranging the blunted snout.*

Then, on August 26, Sutton was shot down in a blazing Hurricane:

*Now, the fluttering of silk above, this swooning through*
    *space —*
*In silence.*
*Silence, except for the sound of a bird. Unashamed I*
    *babble and pray, and hold aloft hands from which*
    *already hang*
*Long skeins of flesh*
*The smell of this singed oxygen mask and my cheeks*
*So God, the last communicant, after so much neglect, and*
    *this bird singing*
*Somewhere below,*
*Alone remain to listen in this quiet.*
*Falling and blazing against the distance haze*
*I saw my shattered, spent, Hurricane,*
*Slowly writhe and smoke its epitaph.*
*Do I care where it falls?*
*I ought, but Dear God I am ashamed.*

"Fried", as was said at the time, Sutton was treated at the RAF Hospital, Halton, and by early 1942 found himself again in action.

Flying with No 135, another Hurricane Squadron, at

Mingaladon as the Japanese drove into Burma and on to India, he edged up his score to a certain 6½, surviving combats in which 22 Hurricanes were lost for the gain of 50 Japanese aircraft. By 1944 Sutton commanded a Wing of Hurricanes and Spitfires and helped to drive the Japanese out of Burma, his long spell of operations being acknowledged with a DFC.

He remained in the RAF, receiving a series of staff appointments and station commands until in 1962 he joined the British Defence Liaison Staff in Australia before returning in 1965 to command RAF Bassingbourn before retirement the following year.

Sutton, who published *The Way of a Pilot* in 1942, is survived at their home in Jersey by his wife and their two daughters.

March 17 1988

# BRIG HENRY CUBITT-SMITH

BRIGADIER HENRY CUBITT-SMITH, one of the most highly regarded and popular officers of the old Indian Army, who has died aged 88, led his regiment, the 1/12 Frontier Force, in the final assault on the Cassino position in May 1944, for which he won the DSO.

This involved crossing the swift-flowing Gari River in canvas assault boats against fierce enemy opposition to establish a vital bridgehead. The success of the operation was a tribute both to his personal leadership and to his meticulous training of his battalion.

Cubitt-Smith managed to weld together the divergent elements under his command, creating high morale and close comradeship in a collection of emergency commissioned officers, Sikhs, Dogras, Punjabi mussulmen and Pathans.

Henry Ernest Cubitt-Smith was born at Tanjore, near Madras, in 1900. Although intended for Winchester, financial disasters left him a penniless orphan at the age of 14.

His father, however, had been a Freemason, and young Henry obtained a place at the Royal Masonic School, Bushey, where he was head of school and captain of rugby, football, cricket and hockey, as well as *victor ludorum*. After training at the military school in Quetta he was commissioned into the Indian Army in 1919.

Following a period in the 53rd Sikhs depot, he joined the 2/4th 2nd Force Dogras for service in Waziristan, where he was mentioned in despatches. In 1921 he joined the 1st Battalion of the 12th Frontier Force Regiment in Kohat.

Most of his early service was spent on the North-West Frontier, either with his battalion or with the South Waziristan Scouts of the Frontier Force. Cubitt-Smith encouraged his junior officers to spend as much time in the jungle as possible, sometimes to shoot tiger and lion, and at others to photograph or study wildlife. Among several encounters with snakes, he liked to recall meeting a king cobra and his queen face to face in thick jungle, and diverting their attention with a shot from his 12-bore.

In the first two years of the Second World War he was senior staff officer to the military adviser-in-chief, Indian State Forces, for which he was appointed OBE. In

1942, he returned to his battalion as commandant and led them through the battles of the Italian campaign.

After the war, as commander of the Peshawar Frontier Brigade Group, Cubitt-Smith was responsible for internal security in the Peshawar District at the mouth of the Khyber Pass immediately before independence. In that capacity he was present at the encounter of Lord Mountbatten and a crowd of 75,000 restive tribesmen in April 1947 – an occasion which helped the last Viceroy to decide that the partition of India and the creation of Pakistan were essential.

After the end of the Raj Cubitt-Smith commanded the North Norfolk sector of the Home Guard, for which he was appointed CBE. He also served his county as a deputy lieutenant and county councillor.

He was to the fore in Anglo-German reunions and commemorations at Cassino in recent years, and in 1986 was awarded the European Peace Gold Cross – only the seventh Briton to receive the cross, which is given for promoting tolerance, understanding and friendship.

Cubitt-Smith had a remarkable repertoire of stories – all of them true – many of which he printed in his book, *Yadagri: Memories of the Raj*. They included that of a well-dined major-general trying to light his cigar with a geranium, and succeeding after a tactful ADC had inserted a lighter from the other side.

He also recalled Gen Gwatkin's first interview with the especially taciturn Lord Wavell, the penultimate Viceroy of India. Gwatkin entered the office, saluted and was motioned to a seat. No word was spoken, so after 15 minutes Gwatkin got up and saluted; Wavell nodded, and Gwatkin marched out.

Cubitt-Smith's first wife, the former Hilda Dobson, died in 1963; and he married secondly, in 1968, the former Patsy Lister, who survives him with a daughter of his first marriage.

June 11 1988

# AIR CDRE "FREDDIE" WEST, VC

AIR COMMODORE "FREDDIE" WEST, who has died aged 92, was the last surviving British VC of the First World War.

When war broke out West was 18, employed as a clerk in the foreign correspondence department of a Zurich bank. Deciding that fist-fights with the German clerk on the next stool were an inadequate response to the Kaiser, he returned home to London to enlist.

He began his service in the Royal Army Medical Corps, but by May 1915 he had been commissioned in the Royal Munster Fusiliers, and in November he arrived in France in charge of 20 men. In 1917, convinced that "trench warfare was for rats, not men", he joined the Royal Flying Corps.

After an air-artillery spotting course at Brooklands he was posted to No 3 Squadron as an observer, then trained as a pilot and joined No 8 Squadron at Amiens, where his commanding officer, Major Trafford Leigh-Mallory, greeted his new recruits with the words: "You gentlemen are just the chickens the red German eagles are looking for."

Leigh-Mallory's warning referred to the famous ace Manfred von Richthofen, the "Red Baron", and his "circus" of red-painted Fokkers, whom West was soon to encounter. One Sunday in April 1918 he was pat-rolling the area of St Quentin-Amiens when his observer spotted three red Fokkers.

To his astonishment, West saw one of the Fokkers fall to the ground. He landed near the crashed enemy machine and was greeted by a jubilant Australian artillery officer who said: "We've had a bit of luck. Guess who we've shot down?" West inspected the dead pilot and found himself looking at the Red Baron, "quite calm in death – he might have died in bed".

He telephoned his commanding officer, who was sceptical: "Don't go and ruin your reputation by originating sensational rumours." Leigh-Mallory had later to eat his words – though the Australian gunner's claim to have bagged the Red Baron was disputed by a Canadian pilot of No 209 Squadron.

On August 10 of that year, flying a two-seater Armstrong F8 reconnaissance machine in the recently formed RAF, West was attacked by seven enemy aeroplanes while on hedge-hopping reconnaissance far over enemy lines. Early in the engagement one of his legs was partially severed by an explosive bullet, falling powerless into the controls and rendering the machine unmanageable.

West managed to extricate his disabled leg, regained control and, although wounded in the other leg, manoeuvred his aircraft so skilfully that his observer, Alec Haslam, was able to open fire on the enemy machines and drive them off.

In the words of the citation: "Captain West then,

with rare courage and determination, brought his machine over our lines and landed safely. Exhausted by his exertions, he fainted, but on regaining consciousness insisted on writing his report."

Ferdinand "Freddie" West was born in London in 1896. After the death of his father in the Boer War, his mother, Countess Clemence de la Garde de Saignes, took him to Italy, where he became trilingual in English, French and Italian – an asset in later postings as a diplomat. He was educated at the Xaverian College, Brighton, the Lycée Berchet and Genoa University, where he read international law.

After the action for which he was awarded the VC, West was treated at the London Hospital and fitted with an artificial leg at Roehampton. Awarded £250 compensation for loss of a limb, he invested £200 in war bonds and went off to Paris, where he paid £20 for a superior wooden leg. Later he was made an even better one by the Swiss tool manufacturer de Soutter, who had also lost a leg.

Although he had been invalided out, within a year West was back in uniform, employed as the RAF's first diplomat at the Foreign Office – where his Navy and Army opposite numbers also had wooden legs. He soon returned to flying, though. He joined No 17 Squadron and was posted in 1928 as adjutant at the flying-boat base in Malta. After commanding No 4 Squadron – he was Douglas Bader's CO when the fighter ace lost his legs – West returned to diplomacy in the late 1930s, when he was appointed British air attaché to Finland, Estonia and Latvia.

After the outbreak of the Second World War he found himself back in Amiens, commanding a wing in the Air Component of the British Expeditionary Force; but shortly after he was appointed air attaché in Rome, as acting air commodore. In June 1940, when Italy came into the war, West was ordered to Switzerland as air attaché – though he was effectively head of British air intelligence.

Freddie West soon became a familiar figure there, limping through the streets of Berne, followed by his White Russian bodyguard. He engaged in a range of covert activities, his most notable coup being the retrieval from a crashed German aircraft of a tin box containing an extensive card index of Luftwaffe dispositions in Italy, which was rapturously received by the Air Ministry.

In 1946 he resigned from his post as head of the Directorate of Foreign Liaison at the Air Ministry, joined the Rank Organisation and became managing director of Eagle-Lion Distributors. Other directorships followed, including chairmanship of a betting shop group.

It was not until 1971 that West acknowledged his disability by selling his house at Sunningdale and moving into a nearby bungalow – and he was still playing golf at 80. His wife, the former Winifred Leslie, died last month. He is survived by his son.

July 11 1988

# BRIG "JOE" VANDELEUR

BRIGADIER "JOE" VANDELEUR, who has died aged 84, was an engagingly stylish and idiosyncratic, if thoroughly professional, soldier.

Tall and ruddy-faced, with his battledress embellished by a Colt .45 and an emerald green scarf, Vandeleur always led from the front, usually accompanied by a huge loudspeaker blaring out such songs as *Praise the Lord and Pass the Ammunition*.

The most dramatic episode in his career came in 1944, when he led the Irish Guards Battle Group in the spearhead on the "Bridge Too Far" at Arnhem, where the 1st Airborne were surrounded and outnumbered by the Germans. Vandeleur's task was virtually impossible, as the ground forces were hampered by canals, narrow roads and resolute German defences. In the briefing before the operation Gen Sir Brian Horrocks, commanding 30 Corps, announced that the Irish Guards would lead the assault.

Vandeleur did not react well to this news. He seemed to say, "Not us again, surely?" "What did you say, Vandeleur?" asked Horrocks. "I said how honoured we all feel, sir," replied Vandeleur. "Yes," said Horrocks, "that's what I thought you said." The scene later reached a wider audience through the film *A Bridge Too Far*, in which the part of Vandeleur was played by Michael Caine (and of Horrocks by Edward Fox).

The son of Lt-Col C. B. Vandeleur, John Ormsby Evelyn Vandeleur was born in 1903 in Nowshera on the North-West Frontier of India, where his father was serving at the time; the family belonged to the Irish Ascendancy, having settled in Cork in 1600.

Vandeleur was educated at Cheltenham and Sandhurst and commissioned into the Irish Guards in 1924. Originally he had planned to join a Highland regiment, but changed his mind because five of his cousins had been killed while serving in the Irish Guards – one in South Africa and four in the 1914–18 War.

From 1928 to 1931 he was seconded to the Sudan Defence Force, where he commanded the Camel Company and the Motor Machine-gun Battery. Vandeleur became most attached to the Sudan and later made several attempts to obtain another posting there, though without success.

Instead he became adjutant of the 1st Bn Irish Guards. He also did a tour as instructor at the machine-gun wing of the Small Arms School at Netheravon, and then as machine-gun instructor to the Egyptian army – he was a fluent Arabic speaker – before serving with the 1st Bn in Palestine.

On his return to Britain Vandeleur became second-in-command of the 2nd Bn. In 1941 he was appointed to command the 3rd Bn, and in 1944 to the Irish Guards Battle Group. He displayed such flair and leadership in the short, sharp battle for Escaut, near Lommel in Belgium, that it was later renamed "Joe's Bridge" by the locals – the name it still bears. Four days after Escaut he was chosen to lead 30 Corps in the attempt to relieve 1st Airborne.

In November 1944 Vandeleur was appointed to command 129 Infantry Birgade, and in July 1945 32 Guards Brigade. For his skill in the North West Europe Campaign he was awarded the DSO twice and also mentioned in despatches. Such was his professionalism that he could use any weapon of any unit: for example, at one point in that campaign he was himself handling a "Crocodile" flame-throwing tank.

He commanded the Irish Guards from 1946 to 1948, and on his retirement in 1951 was granted the honorary rank of brigadier. He then became the Chief Constable of the Ministry of Defence Police.

Vandeleur wrote an autobiography, *A Soldier's Story*, which has less to say about himself than others: exceptionally modest, he attached little value to his own achievements; and he could usually lighten the atmosphere when others became pompous about theirs. In his youth he was a keen sportsman – a good horseman and a useful polo player – and also learned to fly.

He was twice a widower, and had no children.

August 10 1988

# LT-GEN SIR ALEXANDER DRUMMOND

LIEUTENANT-GENERAL SIR ALEXANDER DRUMMOND, who has died aged 87, was a vigorous Director-General of Army Medical Services and earlier distinguished himself in both the Second World War and the Malaya Emergency, being mentioned in despatches six times.

The redoubtable "Alex" Drummond first made his mark in India in the mid-1930s by devising a self-help "iron lung" for a soldier suffering from paralysis of his respiratory muscles after a snake bite. Two large oil drums were welded together with a rubber collar to support the head and neck; pressure for the lung was supplied by an ordinary vacuum cleaner motor and the vent had to be operated manually.

On the outbreak of war Drummond took over the RAF Hospital Sarafand in Palestine, expanding it to 1,200 beds. When Syria collapsed in 1940 and the Vichy French took over, he organised the breakthrough of many medical units belonging to the Poles, the Czechs and the Free French.

Later in 1940 he put together a hospital train running between Palestine and Egypt. In 1942 Drummond went into Iraq and Iran where Indian units were mobilising; at one stage he managed to combine the jobs of Assistant Director Medical Services (Poles) HQ 10 Corps and Officer Commanding 31 Indian General Hospital.

Next he moved on to the Italian campaign, liaising with Gen Clark's American Army until the final push into Trieste. While commanding the British Military Hospital at Taranto, which treated German PoWs and Yugoslavs, he established firm friendships with the latter – language problems were overcome by Drummond holding up his hand in salute with the stumps of his two missing fingers evident.

The commissar of the Yugoslavs did not understand English so Drummond's unit toast was "Balls to the Commissar!" Unfortunately the next commissar turned out to have a greater grasp of the language.

Drummond helped with the rebuilding of the Yugoslav Medical Services and also served in Greece. After the war, following a spell as adviser in oto-laryngology and a brisk stint as officer commanding the Queen Alexandra Military Hospital, Millbank, he took over the difficult job of organising medical services for troops fighting in the Malayan jungle.

Drummond made an immediate impression on reporting to Gen Sir Gerald Templer. "If you don't like my methods," he told that strong-minded commander, "you had better send home for another doctor." Henceforth the two worked together most successfully.

Drummond coped admirably with the generalised ringworm and severe local infections such as scrub typhus, leptospirosis, malaria and encephalitis which plagued the British and Gurkha troops fighting the Chinese Communist bandits. He also helped to set up the Lady Templer Hospital for Gurkhas.

William Alexander Duncan Drummond was born in 1901 at Cape Town where his father was working for the Anglo-American Tobacco Co. The family later moved to England and he studied engineering, losing two fingers of his left hand while working in the Liverpool shipyards.

He completed his education at Dundee and St Andrews Universities, qualifying as a doctor in 1924. He joined the Royal Army Medical Corps in 1925 after working as an ear, nose and throat registrar at Charing Cross Hospital.

As Director-General of Army Medical Services from 1956 to 1961 he worked a seven-day week, insisting that medical training should be expanded to the highest and lowest ranks of the corps. He also formed a pioneering central supply centre for the sterilisation of all dressings and instruments supplied to Army units.

He had a lifelong interest in spreading knowledge of first aid and wrote a textbook of training for the St John

Ambulance Brigade. He was tough and forthright and his demonic energy and enthusiasm were contagious.

He was an honorary surgeon to the Queen and Colonel Commandant of the RAMC, being appointed OBE in 1945, CBE in 1951, CB in 1954 and KBE in 1957. In 1929 he married Mabel Fullegar, a scientist, who survives him.

September 21 1988

# MAJ-GEN MAX SAWERS

MAJOR-GENERAL MAX SAWERS, who has died aged 68, was an imperturbable, cheerful and decisive officer whose adventurous life often took him into situations where all those qualities were required to the full.

When serving with the 81st West African Divisional Signals in the jungle-covered mountains of the Arakan, Burma, in 1944, shortage of transport necessitated that every officer, and British and African soldier, had to carry a minimum headload of 40lb in addition to his personal equipment. Requests for jellied acid for the radio batteries were dismissed by the War Office as "unnecessary" and in consequence acid had to be carried as headloads in carboys, some of which exploded on the unfortunates underneath.

Having been promised a horse or a vehicle, Sawers found at the end of the campaign that instead he had marched 1,000 miles, most of it "straight up or straight down". Eventually his unit was allotted some bullocks for transport. As these were white and would thus attract Japanese attention, they painted them green; however when the beasts proved both "useless and idle on hills" the soldiers ate them and carried the loads themselves.

James Maxwell Sawers was born in 1920 of a military family and was educated at Rugby and Woolwich. He was commissioned into the Royal Corps of Signals a few weeks before the outbreak of the Second World War and served in West Africa, commanding the Gambia Area Signals.

He was then posted to 81st West African Divisional Signals in Nigeria and went with them to Burma in 1943. Sawers served on long-range penetration operations and for several months commanded the regiment when his commanding officer was in hospital; he was then 24.

He was mentioned in despatches in 1945 and 1946. In 1952 he went out to Korea as a squadron commander in the 1st Commonwealth Divisional Signal Regiment. When the campaign settled down to a period of trench warfare, Sawers devised ingenious deception tactics which caused the Chinese to direct their artillery barrages on to unoccupied areas.

Subsequently he was on the staff at HQ Malaya Command before returning in 1955 to become chief instructor at the School of Signals which at that time housed the "think-tank" for future policy planning and subsequently produced new concepts of tactical communication systems.

Later he was closely concerned with the top secret world of Signals Intelligence in BAOR and introduced the new method of area communications, code-named "Bruin", which eventually led to the renowned "Ptarmigan" system.

In 1971 Sawers was appointed Signal Officer-in-Chief (Army) at the Ministry of Defence, where his three years coincided with two general elections, cuts in the defence budget and crises in Northern Ireland, Malta, the Middle East and Honduras.

The numerous demands made on his Corps demanded steady and cheerful leadership, and morale was kept at a high level by his frequent visits to remote units which might otherwise have thought they were forgotten. He also reorganised officer training, introduced reforms in the Corps trade structure, and obtained government approval for the Ptarmigan communications funding.

In retirement Sawers became managing director of the Army Kinema Corporation and managing trustee of the Soldiers' Widows' Fund and Single Soldiers' Dependants Fund. He was also Colonel Commandant of the Royal Signals and honorary colonel of 71 (Yeomanry) Signal Regiment.

Sawers always tackled every situation with a cheerful smile, even when he was diagnosed as suffering from cancer. He was a skilful dinghy helmsman and an enthusiastic skier, golfer, photographer and gardener.

He was appointed MBE in 1953 and CB in 1974. In 1945 he married Grace Walker, who survives him with their two sons and a daughter.

October 1 1988

# AIR MARSHAL
# SIR HAROLD "MICKEY"
# MARTIN

AIR MARSHAL SIR HAROLD "MICKEY" MARTIN, who has died aged 70, was a fearless and brilliant low-level bomber ace who took part in the celebrated attack on the Möhne and Eder dams in May 1943 – portrayed in the film *The Dambusters*.

Later the Australian-born "Mickey" Martin established another reputation as a master of Mosquito aircraft night-intruder operations over enemy airfields in Europe and in low-level marking for heavy bomber attacks. The exceptional effectiveness of his career as an operational pilot was recognised in multiple awards, bringing his tally of decorations to DSO and Bar, DFC and two Bars and AFC.

By the spring of 1943, when he joined No 617, the "Dambuster" squadron of four-engine Lancaster bombers, Martin had already been blooded in No 455, an Australian Hampden bomber squadron and No 50 squadron of Lancasters. But it was in 617 that his outstanding skills in low-level attack reached their apogee.

Gp Capt Leonard Cheshire, at one time his commander in 617, said: "It was only when I met him that I realised all I had to learn. I learned everything I knew of the low flying game from Mick. He was the ideal wartime operational pilot. He had superb temperament, was quite fearless and innovative in his thinking. He was meticulous in his flying discipline and never did make a mistake." Indeed Martin was punctilious to the point of personally polishing every inch of his perspex cockpit canopy.

When Martin joined 617 in March 1943, his commanding officer was Wg Cdr Guy Gibson, whom he had met beforehand at Buckingham Palace when Gibson was there for a DSO and Martin for his first DFC; they had swapped notes on low flying.

On the night of the dambusting raid Martin was in Formation 1, detailed to go for the Möhne dam. As he arrived over the target area Bob Hay, his bomb aimer, seeing the 100ft-thick reinforced concrete, exclaimed: "God, can we break that?"

As he went in, Martin tracked head on for the middle of the dam between its towers as they stood out in the moonlight. Then the flak gunners spotted him and concentrated a curtain of fire where he must pass — between the towers.

"Bomb gone," reported Hay as he released the Barnes Wallis-designed bouncing bomb — the one that skipped the water as in the child's game of Ducks and Drakes — and in that moment two shells hit the Lancaster's starboard wing, one exploding in an inner fuel tank. But Martin was lucky: the tank was empty. At that stage the dam seemed to be still there.

Then, shortly afterwards, Gibson heard Martin shout: "Hell, it's gone. It's gone. Look at it for Christ's sake!"

After the raid Martin was ordered to report to the Royal Australian Air Force in London for an interview for the Australian press. Encountering a dark, attractive Australian girl called Wendy — she was the daughter of the Melbourne artist Ida Outhwaite — he lost interest in the required official "line-shoot" and asked his interviewer to lunch. Shortly afterwards they were married.

Harold Brownlow Morgan Martin was born in 1918 and seemed destined to follow his father into the medical profession. After attending Randwick High School for Boys, Sydney Grammar School and Lyndfield College, he had various adventures in England, including a spell as a gentleman-rider.

On the outbreak of the Second World War he joined the Cavalry Division of the Australian Army before switching to the RAF in 1940 and being commissioned into the RAF Volunteer Reserve the following year. In the autumn of 1941 Martin began his low-flying apprenticeship in 455 Squadron.

One night his Hampden was so low over Kassel that he hit a balloon cable. Had the cable not been carried away and dangled from his wing, his career would have ended there and then. He eventually cleared the cable by diving to 50ft and getting it caught in a tree. On the night of the 1,000-bomber raid on Cologne in May 1942, Martin, in a 50 Squadron Lancaster, had another lucky let-off.

He was awarded his first DFC in this period after a particularly hair-raising exploit in which his Hampden was hit in many places, one engine catching fire.

Martin had commanded 617 temporarily before Cheshire took over, along with the squadron's newly minted motto: *Apres Moi Le Deluge*. Cheshire had voluntarily dropped from group captain to wing commander for the privilege and soon he and Martin were making a formidable team.

In February 1944 Cheshire marked the Gnome and Rhone engines factory at Limoges from a height of 200ft,

supported by Martin and the rest of 617, then demol-
ished the works with extraordinary accuracy.

In operations against V-weapon sites in France,
Martin acted as master or deputy master-bomber. During
an attack on a vital rail viaduct at Antheor, in Italy,
Martin literally flew down the side of a mountain to
mark the target at low level. In this attack his bomb
aimer, Bob Hay, was killed by a cannon shell which
struck his forehead.

During June 1944 Martin moved into the equally
perilous business of low-level night-intruding with No
515 Squadron of Mosquitos and developed a speciality
for baiting flak gunners to draw their fire.

Cheshire said that Martin had an innate sense for
turning up at the right place at the right time. Once,
after their ways had parted from 617, Cheshire broke
silence over the Rhine to inquire about the weather. Out
of the blue and a Mosquito came Martin's voice. "What
the hell are you doing?" Cheshire asked.

Back came the characteristic "Sticking my neck out
for you types." And he was, beating up a night-fighter
airfield to protect the bombers.

After the war Martin flew Transport Command
Stirlings and Yorks and in 1947, in a Mosquito, set a
London to Cape Town record for which he was awarded
the Britannia Trophy and his AFC. The next year, flying
a Mosquito, he nursed six RAF Vampire jets in the first
jet crossing of the Atlantic.

Less at home in the peacetime air force, Martin
nevertheless climbed through a succession of staff
appointments and a post as air attaché in Tel Aviv to a
number of commands. He was Air Officer Commanding
No 38 Group, Air Support Command C-in-C RAF

Germany and Commander Nato 2nd Tactical Air Force; and air member for personnel, Ministry of Defence, until he retired in 1974. He then held posts with Hawker Siddeley.

Martin retained his love of the Turf and owned a racehorse called Amber Call shortly after the war. He also enjoyed polo, as well as pottery and painting, relishing his membership of the Chelsea Arts Club.

Martin, who was appointed CB in 1968 and KCB in 1971, is survived by his wife and two daughters.

November 4 1988

# SIR THOMAS SOPWITH

SIR THOMAS SOPWITH, the early aviator and aeroplane maker who has died aged 101, had an extraordinary career which encompassed the design and production of military machines for the Royal Flying Corps in the First World War, the RAF's first modern monoplane eight-gun fighter in the 1930s and the world's first jump-jet in the 1960s.

The creator of the Sopwith Camel and Pup, he also had overall responsibility for the Second World War Hurricane and the present-day Harrier. As if those achievements were not enough, "Tommy" Sopwith perkily confided to the television cameras in a documentary on his 100th birthday that he had also contested the America's Cup.

Thomas Octave Murdoch Sopwith was born on January 10 1888, the eighth child and only son of a prosperous civil engineer. After being privately educated as an engineer, young Tom indulged the pursuit of speed on water and land. Fascinated by the possibilities of the internal combustion engine, he also gratified a compulsive urge to fly.

In retrospect, the smooth progress of Sopwith's career gives the illusion that it was predestined early in the century and that to succeed he had merely to survive the perils of his pioneer flying exploits. In reality, his success was the result of his personal vision, powers of concentration and talent for employing the right combination of apparently unremarkable men, who just happened to be there when he most needed them.

Under Sopwith's leadership Fred Sigrist, Harry Hawker, Sidney Camm and Frank Spriggs, recruited almost haphazardly, provided the engineering, design and managerial skills of Sopwith Aviation and its successor, Hawkers. In 1910 Sigrist, hired as chauffeur and odd-job man, began to care for Sopwith's part-owned 166-ton schooner, *Neva*, six-cylinder 40-horsepower Napier motor-car, motor-boats and three aeroplanes. By this time Sopwith had already crewed the winning yacht in the 1909 Royal Aero Club race and satisfied a teenage zest for ballooning.

His passion for flying dated from a day in 1910. Putting into Dover from sea he was told that a Bleriot had just landed after crossing the Channel for the first time with a passenger. On finding the pilot in a field seven miles away, he decided on the spot to turn from balloons to aeroplanes.

Within hours he arrived at Brooklands where, inside the concrete motor-racing circuit, flying lessons and joyrides were being offered in a Henry Farman machine. Producing a £5 note, Sopwith booked two circuits.

From that moment he was "terribly bitten by the aviation bug", and paid £630 for a 40-horsepower Bleriot-inspired Avis monoplane built under the railway arches at Battersea. It was delivered to him at Brooklands on October 21 1910, and he crashed it the same day.

Alarmed at the rate at which he was spending money, Sopwith decided to make flying pay by winning prizes. Flourishing his flying certificate (the 31st issued in Britain), he contested the Michelin Cup for the longest non-stop flight by a British pilot in a British machine and, more rewardingly, the £4,000 Baron de Forest trophy for the longest non-stop flight from any point in England to anywhere on the Continent.

By the end of 1910 he had landed both, but not without the indispensable assistance of Sigrist. It was Sigrist who, on December 18 1910, produced the engine-coaxing plan which enabled his employer to bank Baron de Forest's £4,000 after completing 177 miles in 3 hours and 40 minutes to land in Belgium.

Confident that he was now financially and technically equipped to compete in America, in 1911 Sopwith organised a tour of "air meets". At first his arrival, accompanied by his sister, May, was far from welcome in the camp of the pioneer Wright brothers, Wilbur and Orville. They attempted to claim the patent on passenger carrying, which would have ruled out May and her picnic basket of thermos flasks. But the Wrights were appeased when Sopwith, after wrecking his Bleriot, purchased one of their biplanes.

Beginning to win prizes of as much as $14,000 and appearing before crowds of up to 300,000 spectators, he polished his performance in the popular quick start competitions until he could run and jump into the seat of his moving machine in nine seconds.

Having survived a crash into the sea off Manhattan Beach in the autumn of 1911, Sopwith returned to Brooklands where he opened a flying school. Among his earliest pupils were two men whose names were to become better known to the public than that of their instructor.

One was Harry Hawker. Still in his teens and a mechanic since running away from school in Australia, he had hung around the Brooklands perimeter until hired by Sopwith to join Sigrist as another dogsbody. The other was Major Hugh Trenchard, "Father" of the RAF, who urgently needed a certificate before taking up an appointment at the Services' recently established Central Flying School.

As the First World War approached, the nascent Sopwith Aviation Company outgrew its Brooklands shed. Soon Sigrist and Hawker (already Sopwith's test pilot) were chalking the outline of a biplane, known as the Hybrid, on the wooden floor of the disused roller-skating rink Sopwith had bought up-river at Kingston upon Thames.

Early in 1914, Hawker was in Australia demonstrating the Tabloid (a machine which would shortly distinguish itself as a Royal Flying Corps scout). In his absence Sopwith, who had roughed out modifications on the back of an envelope, selected Howard Pixton to fly one of the machines with floats in the Schneider Trophy competition held at Monte Carlo.

Sopwith had designed and built the airframe but selected his engine in France. It was a 100-horsepower

Monosoupape Gnome, which he brought back "almost literally in my suitcase".

Shortly before the outbreak of the First World War Sopwith also designed a side-by-side two-seater modelled on the Tabloid, for Winston Churchill, First Lord of the Admiralty. Called the Sociable, it was popularly referred to as "Tweenie".

As the Tabloid went to war Sopwith stopped flying. It was not a conscious decision, as he later explained: "I was so occupied with design and manufacture that I just didn't have the time to fly and did not pilot an aeroplane for about 16 years."

That was a characteristic understatement which over-looked the continual reinforcement of the RFC, the Royal Naval Air Service and, after April 1 1918, the RAF on the Western Front with Pups, Camels, Triplanes and other machines destined to become museum celebrities.

By the end of the war two of Sopwith's factories were rolling out 90 fighters a week. Sopwith plants had built 16,000 machines in Britain and 10,000 in France. Camel pilots notched up the highest number of "kills" – 2,700.

After the Armistice the market for aircraft contracted almost as rapidly as it had expanded. But amid the gloom one beacon beckoned – the *Daily Mail* Atlantic Flight competition. Sopwith entered the Sopwith B1, which boasted special features designed by Hawker. On May 18 1919, Hawker took off from Newfoundland on the west-east crossing accompanied by Cdr Kenneth Mackenzie-Grieve as navigator.

Less than half-way Hawker was forced to put down in the sea and the pair were presumed lost. King George V sent a telegram of condolence to Mrs Hawker before it was learned that the *Mary*, a small Danish freighter, had rescued the airmen.

A month later John Lacock and Arthur Whitten Brown achieved the first Atlantic crossing in a Vickers Vimy and were knighted. The following year, Sopwith put the company into voluntary liquidation while it remained solvent. Hawker registered the H. G. Hawker Engineering Company and acquired a motor-cycle business.

Shortly afterwards "the gang", as Sopwith called his pioneering team, met up. Sopwith, Sigrist, Hawker and Spriggs were unanimous in their decision: "Let's make aeroplanes again".

In less than a year Hawker was dead. He had crashed his Nieuport Goshawk while testing it for entry in the 1921 Aerial Derby.

Sopwith put his heart and money into developing the Hawker Aircraft Co, which totally eclipsed the name and achievements of the former Sopwith Aviation Co. This meant that designs which might reasonably have been designated Sopwith's have entered history under the name of Hawker, though – to confuse the matter further – coming from the drawing board of Sidney Camm.

In the 1920s and 1930s Sopwith masterminded the gradual growth of the company as its military and civil designs found markets at home and abroad. The Hawker Hart, Hind, Demon, Fury, Hornet, Audax and Hotspur are merely a few of the best remembered names. There was also the little Tomtit trainer for which Sopwith – and the Duke of Windsor – always had a soft spot.

Sopwith told a favourite anecdote about it. George Bulman, his chief test pilot, was about to fly the Tomtit to Martlesham Heath for assessment by the RAF when

Sopwith climbed in and told Bulman: "Today you are my passenger."

Then, no longer the occasionally impetuous pilot of his youth, he reflected: "George, you had better take her off."

In 1930 Sopwith was elected to membership of the Royal Yacht Squadron. An outstanding helmsman, he sailed *Shamrock V* (which he had bought from the executors of the tea merchant, Sir Thomas Lipton), to win the King's Cup at Cowes in 1932. In 1935 he won it again in *Endeavour I*.

Sopwith was ambitious to repair Lipton's failure to win the America's Cup, but *Endeavour I* was foiled in 1934. His professional crew walked out after a pay dispute and he lost 4–2 to Harold Vanderbilt's *Rainbow*. *Endeavour II*, a new J-class boat, was defeated in four races by Vanderbilt's Ranger in 1937.

As *Endeavour* was being towed back to Newport a motor launch came alongside, and the helmsman called out: "You Sopwith? – I'm Fokker." Over a drink aboard *Endeavour* the former plane-making adversaries exchanged 1914–1918 reminiscences.

From 1935 Sopwith was chairman of the Hawker Siddeley group which he had put together with the help of the financier Philip Hill. The merger and reorganisation established Sopwith as Britain's foremost aircraft constructor.

After bringing Glosters, Armstrong Whitworth and A. V. Roe, builders of the Lancaster bomber, into the Hawker family Sopwith provided a foundation for the future British Aerospace. De Havilland was incorporated later.

Hawkers' consolidation and growth owed everything

to Sopwith's good judgment and imperturbable coolness. Enigmatic and rarely on the spot (he revelled in nautical and country pursuits), Sopwith maintained control by operating through an ubiquitous managing director, his former sweeper and office boy, Spriggs. Meanwhile, Sigrist, dogsbody at the start, had become the hard man of Hawkers, troubleshooting and dealing with any unpleasantness.

As the business grew Sopwith encouraged each aircraft company to retain its individuality, enabling Camm and his associated designers to produce the fruits of their particular creative talents. His genius for knowing what was going on without interfering is best illustrated by his relationship with Camm.

If at times Sopwith recoiled at Camm's authoritarian manner in the drawing office, he bit on his pipe and remembered that unemployment obliged Camm's men to put up with him. The end product was K 5083, the prototype of the Hawker Hurricane, financed by the company as a private venture.

In October 1935, George Bulman tested her at Brooklands. The Government dallied until the following summer before issuing a first contract for 600 Hurricanes.

Sopwith's investment and belief in the interceptor monoplane, at a time when the Air Ministry still favoured biplane fighters and afforded priority to bombers, reaped its reward in the Battle of Britain. At that stage the Hurricane far outnumbered the Spitfire in RAF fighter squadrons.

As the war progressed and peace came other aircraft followed, the Typhoon, Tempest, Meteor and Hunter each being destined to become part of aviation archaeology in Sopwith's lifetime. Even the revolutionary jumpjet

Harrier, which Sopwith and Camm initiated, could be said to be anticipating obsolescence while Sopwith lived.

Always a man of few words, Sopwith observed the motto on his coat-of-arms, "work without talk", to the letter and to the end. But on his 100th birthday, speaking sparingly on television from Compton Manor, his Hampshire estate near Winchester, he acknowledged the tributes of aviation's great and good as they banqueted at Brooklands in celebration.

Blind, and walking on the arm of a nurse in his garden, he lifted his head towards the sound of a replica Sopwith Pup as it circled overhead in salute. Repeating a favourite aside, he murmured: "You know, they were all done off the cuff."

Sopwith was appointed CBE in 1918 and knighted in 1953. He married first, in 1914, Beatrix Hore-Ruthven (who died in 1930), daughter of the 8th Lord Ruthven.

In 1932 he married secondly, Phyllis Brodie Gordon (who died in 1978). Their son, Tommy, also an adventurous all-rounder, survives him.

January 28 1989

# "DIXIE" DEANS

"DIXIE" DEANS, who has died aged 75, was an RAF sergeant pilot whose exploits and leadership as a prisoner of war eclipsed the contributions of many senior officers.

He had baled out when his twin-engined Whitley bomber, one of six aircraft raiding Berlin on the night of September 10 1940, battered by flak, gave up the ghost over the Dutch border. Thereafter Deans spent the remainder of the Second World War in Europe in a succession of prison camps, where he created and supported escape opportunities, as well as keeping up the morale of fellow prisoners.

As Allied and Russian advances squeezed Germany from west and east, Deans, in a remarkable prisoner of war election, was voted leader of 10,000 of his fellows. He was unflagging in his efforts to fulfil such confidence and figured in a series of exploits on their behalf until, finally, the German colonel in charge surrendered to him.

James Alexander Graham Deans was born in Glasgow in 1914 and educated at North Kelvinside Secondary School before joining the RAF in 1936. Although he was taken prisoner so early in the war he was one of Bomber Command's more experienced pilots, the Berlin raid being his 25th operation.

"Dixie" Deans – a barrack-room adaptation of the name of the famous footballer Dixie Dean – soon established his natural authority at Stalag Luft I in Barth, north Germany. Whereas it was normal practice to elect the senior officer or NCO as leader, "King Dixie" was voted in by acclamation.

When in early 1942 the Germans concentrated most of their RAF prisoners in Stalag Luft III at Sagan in Silesia he remained leader in the NCOs' compound.

After his next move in mid-1943 to a new camp, Stalag Luft VI at Heydekrug on the Memel peninsula, Deans was at the centre of a campaign of bribery and blackmail, infiltration of enemy security and, with the help of the Polish underground, establishment of an escape line to the Baltic ports.

In the camp Deans kept discipline effortlessly and

was able to control several thousand restive men on the parade ground without a word or a movement. When the Germans called a parade to announce the deaths of 50 officers recaptured after the Great Escape from Stalag Luft III, Deans defused a potentially ugly situation by the sheer force of his personality.

In his dealings with the Germans he was tactful and shrewd. When they ordered Jewish prisoners to be segregated he refused and argued strongly until they gave in.

Never too busy to listen to a personal problem, he also defended men court-martialled by the Germans. On one occasion when a PoW, bent on suicide, leapt the warning wire and charged the barbed wire fence, Deans gallantly pursued him and persuaded the man to return.

In 1944 the advancing Russians enforced the transfer of prisoners from Stalag Luft VI to Thorn in Poland, where they joined Army NCOs. Shortly afterwards all 10,000 Army and RAF prisoners were marched to Stalag 357 at Fallingbostel near Hanover. It was here that, after at first deferring to the senior regimental sergeant-major, Deans was elected leader.

As the enemy sought to march the 10,000 into their northern redoubt with a view to holding them hostage, Deans pedalled an ancient bicycle from village to village, column to column of marching men, encouraging the weary, seeking out those who were ill and insisting the Germans find transport for them

He persuaded the commandant, Col Ossmann, to drive him to Lubeck where there were Red Cross stores and arrange for truckloads of food parcels to be sent immediately. When one of the columns was strafed by the RAF and some 60 were killed he helped identify the dead and dig a mass grave.

Realising that the hard-pressed Germans could not cope with so many wounded, Deans persuaded the commandant to give him a safe conduct through their lines. He bicycled through the fighting to obtain a promise of ambulances from a British general and returned to the prisoners in a Mercedes Benz.

But the British advance became so rapid that ambulances no longer mattered and finally he persuaded German troops to lay down their arms. Col Ossmann surrendered formally to Deans, remarking that his honour demanded no more.

Warrant Officer Deans was appointed MBE in 1945. His fellow survivors felt this was insufficient recognition, but took some consolation in the unusual ending to the citation: "He was loved by all."

Afterwards he went up to Oxford and later worked in an administrative job with the London School of Economics, from which ill-health compelled him to retire in 1969.

Deans suffered for most of his post-war life from multiple sclerosis, but as president of the RAF Ex-PoW Association he continued to care for his fellows, and, though in a wheelchair, attended reunions in North America and Australasia.

He is survived by his wife, Molly, a son and a daughter.

February 21 1989

# PAT O'LEARY

MAJOR-GENERAL COUNT ALBERT GUERISSE, alias
PAT O'LEARY, who has died in Brussels aged 77, was the
remarkable Belgian medical officer who ran the O'Leary
Escape Line along which at least 600 Allied servicemen
made their way to Britain during the Second World
War.

The extraordinary saga was made possible by the
chance that Guerisse tumbled out of a skiff off the French
Mediterranean coast and attempted to pass himself off as
a French-Canadian airman requiring rescue. At the time
he was serving in the Royal Navy as a lieutenant-
commander, although until May 1940, when Belgium
was overrun, he had been serving with a Belgian cavalry
regiment as a doctor.

Later in the war, in 1943, Guerisse was captured by
the Germans, imprisoned and tortured, and sent to a
series of concentration camps including Dachau. Afterwards he returned to the Belgian Army.

While serving in Korea in 1951 as a member of the
Belgian Volunteer Battalion he was to the fore in an
open battlefield rescue, under fire, of a wounded man
which was every bit as valiant as any of his earlier
exploits. It earned him a Korean gallantry medal – an
award which he added to his George Cross, DSO and
numerous Belgian, French and other continental
decorations.

Albert Marie Edmond Guerisse was born in Brussels
in 1911, and educated at Louvain and at Brussels
University. He served as medical officer with the 1st

Belgian Lancers but after Belgium's capitulation he was evacuated from Dunkirk in the trawler *Westward Ho!*

The strength of his personality helped to obtain him a commission in the Royal Navy, and by the autumn of 1940 he was a lieutenant-commander on the "Q" ship *Fidelity* (a 1,500-ton French cargo vessel renamed and used by Special Operations Executive) under the *nom de guerre* of Patrick Albert O'Leary.

In April 1941 Guerisse/O'Leary helped to put two agents ashore just north of the eastern end of the Pyrenees when the skiff in which he was returning to his ship capsized. He swam ashore.

On being arrested by a *gendarme* he explained that he was a French-Canadian airman. He was then imprisoned near Nimes where he was contacted by Ian Garrow, a captain in the Seaforth Highlanders working for the London escape organisation MI9.

O'Leary himself duly escaped and was recruited to MI9, but that autumn Garrow was arrested by French police. Hitherto O'Leary had listened to BBC broadcasts for Garrow and acted generally as his dogsbody; now, perforce, he took over and the "Pat Line" was in business.

He found himself based at Marseilles at the head of a network of secret agents and called upon to help an increasing tide of escapers. Capable of intense concentration, highly disciplined and radiating great charm as part of his persuasive armoury, O'Leary faced up to his principal problem: money.

He needed cash to pay Spanish guards to escort escapers across the Pyrenees and to buy food for them. On average it cost £200 to get each prisoner home. O'Leary persuaded the French representative of J & P

Coats, the spinners, to part with a fortune in francs belonging to the company, on the promise that it would be reimbursed in London in sterling.

Inevitably, there was a farcical quality about some of the Pat Line's activities. On one occasion Sqn Ldr Jimmy Higginson had been in hiding at Monte Carlo and it was essential that the "parcel" (as escapers were coded) be well disguised on the perilous rail route to Marseilles. O'Leary borrowed a spare suit of clerical black from a Polish priest who was also escaping and boarded the train with them both. Higginson took the only seat available and was soon pestered by an elderly French woman.

Finally, frustration getting the better of him, the RAF pilot yanked at the real Polish priest who was standing with O'Leary in the corridor and whispered, "For God's sake, lend me your Bible."

He then buried himself in the Latin text as if his life depended on it. The Pat Line got Higginson home.

In March 1943 the Gestapo net closed on O'Leary and, betrayed by one of his own agents, he was arrested at a café in Toulouse. On searching him, his captors discovered the requisite tiny phial of potassium cyanide sewn into the hem of his jacket.

During interrogation he was locked in a large refrigerator for four hours. Beatings and solitary confinement followed.

Finally, pretending to volunteer information, he managed to fox the enemy with a load of false information. The Germans compiled a vast dossier of nonsense before despatching him to Dachau and other concentration camps.

Of the 600 or so Pat Line escapers O'Leary had personally conducted more than 250 to safety. His top individual score of "parcels" was the 48 Allied military personnel he sprang from the prison at La Turbie near Monte Carlo, scattering the parcels throughout the countryside and sending 36 out of France.

When his exceptional wartime career was recognised in 1946 with the award of the George Cross, the *London Gazette* stated that the award was made "for his exceptional work organising the escape of Allied officers and men from France; for his refusal under torture to betray his comrades when he was captured by the Gestapo; and for his great moral and physical encouragement of his fellow prisoners in various concentration camps".

After the war he soldiered on in the Belgian Army, eventually retiring in 1970 as Director-General of the Medical Service of the Belgian Forces.

In 1988 Guerisse was much distressed by Thames Television's transmission of an Australian-made dramatisation of the story of Nancy Wake, a Resistance figure. The programme implied that he broke down under torture and gave information which led to arrests. An apology was subsequently transmitted and a video of it delivered to Guerisse in Brussels.

He was awarded the DSO in 1942 (under the name of O'Leary) and appointed an honorary KBE in 1979. In 1986 he was admitted to the Hereditary Nobility of Belgium with the personal title of Count granted by the King of the Belgians.

His wife, the former Sylvia Cooper Smith, died in 1985 and he is survived by a son who has followed him into the medical profession.

March 29 1989

# MAJ-GEN JOHNNY WITT

MAJOR-GENERAL JOHNNY WITT, who has died aged 92, was commissioned in 1914 into the Army Service Corps, then jocularly known on the Western Front as "the Jam Stealers".

At that time the ASC was required to transport huge quantities of Tickler's Plum and Apple Jam in its rations, and because no other recipe ever seemed to reach the troops it was assumed – incorrectly – that the ASC had extracted all the more tasty varieties.

The ASC also, of course, transported much more dangerous cargoes than jam and had the hazardous task of moving over exposed and heavily shelled roads conveying ammunition and other explosives to the trenches. Although the courage of the ASC was regarded with awe by infantrymen (who at least could retire behind parapets or into dug-outs), the Corps was still trying to shrug off the reputation it had acquired in earlier times of being simply a transport unit operating well out of danger – a reputation which would bring a wry smile to the driver of a petrol tanker in a war zone.

Witt did much to enhance the ASC's good name and in the critical days of 1918 he won an MC for outstanding gallantry, managing to get through a vital ammunition convoy.

Curiously enough, although he had become a captain at the age of 18, Witt remained in that rank for 22 years – in spite of serving throughout the 1914–18 War in France.

John Evered Witt was born on January 15 1897, the

son of an Army chaplain then stationed at the Curragh. He was educated at King's School, Canterbury, and Sandhurst.

From 1919 to 1921 Witt served in the British Army of the Rhine where periodically his duties as an adjutant required him to ride a white horse at the head of a parade. The mount requisitioned for this purpose had previously been a circus horse and when touched underneath would promptly lie down.

In Cologne when the Adjutant stood up in his stirrups momentarily to make sure the column was moving properly he inadvertently contacted the critical spot with his toe. The horse naturally lay down and would only rise to its feet when given a command by its former groom, who was located with some difficulty.

After two years of home service Witt did a second tour in BAOR before proceeding to India and then to Egypt, where he served until 1932. As OC Troops, Port Said, his task was to greet passing ships and supervise the loading of rations.

These included supplies of meat which were graded for quality and origin with two sets of numbers 1–20. Soldiers receiving bags stamped 19 and 10 refused to believe that this was extra meat from, say, Kenya, and could not be persuaded that the unfortunate animal had not been slaughtered in 1910 and been in store for 20 years or more. All Witt's attempts to enlighten them were received with stony disbelief.

At the beginning of the Second World War Witt was in charge of vehicles hastily acquired for transport in France and, as he recalled, "a weird and wonderful collection they were".

His next posting, in 1940, was to command

an Officer Cadet Training Unit in Kent, which was also entrusted with the ground defence of the RAF airfield Manston. For this purpose they were allocated one rifle for every five men and 10 rounds for every rifle.

In 1944 Witt served at the War Office, engaged in logistical planning for the North-West Europe campaign and was afterwards successively Director of Supplies and Transport – first in BAOR for two years, then in Singapore for a further two years and then in Egypt for a further three years. He was mentioned in despatches in 1949 and retired in 1953.

Johnny Witt was an efficient but tolerant man who could invariably bring out the best in those working with or under him. He had been an excellent horseman in his youth and was a first-class shot and a good and patient fly-fisherman. He was also a canny golfer and at the age of 80 achieved a hole in one.

He was appointed CBE in 1948 and CB in 1952. His first wife, the former Kathleen Outram, died in 1968; and his second, the former Mrs Cynthia Reynolds (*née* Eden), in 1982. He is survived by a son of the first marriage.

May 24 1989

# CDR DAVID WEMYSS

COMMANDER DAVID WEMYSS, who has died aged 89, was one of the most decorated and successful "U-Boat killers" of the Second World War.

He won a DSO, a DSC and two Bars, and was mentioned in despatches four times — all for operations against U-boats.

Commanding the sloop *Wild Goose*, he was the second-in-command and right-hand man of the legendary Capt "Johnnie" Walker, whose 2nd Support Group of sloops and frigates sank 23 U-boats between June 1943 and March 1945.

In one "purple patch" early in 1944, they sank six U-boats in one trip to sea, three of them in 24 hours. On their return Walker's ships were cheered back into their base at Bootle, with the signal flying "Johnnie Walker Still Going Strong".

Wemyss and the other captain in Walker's group relied on hard training and excellent teamwork, under Walker's inspiring leadership. Together they evolved a particularly sinister manoeuvre known as the "Creeping Attack".

One ship would follow a dived U-boat at some distance, "pinging" on its Asdic, but making no attempt to attack, thus lulling the U-boat captain into a false sense of security. Meanwhile, a second ship would steam ahead and, directed by the first, fire a full pattern of depth charges. The unsuspecting U-boat would steer onwards into a carpet of sinking depth charges which then exploded all around it.

The method was deadly accurate. The attacking ship fired a marker with the middle charge. More than once oil, smashed debris and human remains from the U-boat came to the surface all round *Wild Goose*'s marker.

Morale in Walker's group was always spectacularly high. His ship sailed to the strains of *A Hunting We Will*

*Go*, played over the loudspeakers. Walker signalled "Splice the Mainsbrace", with an extra tot of rum all round, every time a U-boat was destroyed.

As an ex-submariner himself, Wemyss had, as he said, "a strong objection to being stared at through periscopes". And true to her motto "Alert to Evil", *Wild Goose* was responsible for the first detections of seven U-boats and was involved in the kills of 10.

She had her own Jolly Roger flag, with the ship's crest and 10 empty rum kegs, one for each sunk U-boat, sewn in a row. But in one corner there was a red cross on a white circle, marking the day *Wild Goose* inadvertently hit a distant hospital ship with a stray round during a practice shoot. The flag also bore a polar bear, for one convoy to Russia, and a crown commemorating the visit of King George VI and Queen Elizabeth to *Wild Goose* in 1945.

After Walker died suddenly in July 1944, Wemyss saw that spirits in Walker's own ship, *Starling*, were very low. *Wild Goose* was in dock, so Wemyss himself took *Starling* and the group to sea and was rewarded with yet another U-boat kill. He then took over command of the group for the rest of the war.

A scion of the Wemysses of Wemyss Hall, Fife, and the maternal grandson of Capt Thomas Young, RN, who won a VC in the Indian Mutiny at Lucknow, David Edward Gillespie Wemyss was born in Sweden on February 21 1900. He joined the Navy as a cadet in 1913, going to Osborne and Dartmouth.

He was a midshipman in the battleship *Valiant* at the Battle of Jutland in May 1916, his duty being to keep the deck log of the ship's movements in action. Wemyss joined submarines in 1920 and commanded six submarines in all – his first being *H-28* and his last, from 1933 to 1934, being *Oberon*.

After going back to general service he was first lieutenant of the cruiser *Diomede* on the Northern Patrol when war broke out in 1939. In 1941 he commanded the sloop *Folkestone* on convoy duties.

Although Wemyss had been much praised in the submarine service for his leadership, staff work, and his ability to overcome difficulties, he was actually passed over for promotion as a lieutenant-commander. But he was specially promoted to commander for his war service in December 1944, and he was amused to see that the lieutenant-commander next to him on the promotion list was 10 years his junior.

He retired from the Navy in 1950 and went to live in his ancestral county of Fife, where he served for a time on the county council.

Although Wemyss once attended the celebrations by "Johnnie Walker's Old Boys" (held annually in Bootle during the May weekend of the Battle of the Atlantic Service in Liverpool's Anglican Cathedral) and he went to *Wild Goose* reunions in Leeds, he was not a man for reunions. He was, however, always interested in Naval history. When *Valiant* was broken up in 1948, he managed to secure her deck log – "because nobody else seemed to want it". For years it had been kept in a glass case on the quarterdeck, opened permanently at the Jutland page where Wemyss's own handwriting recorded the ship's doings that day.

He also obtained *Wild Goose*'s ship's bell. After all the scenes of violence and death at sea the bell had witnessed, it was now used to summon people in from the garden for meals or to answer the telephone.

He wrote of his experiences as a midshipman in the Grand Fleet – "a war baby", as he called himself – for *Blackwood's Magazine*. In 1948 the Liverpool *Daily Post* published his book *Walker's Groups in the Western Approaches*, a vivid first-hand account of the Battle of the Atlantic, later republished as *Relentless Pursuit*.

In 1924 he married Edith La Touche, the middle one of three sisters. When she died in 1930, he married her elder sister, Avice, and when she died in 1961 he married Lynette, the youngest, who had earlier been bridesmaid to her two elder sisters.

His third wife died in 1979. Wemyss is survived by two sons from his first marriage, who both followed their father into the Royal Navy.

June 3 1989

# MARIE-MADELEINE FOURCADE

MARIE-MADELEINE FOURCADE, who has died in Paris aged 79, was one of the most celebrated heroines of the French Resistance during the Second World War; *Hérisson*, as she was known ("Hedgehog"), was caught four times by the Germans but on each occasion was either released or escaped.

Mme Fourcade was the only woman to direct the important Resistance section known as the *Alliance* or Noah's Ark. The Fall of France in 1940 found her in the foothills of the Pyrenees, where she immediately became involved in establishing the network. She worked first with Commandant Loustaunau-Lacau, then with Commandant Louis Faye and after both were arrested carried on alone.

*Alliance* smuggled General Giraud to North Africa and passed a huge amount of information to the British. This included details of V1 rocket emplacements, and the sorties of submarines from Brest and Lorient. It is said that a member of the network proposed the kidnapping of Marshal Petain.

The organisation, which at one point numbered 3,000 members, paid dear for its valuable work. Some 600 were arrested and tortured, and died in concentration camps or were executed by firing squads. A group of more than a hundred was executed in September 1944, at the Struhof camp in Germany.

Between 1940 and 1944 Mme Fourcade roamed France, from Marseille to Paris to Pau; she became adept at disguises and surfaced at different times as secretary, nurse and charwoman. She crossed to Spain and back hidden in a postal sack, with the code names of members – like "Hedgehog" they were all names of animals – sewn into the hems of her clothes.

In 1942 Mme Fourcade was arrested at Aix-en-Provence but escaped from jail. A year later she was flown into England, where the British were astonished to discover that agent POZ55 was a beautiful young woman. She returned to France after six months, was once again arrested and once again escaped.

She was born Marie-Madeleine Bridou on November 8 1909, into a family of the Marseille *grande bourgeoisie*. A gifted musician, she considered a professional career as a pianist before taking up journalism.

She emerged from the war a fervent Gaullist. She

became secretary-general of the Action Committee of the Resistance, was one of the founders of the UNR (Union for the New Republic), and worked assiduously for the General's return to politics in 1958.

A member of the Committees for the Defence of Human Rights and of the League Against Racism and Anti-Semitism, Fourcade was one of the moral witnesses called at the trial in Lyons of Klaus Barbie in 1987. Only weeks before her death she was at her desk, although ill, working for the rescue of refugees from Lebanon.

Her decorations included the Rosette of the Resistance, Commander of the Legion of Honour and the Croix de Guerre of France and Belgium. In 1968 Fourcade published a book, *Noah's Ark*, about her time in the Resistance.

She was married twice: first to a soldier, Edouard Meric, whom she divorced after the war; and then to an industrialist, Hubert Fourcade. She is survived by her husband and their five children.

July 22 1989

# WING CDR BENTLEY BEAUMAN

WING COMMANDER BENTLEY BEAUMAN, who has died aged 98, was one of the first naval aviators and a distinguished mountaineer, whose experiences in the Himalayas in the 1930s persuaded him of the existence of the Abominable Snowman.

Commissioned as a sub-lieutenant in the Royal Naval

Air Service on Aug 3 1914, the day before the First World War began, he reported on Aug 5 to Cdr Samson at the Naval Air Station at Eastchurch on the Isle of Sheppey. Samson's welcome left an indelible impression.

"Can you fly a Caudron?" Samson asked. "No sir." "Do you know the way to Hendon?" "No sir." "Very well, at dawn tomorrow you will fly a Caudron to Hendon."

After a forced landing Beauman duly arrived at Hendon, where he reported to Capt Murray Sueter, director of the Air Division at the Admiralty. Sueter told him: "You are now the defence of London from air attack."

Beauman replied: "I haven't got an observer or any armaments. What could I do if a Zeppelin does come over?" Sueter answered: "I leave that to you."

The remainder of Beauman's war was more conventional, involving search and anti-submarine flying boat patrols at home and overseas; he was mentioned in despatches.

Small, thin and wiry, he was ideally suited for the cockpits of early flying machines; and when he learned climbing in Switzerland he found that his compact physique was equally suitable for mountaineering. After scaling the Matterhorn five times by different routes, and much rock climbing in England and Wales, Beauman put his skills to the extreme test as a member of Frank Smythe's six-man expedition up the Himalayan peak of Kamet – at 25,447ft the highest mountain then to have been climbed.

Tracks observed in those frozen wastes set Beauman on the trail of the Abominable Snowman, on whom he brooded ever after, writing measured letters to newspapers on the subject and calling, unsuccessfully, for scientific hunting expeditions.

The son of a stockbroker, Eric Bentley Beauman was born at Paddington, London, on February 7 1891 and educated at Malvern and Geneva University.

In 1913 he obtained the Royal Aero Club's pilot's certificate; eager to join the RNAS, he improved his skills – paying £50 for 10 hours – at the flying school of the French pioneer Bleriot at Buc, near Versailles.

When the RNAS and the Royal Flying Corps were amalgamated in 1918 Beauman was commissioned as a major in the RAF. After attending the first course at the new RAF Staff College at Bracknell in 1922 he embarked on a routine round of peacetime postings, interspersed by various expeditions.

In 1934 he was a member of Sir Norman Watson's pioneer crossing of the Coast Range in British Columbia, on which his ski-ing skills – he was president of the Alpine Ski Club – proved invaluable.

During the Second World War Beauman established a close liaison between the Air Ministry and the BBC and introduced a weekly series of broadcasts about the air war. He also published a series of books extolling the exploits of Battle of Britain pilots. His other publications included *Winged Words*, *We Speak from The Air* and *The Boy's Country Book*.

In 1940 Beauman married Katherine Miller Jones, who survives him with their son.

July 28 1989

# "RORY" MOORE

LAURENCE "RORY" MOORE, who has died aged 90, was closely associated with Lawrence of Arabia in desert operations from 1916 to 1918 as a member of the Imperial Camel Corps.

Moore was, in fact, the first member of the Camel Corps to encounter T. E. Lawrence, whom he described as "a fair, smallish-built man with rather a large head, clothed in a brown Arab *aba*, covering an immaculately white undergarment: on his head he wore the usual Arab headcloth held down by a head rope which the Arab takes off at night and uses to hobble his camels' legs. Lawrence's head rope was bound with gold wire." Moore used to recall that however dirty the conditions Lawrence always seemed to remain immaculate. Once, when there had been arguments between some of the local Arabs and the British, Moore, who spoke Arabic, was called in to intervene. Asked who he was by the Arabs he replied: "*Ismi Hurrence*". One of the Arabs then said: "Yes, the same mad blue eyes, the same red face. Verily this is the brother of Lawrence." Friendship was restored immediately.

On this and on other occasions Moore was astonished to find how great was Lawrence's reputation with Arabs who had never even seen or met him.

Forty years on Moore became editor of *Barrak: The Irregular News-Letter of the Old Boys of the Imperial Camel Corps*, which had first been published in Beersheba in 1917. "*Barrak*" is the command given to a camel when it is required to kneel down and be hobbled.

Moore became an expert on camels (theirs were the one-humped Arabian dromedary type). There were 18 camel companies of which 17 had bull camels; the 18th Cow Camel Company lived at a considerable distance.

He did not find camels aggressive or smelly but noted that if a camel became annoyed it would spray the cud it was chewing all over the offender. In season the camel became singularly determined and undiscriminating.

In the issue of *Barrak* for summer 1989 Moore reprinted the programme for the regimental sports in 1918 in Palestine. It had a dignified cast of judges, stewards and other officials and included such esoteric pastimes as "camel scurry" egg-and-spoon races.

Laurence Moore was born in 1898 of a family traditionally in the coal trade. He was educated at the Northern Institute in Leeds, a commercial school which had a French headmaster who taught Moore French and German and instilled in him a liking for languages.

In 1914 the 16-year-old Moore tried to enlist in the Yorkshire Hussars and other regiments but was inevitably detected and sent home. He was eventually allowed to join the East Riding Yeomanry, taught riding by the Scots Greys and then sent to Egypt to join the Imperial Camel Corps which had just been formed from members of yeomanry regiments by Lt-Col Leslie Smith, VC.

The task of the Corps was to patrol the Western Desert and Northern Sudan and maintain contact with the friendly tribes of Senussis. Originally it had 30 officers, 800 NCOs and men, and 1,000 camels.

Three-quarters of its strength was made up of Australians and New Zealanders; it also included Sikhs from Hong Kong and Singapore, Rhodesian volunteers from their mounted police, a South African mine prospector who had fought against the British in the Boer War, a Canadian from the Rockies, a pearl fisherman from Queensland, a noted polo player from the Argentine and even an American.

Although the cavalry was sceptical about the idea that a camel corps could replace it, it was already all too clear that the task of patrolling the desert was beyond the capabilities of horses.

Moore, who was a qualified signaller, usually working with a heliograph, took part in many skirmishes. He was in charge of Brigade Signals with the Hejaz Assault Column when Gen Allenby loaned 300 men and 400 camels to T. E. Lawrence for operations against and beyond the Hejaz railway. Subsequently the Corps took many Turkish prisoners, sabotaged numerous Turkish installations, such as bridges and viaducts, and destroyed the enemy's water supplies.

Moore thought that Lawrence was resourceful and very brave but after reading *The Seven Pillars of Wisdom* he found a number of inaccuracies which caused him to revise some of his former high opinions. He felt that David Lean's film on Lawrence was completely wrong and later told Peter O'Toole, whom he had originally advised on playing the part, what his thoughts were.

After demobilisation Moore, like Lawrence, found himself restless and discontented but recovered his self-confidence after rescuing from drowning a boy who had fallen off the pier at Blackpool. He was awarded the Royal Humane Society Medal.

During the Second World War Moore was Chief Air Raid Warden in his district and an adviser to the Ministry of Fuel, for which he was appointed MBE in

1952. He became president of the Yorkshire Coal Exchange and Yorkshire Federation of Coal Merchants, as well as chairman of the Coal Utilisation Council for the North-Eastern Region for 21 years.

He was a keen philatelist and became a Fellow of the Royal Philatelic Society; he exhibited his collection of Swiss stamps and postal history all over the world. He also founded the northern group of the Helvetia Philatelic Society.

He was twice married.

August 18 1989

# MARJORIE COUNTESS OF BRECKNOCK

MARJORIE COUNTESS OF BRECKNOCK, who has died aged 89, was a redoubtable figure with an outstanding record as a Senior Commander in the ATS during the Second World War and subsequently as Superintendent-in-Chief of the St John Ambulance Brigade.

In the latter post she succeeded her cousin and closest friend, Edwina, Countess Mountbatten of Burma, who died while on service with the Brigade in North Borneo in 1960. Marjorie Brecknock, who had accompanied Lady Mountbatten on numerous foreign tours around the world in both war and peace, published a vivid pictorial memoir, *Edwina Mountbatten* (1961), the proceeds of which she gave to the Edwina Mountbatten Trust and the Save the Children Fund.

The two ladies were related through the Cassel

family, Marjorie being the only child of Col "Teddy" Jenkins of the Rifle Brigade by his wife Anna, a niece of Sir Ernest Cassel, the German-born financier who was Edwina Ashley's grandfather.

Marjorie Minna Jenkins was born on March 28 1900 and educated at Heathfield. Part of her childhood was spent "following the drum" with her parents and part sharing a governess with her cousin Edwina.

Eventually the Jenkins family settled at Wherwell Priory in Hampshire, a gift from Sir Ernest Cassel, which was to remain Lady Brecknock's home all her life. During the First World War, when the estate mechanic was called up, young Marjorie, who always had an intensely practical approach, took over the running of the electricity at Wherwell.

She also worked in a convalescent home for soldiers at Marsh Court, Stockbridge. In 1920 she married the Earl of Brecknock, elder son and heir of the 4th Marquess Camden. The marriage was dissolved in 1941, two years before Lord Brecknock succeeded to the marquessate.

Between the wars Lady Brecknock was a spirited socialite. In 1928, together with Edwina Mountbatten and Lady Alexandra Metcalfe, she opened an all-women's club, called Masters, in Savile Row – somewhere, as a contemporary gossip columnist put it, "where they could have cocktails, luncheon and perhaps dinner before the theatre". Subsequently men were also reluctantly admitted, "being necessary and desirable for financial as well as other reasons".

Marjorie Brecknock and Edwina Mountbatten also undertook a series of exotic expeditions. They traversed the wilds of Mexico, Guatemala and Honduras to study Mayan art and civilisation in the Yucatan peninsula; and subsequently to Chile and by train to La Paz in Bolivia, where they suffered from mountain sickness and became involved in a local uprising.

From 1937 to 1939 Lady Brecknock was a Lady-in-waiting to Princess Marina, Duchess of Kent, and it was during this time that she made her first contact with the St John Ambulance Brigade. In 1938 she joined the FANYs (later to be embodied in the ATS) as a private and during the Second World War she served first with motor companies, then with the anti-aircraft artillery. By the end of the war she was the senior ATS woman officer at Supreme HQ Allied Expeditionary Force in France.

In 1945 she was mentioned in despatches and awarded the American Bronze Star. Lady Brecknock was celebrated for her driving and mechanical skills. A wartime story is told of a major who could see only the behind of a female corporal working under the bonnet of his brigadier's staff car. He diffidently asked if he could be of any help whereupon Lady Brecknock's oil-bespattered face turned to him: "I'm perfectly capable of coping with the engine, but you *could* post this letter for me."

On leave during the war Lady Brecknock accompanied Edwina Mountbatten on a tour of hospitals and other units in Europe for the Joint War Organisations of the Red Cross and St John. On one flight in a small aircraft they found themselves under fire above German lines.

In 1946 Lady Brecknock joined St John HQ as staff officer to Lady Mountbatten, the Superintendent-in-Chief. Four years later she rose to become Assistant Superintendent-in-Chief (Overseas), a title later changed to Controller of the Overseas Department. Lady Brecknock held this position until 1960, when she became Superintendent-in-Chief in succession to Lady Mountbatten. During her 10 years in the top job she indefatigably visited St John units throughout the Commonwealth – always at her own expense.

After trips to India, Ceylon, Malaysia, Singapore, Hong Kong, Australia, New Zealand, Sabah, the West Indies, East and West Africa, Mauritius, Malta and Cyprus she undoubtedly knew more than anyone about the Brigade overseas. The ground she covered and the amount she achieved on these extended tours were phenomenal.

In 1970 she arrived in Cambodia for a sight-seeing visit to Angkor the day before the *coup d'etat*. On her return to London her only comment on being caught in a revolution was the inconvenience of not being able to leave the country as planned (she was delayed two days), and the disappointment at not having seen anything exciting.

Lady Brecknock continued to play an active role in the St John Ambulance Brigade as Chief President from 1972 to 1983. She was made a Dame of the Order in 1958, Dame Grand Cross in 1971 and made a member of the Order of Mercy.

From 1948 to 1954 she commanded 310 (Southern Command) Battalion of the WRAC (TA).

At home in Hampshire she ran the Wherwell estate with the same energy and know-how as she applied to the St John Nursing Corps and Divisions, characteristically taking her turn at the wheel of an enormous combine harvester. Her recreations were gardening, fishing and music; she was also an extremely good shot.

Lady Brecknock was appointed DBE in 1967. She is survived by a son, the present Marquess Camden, and a daughter.

August 26 1989

# THE REV KEITH ELLIOTT, VC

THE REVEREND KEITH ELLIOTT, VC, who has died at Lower Hutt, New Zealand, aged 76, won the Victoria Cross in 1942, as a sergeant in the Western Desert, for bayonet charges in which he and a handful of men captured 130 prisoners, five machine-guns and an anti-tank gun.

After the Second World War Elliott, a rugged, short, thickset man who had been wounded four times in the action on Ruweisat Ridge, went back to his dairy farm in New Zealand. But in 1947 he was ordained an Anglican priest; a comrade-in-arms recalled that "even in the desert, he'd get down on his knees and pray".

An outspoken and controversial cleric, Elliott ran a mission for down-and-outs in Wellington, served as a prison chaplain and campaigned passionately for the rights of the Maori minority. Because Maoris were excluded from New Zealand's All-Black rugby team to tour South Africa in 1960, he declared that he would never wear his VC again.

Keith Elliott was born on April 25 1913, one of nine children. During the war he came to England with the

New Zealand Expeditionary Force, leaving the family dairy farm in the care of his parents.

After service in Egypt he fought in Greece and Crete and was wounded in the arm. During Auchinleck's desert campaign he was captured, but freed when South African forces took Bardia in 1942.

That summer, on July 15, Elliott's battalion was attacked on three flanks by tanks. Under heavy tank, machine-gun and shell fire, he led the platoon he was commanding to take cover of a ridge 300 yards away, and was wounded in the chest in the process. Here he re-formed his men and led them to a dominating ridge 500 yards away, where they again came under machine-gun and mortar fire. Elliott led a bayonet charge across 500 yards of open ground in the face of heavy fire, capturing four machine-gun posts and an anti-tank gun, killing a number of the enemy and taking 50 prisoners.

Single-handedly he charged another post, killing several of the enemy and taking another 15 prisoners. In these two assaults he was wounded three times in the back and legs. Although now badly wounded in four places Elliott refused to leave his men until he had re-formed them and arranged for them to rejoin the battalion, handing over his prisoners, now totalling 130.

The citation for his award for valour said: "Owing to Sgt Elliott's quick grasp of the situation, great personal courage and leadership, 19 men who were the only survivors of B Company of his battalion captured and destroyed five machine-guns, one anti-tank gun, killed a great number of the enemy, and captured 130 prisoners."

Elliott took the only casualty among his men to an advanced dressing station. He was invested with the VC by Gen Montgomery that November in the Western Desert.

Later he told war reporters: "Don't play me up as a hero. Thank the boys for what they did. I couldn't have done any of it without them. When we were going for the Italian machine-gun nests I saw one of my boys knocked clean over by an Italian grenade. I thought it was all over, but he picked himself up and waded into them again. They were all like it. You couldn't stop them.

"I hardly felt any of the wounds at all, although I knew I had been hit, because when the bullet strikes its velocity shakes you. I was not conscious of pain, so I was able to carry on. I think my paybook did me a good turn." And he showed the leather cover of the paybook which had been cut by a splinter from an explosive bullet.

October 10 1989

# SIMON JERVIS-READ

SIMON JERVIS-READ, who has died aged 67, was an adventurous leader of tribal guerrillas behind Japanese lines during the Second World War in Burma.

He was dropped into Burma as a member of Special Operations Executive's Force 136 and landed by submarine on the Malayan island of Penang, where his exploits won him an MC in 1944 and attracted the attention of SOE's American opposite number, the Office of Strategic Services. At one point he was part of the US Army's Detachment 101, the OSS Unit in Burma, and of

Merrill's Marauders, a long-range penetration regiment which took its name from its American commander Brig-Gen Merrill.

Six foot four inches tall, lean and tough and with a considerable reach as a squash and racquets player, Jervis-Read cut a splendidly rakish figure in the jungle: his comrades-in-arms the Kachins found his monocle quite riveting. On one parachute jump over the jungle he forgot to remove the eyeglass. The force of the wind jammed and embedded it in an eye socket; its retrieval was painful and difficult.

Guerrilla operations at the head of Kachin or Karen raiding parties were hazardous. Hit in the thigh during an ambush of Japanese troops, he was fortunate to survive a 10-day journey on an improvised bamboo stretcher.

Sometimes it was essential to lighten his pack. On one occasion it grieved him to abandon a satchel containing a large sum of operational gold. He took bearings of the spot, intending to return after the war to recover the treasure; but, although his children were brought up on the story, he never went back.

A stockbroker's son, Simon Holcombe Jervis-Read was born at Farnham Royal, Bucks, on February 7 1922 and educated at Winchester. In 1940 he enlisted as a private in the Essex Regiment and the next year was commissioned into the 10th Baluch Regiment of the Indian Army.

This led to his recruitment by SOE and employment in Burma, Malaya, Thailand, Cambodia, Indo-China and China. In 1946, released as a major, he joined the Foreign Office.

He served in Singapore, Thailand, Hong Kong, Iran and Berlin, and at the Foreign Office in London until

1977, when he retired and was appointed secretary of the Game Farmers' Association. It amused him, in the light of this appointment, to recall that Force 136's formal record of Japanese casualties was called "The Game Book".

Throughout his postings Read maintained a lifelong recreational interest in natural history and ornithology. When in Iran he published a check-list of the country's birds. He collected bird specimens, keeping them in his refrigerator until ready to stuff them, and he later presented his collection to Teheran University. Shooting, particularly wildfowling, was another favourite pastime.

Jervis-Read was appointed CBE in 1977. He was a popular member of the Special Forces Club.

His first marriage, to Bridget Dawson, was dissolved in 1959 and he married secondly, in 1960, Coelestine von der Marwitz, who survives him with two sons and a daughter of the first marriage.

November 8 1989

# Major Harry Edmonds

MAJOR HARRY EDMONDS, who has died aged 98, had a life of remarkable adventure which included being wounded and gassed in the First World War and spending a night as a prisoner in the Tower of London.

He went to sea before the mast at the age of 15 and rounded the Horn three times; joined the Territorial Army at the age of 17 in 1908, in the first year of its existence, as a Royal Engineer, and subsequently transferred to the Royal Field Artillery. Then he became an instructor in the Australian Army, which he joined on Anzac Beach, Gallipoli, in 1915.

Later he served with Naval Intelligence; worked on the airship R101; and in his mid-nineties was flying gliders. He was the founder of the Wagner Society, and the author of some 15 novels, many of them signally prophetic, as well as a number of poems.

Harry Moreton Edmonds was born in 1891 at Merthyr Tydfil, where his father edited the *Merthyr Express*, a paper owned by his maternal grandfather, H. W. Southey – a descendant of the poet Robert Southey. The family moved to London where his father became editor of *London Opinion*, a humorous, *Punch*-type paper which lasted until the 1950s.

Young Harry was educated at Alleyn's School, Dulwich, before going to sea. In 1908 his father was told by the chairman of the Elder Dempster line that there was no future in sailing ships so the boy became a marine engineering apprentice with Thornycroft's shipyard.

Having also joined the Territorials, he learned to ride and drive six-horse teams, one of which he drove in the Lord Mayor's Show in 1911, the year of King George V's Coronation. The next year he was transferred to the Royal Field Artillery and when, in 1913, his firm sent him to New Zealand for two years, he helped to train the local regiments there.

On returning to England in 1914, he was commissioned in the RFA and saw action at Neuve Chapelle in 1915. He was then persuaded to join the Australian Army as an instructor.

After a brief period in Gallipoli he was sent on to Australia but in 1916 he returned to France via Egypt. That year he flew for a while as an artillery spotter with the Royal Flying Corps, where his CO was Kenneth Dowding (youngest brother of "Stuffy", who was to lead Fighter Command in the Battle of Britain in 1940).

Edmonds was back again on the ground in the Battle of the Somme in 1916. Later he learned that at one stage he had been serving opposite Cpl Hitler in the Bavarian Jager Division.

In the Battle of Fromelles in July 1916, he recalled watching the infantry as they sustained 6,500 casualties in an abortive attack over open ground. He was then in Delville Wood where the trees had all been replaced by mud, shell holes and corpses.

During the long and severe winter on the Somme he recalled ensuring that his men all rubbed their feet with whale oil to prevent frostbite. In April 1917 at Lagincourt when the Germans broke through the British line during a snowstorm, they did not realise their success, and were soon pushed back, mainly by heavy shelling from Edmond's battery.

He was promoted major on the battlefield of Passchendaele in 1917, was wounded in the face and also gassed, but he managed to return to his battery after 10 days in hospital. After the battle, his CO – with whom he had many disagreements – refused to acknowledge the vital part that Edmonds's battery had played in the Lagincourt battle the previous April and refused to recommend him for promotion.

Edmonds was advised by friends to apply for an official inquiry but when told that it would not occur, asked to resign or be court-martialled. This led to his temporary incarceration in the Tower.

He was then sent to the Maudsley Hospital, after which he was offered six months' leave. He refused the leave as he said he wanted to get back into the war, and he managed to gain a place in the Naval Intelligence Division as a lieutenant RNVR. Here he worked closely with Adml Sir Reginald "Blinker" Hall in the legendary Room 40.

After the First World War Edmonds returned to engineering and also took up authorship, one of his books selling more than 100,000 copies. In 1936 Naval Intelligence sent him to Germany on a special mission to study the performance of the new German airships *Graf Zeppelin* and *Hindenburg*.

During his time in Germany Edmonds made many friends, including descendants of the composer Wagner. He became such an enthusiast that after his return he founded the Wagner Society of England.

During the Second World War he worked with the Australian Red Cross. Afterwards he helped to market his wife's flower pictures from *La Nive* studios and also became chairman of a wine exporting company.

At the age of 75 he took up gliding and he celebrated his 80th birthday by making a record solo flight. He was said to be the oldest glider pilot in the world; with difficulty he was persuaded not to take up hang-gliding in his nineties.

Harry Edmonds was a man of many friends, from the set of "Boney" Fuller and Lord Hankey to the least distinguished of people; children adored him. He was a keen all-round gamesplayer, particularly of rugby football.

He is survived by two sons.

November 11 1989

# LT-COL "BUSTER" KEENE

LIEUTENANT-COLONEL "BUSTER" KEENE, who has died aged 83, had a military career of considerable variety which included being second-in-command of the Abyssinian contingent of 5/14 Punjabis in Addis Ababa in the Abyssinian-Italian war of 1935; Assistant Commandant of the Assam Rifles on the Tibet-China border from 1939 to 1943; and commander of the 3rd Battalion in the Naga Hills in the Burma campaign from 1943 to 1945.

Keene was wounded and mentioned in despatches in the battle for Kohima, when the Japanese were making a desperate effort to break through into India in April 1944. The fighting round that area was so fierce and the Japanese casualties so high that no one was surprised when the ghost of a Japanese soldier, complete with steel helmet, was subsequently observed charging forward on a number of occasions before suddenly vanishing in the Naga village.

Kohima was the depot for the 3rd Battalion of the Assam Rifles, which Buster Keene commanded. The battalion, mainly recruited from Gurkhas, wore Gurkha uniforms and was armed with rifles and *kukris*. Under normal conditions it acted as a form of gendarmerie, maintaining law and order among the hill tribes.

Normal duties did not include confronting several thousand battle-hardened Japanese, but when these arrived the Assam Rifles left many of their visitors with their skulls split in half. The Rifles used "line boys", aged 10 upwards, as messengers.

At that time Keene was married to the matron of the 49th Indian General Hospital, which was on an important spur on the ridge. Behind Keene's bungalow lay the celebrated tennis court, where the two armies later fought a battle separated only by its width.

The Assam Rifles were not on the regular establishment and had not been issued with shovels or entrenching tools, so as the days passed they were surrounded by a growing mound of corpses and attendant flies. As the battalion, short of sleep and water, repelled attacks day after day, Keene moved around, quietly encouraging the different platoons, always accompanied by his shaggy little Tibetan Lion Dog, Judy.

Finally, the Japanese gave up their costly struggle and retreated. It was said of the action: "If the Royal West Kent were the dominant unit, the Assam troops were little behind them and many of them not in the least behind in valour. The Assam regiment saved Kohima by its resolute defence at Jessami; when it got back to the ridge, it was dismembered, short of officers yet, together with their friends of the Assam Rifles, extemporised successfully in many an emergency and held the tennis court in a fine example of soldierly conduct."

Geoffrey Abbot Exshaw Keene was born at Taunggyi, Burma, on May 17 1906 and educated at Elizabeth College, Guernsey, and Sandhurst. Commissioned into the 16th Punjabis in 1925, he was attached to the Cameronians (Scottish Rifles) for a year, serving in Baluchistan, then in the Punjab Waziristan and Baroda.

From 1931 to 1933 he was physical training instructor to the Indian Army. After the Abyssinian war Keene returned to India and became successively officer-in-charge of a jungle training course and a mountain warfare course.

In 1943 he was appointed MBE for evacuating refugees in the north-east of Burma under appalling conditions. Keene retired from the Army in 1948 and was attached to the Foreign Office to work as an interpreter to the Tibetan Trade delegation.

In 1951 he was attached to the Colonial Office for anti-terrorist work in Malaya. Subsequently he became the honorary treasurer of the Kent Discharged Prisoners Aid Society; he also held various retired officer appointments at headquarters in Canterbury, Colchester and Bassingbourn.

Buster Keene lived life to the full, taking part in all games and subsequently umpiring and judging hockey, boxing and wrestling. He spoke Urdu, Pushtu and Gurkhali and was a first-class rifle shot.

He is survived by his wife, Patricia.

November 17 1989

# TOM MAPPLEBECK

TOM MAPPLEBECK, who has died aged 95, played a crucial role in the coup which overthrew the increasingly pro-Axis government of Prince Paul of Yugoslavia in 1941.

Mapplebeck was assistant air attaché at the Belgrade legation and a fluent speaker of Serbo-Croat, but refused to join MI6 because it would mean spying on old friends. He agreed, though, to pass on any information to the British government. For a year this had included summaries of Yugoslav intelligence reports supplied by Brig-Gen Bora Mirkovic, chief of the air staff, whom he had long known through selling aircraft to the Yugoslav air force.

As Germany prepared to launch an attack on Greece – which made Yugoslavia's reliability essential – the anglophile Prince's government started to waver in its neutrality. But on the day the Tripartite Pact with Germany and Italy was signed, Mapplebeck urged Mirkovic to act. He won the promise that a long-planned coup would go ahead to replace the Prince with the 17-year-old King Peter.

In retaliation Hitler launched Operation Punishment, which led to 17,000 deaths in Belgrade in three days. The move – once believed to have delayed the German attack on Russia by a crucial five weeks – was claimed as a significant achievement by the fledgling Special Operations Executive, although it was only marginally involved.

Mapplebeck – whose brother-in-law, the Zagreb police chief, was murdered in the invasion – was closely involved in the consequent withdrawal. He removed the British embassy's transmitters in his own car and later found a boat for 60 pilots in Greece who wanted to escape to Cairo.

He rowed out to a ship and at first met with a refusal by the master, who said there were neither blankets nor water for so many. Mapplebeck replied that the blankets did not matter and he would see to the water, returning soon after aboard a water-carrying boat.

He himself eventually arrived in Cairo aboard an aircraft carrying Yugoslav gold reserves. But his urging that the demoralised Yugoslavs should put their full effort into the hostilities, and his strong support of Mirkovic's faction, eventually led King Peter to dismiss him as liaison officer.

Although these dramatic events took him into the murky world of politics, Mapplebeck spent most of his life, apart from the two world wars, as a commercial agent.

The son of a Liverpool dentist, Thomas George Mapplebeck was born on October 15 1894 and educated at King William's School, Isle of Man, which he had to leave at 14 because of family bankruptcy. His first job was to watch over an untrustworthy farm manager for absent owners in Cheshire, then he went to work with a Smith-field meat merchant who took him on a visit to Kiev.

In 1910 he was a special constable in Scotland Road during the Liverpool dock strike, a task he performed after shovelling coal for eight hours at a power station.

On the outbreak of war in 1914 Mapplebeck, who had been working for an agent in Hamburg, immediately joined the 4th Battalion of the King's Liverpool Regiment. He was wounded in the head at the second battle of Ypres, which he had foreseen in a dream the night before. When he recognised the terrain he gave his batman careful instructions about what should be done if he was killed or only wounded.

Having recovered, Mapplebeck joined the Royal Flying Corps, in which his brother had won one of the first DSOs of the war, and was shot down in an SE8 by a sniper after accounting for a balloon on the Somme in November 1916.

He spent two years as a prisoner in Germany. On his one successful escape, his fluent German enabled him to persuade police that he was an Argentinian sailor who wanted to volunteer, but he was then recognised by a guard from his camp. At the Armistice he proceeded to Hamburg, where he booked into the best hotel and began to help with the embarkation of returning troops.

Soon afterwards he also proved himself invaluable to a group of war correspondents who could find no cloakrooms at Cologne railway station. He obligingly showed them the Kaiser's velvet-seated WC.

Sent out to Yugoslavia as part of the British economic mission, Mapplebeck settled down as a commercial agent. The British abandonment of the Gold Standard in 1929 almost bankrupted him because the Yugoslav government declared a moratorium on peasants' debts. But he soon began the more profitable business of selling aircraft. On one occasion he hurried home to tell Tommy Sopwith (*qv*) that sales of the Hawker Fury would be lost unless an extra 20 mph was added to its speed.

After his links with the Yugoslavs ended in 1942, Mapplebeck rejoined the RAF, serving in Luxor, Baghdad, Jerusalem and Turkey, where he upset his superiors on taking command of a secret radar station by sending a coded message: "ALL ARRIVED SAFELY MOUTHS SHUT BOWELS OPEN". But by the end of the war he was Group Captain in charge of welfare for the whole Middle East.

Staying on in Cairo, Mapplebeck settled down as an agent specialising in defence equipment. He had his property confiscated during the Suez crisis and, with accusations of being Britain's chief spy ringing in his ears, settled in Beirut for the next 20 years.

By his return to Egypt in 1975, he was a near-legendary figure, known for his scrupulous honesty, five marriages and such meticulous habits as reading his London newspapers in daily succession even when a week's supply arrived at once. In 1985 his success in selling a large consignment of Land-Rovers earned him the appointment of OBE.

On returning to Britain at the age of 92 he continued to conduct business from his London old people's home, in which he had an office equipped with telex and typewriter. He also found a happy diversion in the steady stream of letters sent to *The Daily Telegraph*.

Writing in lucid, brief paragraphs he proffered sensible, genial views – on the national debt, the use of the stocks for punishment and the footballing skills of Gurkhas at the battle of Neuve Chapelle in 1915 – that make his failure to complete an autobiography regrettable.

January 25 1990

# GP CAPT FRED WINTERBOTHAM

GROUP CAPTAIN FRED WINTERBOTHAM, who has died aged 92, masterminded the deployment of Ultra intelligence – the greatest Allied secret of the Second World War.

Indeed, his contribution to the Allied victory exceeded that made by many of his seniors. As Marshal of the Royal Air Force Sir John Slessor commented in his foreword to Winterbotham's book, *The Ultra Secret* (1974), it was "a curious reflection on our system of honours and awards that he should have finished up after the war as a retired Group Captain with a CBE on a quiet farm in Devon".

Ultra's decrypts – known to some simply as "Fred" – of the enemy's "unbreakable" Enigma code signals often put Allied leaders ahead of the game in critical strategic and tactical situations. Outstanding examples of Ultra's influence on the successful outcome of campaigns are to be found in the Battle of the Atlantic, Montgomery's victory at Alamein, the D-Day invasion of Normandy and subsequent advance into North-West Europe.

Churchill set such store in Ultra and its begetter – he sometimes referred to it as his "golden eggs" – that Winterbotham received personal telephone calls from the Prime Minister and had ready access to him. The great man also marked Winterbotham's card with C-in-Cs and supported his visits to operational theatres to ensure that maximum use was made of Ultra intelligence.

It was essential that secrecy should be maintained, and Winterbotham was ruthless in restricting to a minimum those receiving Ultra or knowing about it. He established teams, known as Special Liaison Units – initially composed of specially trained RAF officers and sergeants, later of Army personnel – to provide and interpret decrypts.

To British and American military leaders Ultra seemed like manna from Heaven – though some were more gracious in their acknowledgments than others. Montgomery, for example, niggled that it was largely an RAF show, tended to keep his Special Liaison Unit at more than arm's length and ascribe results gained from its service to his own vision.

A Stroud solicitor's son, Frederick William Winterbotham was born on April 16 1897. His mother engaged a French nursemaid and encouraged young Fred to speak

French, a language to which he was to add some German during his spell as a prisoner of war in 1918.

Another early influence was his grandfather, with whom he built a box kite to fly on Minchinhampton Common. He was educated at Charterhouse and after a bout of measles at the age of 16 he was packed off on a recuperative world tour – "brilliant preparation for what lay ahead," he used to say, not forgetting a visit to the red light district of Yokohama.

In 1915 Winterbotham was commissioned into the Royal Gloucestershire Hussars Yeomanry, but when its horses were withdrawn the next year he was issued with a bicycle. He then volunteered for the Royal Flying Corps and was accepted on the evidence of having good hands for a horse.

He was posted to No 29 Squadron, flying Nieports in France, where his talisman was a blue silk garter he had "won" on a night out in Amiens. On July 13 1917 he took up a borrowed fighter without the garter adorning his compass and was shot down behind enemy lines.

After the war he went up to Christ Church, Oxford, where he acquired some riding gear from Prince Paul of Serbia, a fellow undergraduate, and rode to hounds as well as playing polo. Subsequently he farmed in the Cotswolds until he decided to take a salaried job at the Air Ministry in RAF Intelligence at the end of the 1920s.

He also became involved with the Secret Intelligence Service in an extraordinary chain of events which led to Ultra. First he set about ingratiating himself with prominent Nazis in Berlin.

After befriending Alfred Rosenberg, the editor of the Nazi party newspaper, Winterbotham was introduced to the Führer himself in 1934. The conversation began with pleasantries about Winterbotham's time as a PoW and the chivalry of Anglo-German "dogfights" in the 1914–18 War. Then Hitler talked freely about the new Luftwaffe and smoothed the way for Winterbotham to meet some of the military leaders such as Generals Kesselring, von Reichenau and Lörzer.

When the Luftwaffe Club was founded in Berlin in 1935 Winterbotham received honorary membership and did not miss the opportunity of chatting with young pilots. It was in the club that, in 1936, he heard about the new Stuka dive-bombers, the aerial artillery of *blitzkrieg*, which duly featured in his invaluable intelligence reports.

To augment such intelligence Winterbotham arranged the purchase of a Lockheed executive aircraft from America, and recruited the colourful Australian aviator Sydney Cotton for a series of elaborate adventures. Cotton posed as a film tycoon surveying possible locations while managing to photograph Italian bases in North Africa and German installations: this led to the introduction of the RAF's first Photographic Reconnaissance Unit.

Winterbotham had hoped to command the unit, but in April 1940 he was asked instead to organise the translation, distribution and security of Ultra. He then set up his own intelligence hut – No 3 – at Bletchley Park, otherwise "Station X", the war section of the Government Code and Cypher School. Here a brilliant concentration of academic talent, including many Cambridge mathematicians, broke the Enigma codes. Winterbotham organised a team of German-speaking RAF officers to translate Luftwaffe signals.

An early Special Liaison Unit occupied a cubicle next

to Fighter Command's operations room at Bentley Priory and made a modest contribution to Dowding's intelligence in 1940.

Winterbotham soon found himself with the job of sorting out the decrypts for the Prime Minister each day and then telephoning them to him. On the morning of Sept 17 1940 Ultra disclosed the preliminary dismantling of Operation Sealion, Hitler's plan to invade Britain. Winterbotham sent it to Churchill's underground war room in Whitehall and in the evening he visited the Prime Minister with the head of MI6 and confirmed that in his opinion the invasion threat was over.

It was now time to consolidate the flow of decrypts, and Winterbotham expanded the Special Liaison Units – though the Navy ran its own show on his establishment, since for security reasons an HMS *Bletchley* was taboo.

There followed coup after coup, including the news that Rommel had arrived in North Africa. Winterbotham had hoped to brief Montgomery personally in Churchill's presence but was dissuaded on the grounds that the leader of the 8th Army did not like RAF uniform, or being told what he could not do. Ultra also put warships of the Mediterranean Fleet on course to disrupt Rommel's supply convoys. When Winterbotham met a submarine commander in Malta, secrecy forbade him to disillusion the sailor about his "luck" in always seeming to surface astern of an enemy convoy.

As the invasion of Normandy ("Overlord") approached Winterbotham anticipated the necessary expansion of Ultra to satisfy many new customers – particularly the Americans. Eisenhower, who had benefited from Ultra's intelligence for the earlier North African landings, was an especially enthusiastic recipient.

After the Second World War Winterbotham was offered an Air Ministry civil service job "at a pretty low grade". Instead he joined BOAC in an executive capacity, from which he afterwards moved to the Colonial Development Corporation.

In 1952 he returned to farming, and 20 years later he received government approval for his remarkable book which became an international bestseller. His other publications were *The Nazi Connection* (1978) and an autobiography, *The Ultra Spy* (1989).

He was appointed CBE in 1943.

January 31 1990

# MAURICE SOUTHGATE

MAURICE SOUTHGATE, who has died in France aged 76, led one of Special Operations Executive's most successful subversive teams during the Second World War and turned his talents for spreading confusion to brilliant purpose against the Nazis.

Of British parentage, Maurice Southgate was born in 1913 and brought up in Paris. He began his war in the Army, and survived the sinking of the troopship *Lancastria* during the fall of France in the early summer of 1940. He was then recruited into SOE by Col Buckmaster (*qv*) and given an honorary commission in the RAFVR.

It is part of SOE folklore that some clerical delay

attended the transfer and – not quite knowing to which service he belonged – Southgate wore Army and RAF uniforms alternately while staying with his mother in London. A neighbour observed to Mrs Southgate: "I never see your two sons go out together."

Southgate was teamed up with Jacqueline Nearne, who was part of an SOE family – her sister and brother also served in the organisation. During her parachute training Miss Nearne knitted socks for use in France because the enemy could distinguish the weaves of manufactured socks – and she became known as "Jackie Red Socks".

In 1943 Southgate and Jackie Red Socks were parachuted into France, in the full knowledge that on this occasion there would be no resistance reception committee to help them. The absence of welcome and guidance was nearly Southgate's undoing. During a four-hour march he encountered a peasant and so forgot himself that he asked in English when there would be a bus.

Eventually the pair caught a train, on which they sat next to a German soldier. They alighted at Clermont-Ferrand, where there was a safe house. Joined there by the agent Pearl Witherington, and the Mauritian Amédée Mainguard as radio operator, they embarked on a triumphant course of subversion.

Jackie Red Socks posed as a commercial traveller while she carried essential messages, found dropping zones and arranged reception committees. Southgate (code name "Hector") organised arms training and sabotage. Once he asked her to take a message by train, an impossible mission because on the night before he had blown up the points on that line. When she returned, mission unaccomplished, he could only apologise.

On another occasion Southgate was talking to some French workers as a German aircraft took off. As it left the ground he said: "I bet it's going to blow up." When it did there was much head scratching: he had placed a bomb on the aircraft during the night.

After some months Hector and Jackie Red Socks were recalled for briefing, and in October 1943 Southgate returned to France with a price of one million francs on his head. He was seized, as a result of treachery and torture, and sent to the concentration camp at Buchenwald. Many members of SOE perished in such camps, but Southgate, working as a tailor, managed to survive. His DSO, as a squadron leader, was gazetted while he was there.

Southgate's arrest affected D-Day plans, since the main lines to Normandy ran through his sector and he was a key figure in arrangements to disrupt them.

After the war he resumed his woodwork, furniture designing and interior decorating business in Paris.

He is survived by his second wife.

March 17 1990

# MAJOR PAT REID

MAJOR PAT REID, who has died aged 79, was the most celebrated escaper of the Second World War, the mastermind of three escapes from Colditz, two of them successful.

"No sport," he said, "is the peer of escape, where freedom, life and loved ones are the prize of victory, and death the possible, though by no means inevitable price of failure." Through his books about Colditz Reid later shared this excitement with millions; the books spawned a film and a television series, and an industry of toys and board games.

Reid was taken prisoner during the fall of France and sent to Oflag VIIC at Laufen near Salzburg, from which he escaped disguised as a German peasant woman. Recaptured, he was incarcerated at the forbidding Saxon castle of Colditz.

Powerfully built, Reid gave "an impression", as his fellow prisoner Airey Neave later described it, "of concentrated power, enhanced by a quiet deliberate speaking voice." Reid did not make his own successful escape until his organisational skills and resourcefulness had first enabled other prisoners-of-war to get away.

He was none too keen on fancy plans after recapture at Laufen and a first Colditz fiasco, and the plan for his successful Colditz escape eschewed the laborious process of tunnelling. After cutting the bars of a window, Reid and three fellow officers darted across brilliantly lit paths while sentries' backs were turned and struggled through a cellar flue to freedom. All four reached Switzerland.

A civil servant's son, Patrick Robert Reid was born in India on November 13 1910 and educated at Clongowes College, Co Kildare, Wimbledon College and King's College, London. After serving an engineering pupillage with Sir Alexander Gibbs & Partners, he was commissioned into the Royal Army Service Corps.

As a boy Reid had been gripped by the best escape

books of the First World War – *The Road to Endor, Within Four Walls* and, an especial favourite, *The Escape Club*. These epics, he later wrote, "lived long in my memory, so that when the fortunes of war found me a prisoner in an enemy land the spirit enshrined in them urged me to follow the example of their authors."

British officers held in Colditz counted previous PoW camps as prep schools, the Common Entrance qualification for transfer to Colditz being at least one escape. Reid's prep school was Laufen, where he arrived in 1940, head shaven, to be issued with a small aluminium disc declaring him Kriegsgefangennummer 257. Within a week he was plotting escape.

On September 5 the required tunnel was ready. Attired as a peasant woman, Reid broke out with two fellow officers. Once clear of the camp he had planned a quick change into a Tyrolean hat and clothes run up by a PoW who had been a tailor in civilian life, but to begin with there was not the opportunity.

The deception worked, though, and soon he was on the open road. Separated early on from his fellow escapers, he was reunited with them within an hour and they set off for Yugoslavia, 150 miles distant.

After five days they were recaptured. Punished with periods of solitary confinement and bread and water, in November they were transferred to Colditz.

In the New Year of 1941 Reid assumed responsibility for escape planning and organised the construction of a tunnel from below the floorboards of the canteen to beyond the outer wall on the eastern side of the castle. German-speaking British officers picked out a sentry they believed could be bribed with money, cigarettes and chocolate to look the other way as the escapers cleared the tunnel. The "goon" accepted the bribes and promptly betrayed his benefactors. Reid was caught red-handed.

A year later he master-minded another escape, this time a successful one – though there were stressful moments. After spiriting Airey Neave (then a Royal Artillery lieutenant) through a disused passage to an attic above the guardhouse, Reid took an agonising 10 minutes to pick the lock of the attic door before he could send Neave and Tony Lutyn, a Dutch officer, on their way.

Dressed in imitation German uniforms, the escapers returned the salute of the sentry outside the guardroom door and strolled past the married quarters to freedom. In little more than 48 hours Neave was safely in Switzerland.

Reid's preparations for his own escape were characteristically painstaking, though on this occasion he gave the tunnel of his boyhood imagination a miss, resorting instead to more cerebral ruses. One was to have Douglas Bader, who was conducting an orchestra on the night of the escape, vary the music to signal the movements of a sentry.

By the night of October 14 Reid and three fellow escapers – Lt-Cdr Billie Stephens, a naval survivor of the St Nazaire raid, Maj Ronnie Littledale, KRRC, and Flt-Lt Hank Wardle of the RCAF – had loosened the bars on the window of the prisoners' kitchen. This was accomplished with the help of a saw – which had been smuggled into the castle in private food parcels, along with other tools and a detailed floor-by-floor plan of the castle, found in the British Museum. The source of such manna was MI9, the escape and evasion organisation into which Airey Neave was recruited on his return to London.

Just after 9 pm Reid and Wardle removed the bars, climbed out on to a flat roof and dropped some 10 feet to the ground; Stephens and Littledale followed.

Darting across illuminated paths while sentries' backs were turned, they found a cellar from which a narrow flue ran at ground level to a series of three terraces on the outer side of the castle. Twice as they climbed down an Alsatian barked, but the goons failed to respond, and the escapers reached a road passing between the German married quarters. They walked up to it and scaled a gate in the wall at the end.

It was now 4.15 am. As planned they split into pairs, each pair travelling by road and train towards the Swiss frontier, but by different routes. Reid was stopped – but a passport, forged with a rubber stamp carved out of linoleum, passed muster. With Wardle he reached Switzerland three days later, followed by Stephens and Littledale the next day.

Reid's courage was soon acknowledged with the award of an MC. He was then appointed assistant military attaché at Berne, where Air Cdre Freddie West (*qv*) was already supervising escape routes and running a flourishing intelligence business.

When the war ended Reid remained in diplomacy, being appointed first secretary for commercial affairs at the British Embassy in Ankara in 1946. Three years later he was posted to Paris, as chief administrator in Paris of the Marshall Aid plan.

He then took an unsuccessful stab at politics, nursing Dartford and Erith from 1952 to 1955 as prospective parliamentary candidate for the Conservative party. Reid also became a director of the engineering firm of W. S. Atkins and established Kem Estates to build houses in the neighbourhood of Possingworth, his Jacobean manor at Blackboys near Uckfield in Sussex.

He published *The Colditz Story* (1953), *The Latter Days* (1955), *Colditz* (1962), *Winged Diplomat: a biography of Freddie West, VC* (1960), *My Favourite Escape Stories* (1975), *Prisoner of War* (1983) and *Colditz: The Full Story* (1984).

Inevitably Reid encountered sour grapes for cashing in on his experiences: he replied that 10 years separated his escape from the first book, and that it had been open to any other Colditz old lag to beat him to it.

He was appointed MBE in 1940.

Reid was married three times. First, in 1943, to Jane Cabot (of the Boston family); there were three sons and two daughters. The marriage was dissolved in 1966, and in 1977 he married, secondly, Mary Stewart Cunliffe-Lister, who died the next year. In 1982 he married Nicandra Hood.

May 24 1990

# "MICHETTE" ROSENTHAL BOROCHOVITCH

"MICHETTE" ROSENTHAL BOROCHOVITCH, the French Resistance fighter and staunch Gaullist who has died in Paris aged 65, was one of the most daring as well as one of the youngest women to join the South-Eastern *Maquis* in the Upper Alps in 1943.

These were perhaps the largest strongholds of the Resistance in Nazi-occupied France: free enclaves of sometimes more than 10,000 fighters which held several German divisions during the winter of 1943–1944.

Michelin Rosenthal was born in 1925 and joined the Resistance at the age of 17, barely two years after having sworn to avenge the murder of her father, Adolphe Rosenthal, a prominent Parisian jeweller. Rosenthal *père* had been shot by the Pétainiste *Milice* a few hours after having been arrested at his house and his body, thrown out of a *Milice* car, had been found lying in an underway road passage in Paris.

She first organised the transport of guns and wireless sets for the Haute-Savoie *Maquis* with the help of the Megève *gendarmerie*, where weapons and wireless sets used to be hidden for a while – the last place, she explained, where the Germans would be expected to look. They were then carried into the mountains in a lorry: she would throw a piece of canvas over them in the back and lie down on it, pretending to be a casual hitch-hiker at road checks.

The Gestapo on her scent, and with her name and description sent out to all police stations, she left Haute-Savoie in November 1943 for the larger *Maquis* of the Ain and Haut Jura, to the north.

Here she became a liaison and intelligence agent for the legendary Col Romans-Petit, running dangerous mountain routes and trails, carrying information and orders to all Romans-Petit's outposts. Sometimes she was sent down to the occupied valleys – a blonde, blue-eyed girl riding a bicycle, gathering information on the Germans and *Milice* movements in the area. She was once caught at a German roadblock while walking to the local

*Kommandantur*, but managed to swallow the three incriminating documents that she was carrying to the Resistance in the village. She recalled later that, with her throat almost blocked, she had requested a glass of water from the German officer in charge, who gave it unthinkingly to her, and shortly afterwards released her for lack of evidence.

During the winter-long fierce fighting for the *Maquis* des Glières (which was eventually overtaken by thousands of *Milice* and German troops, who killed the handful of survivors of this 400-strong position on March 25 1944), Michette operated the liaison between the Glières commanding officer, Tom Morel, and Col Romans-Petit. She managed to avoid six or seven different enemy checkpoints each time for the whole winter, being finally cut off from Morel a few days before the final bloody onslaught. She stayed in the *Maquis* until the liberation of France.

In early 1945 Michette was posted to Calcutta as a lieutenant with the French Expeditionary Corps, then organising the fighting for occupied French Indo-China under the Supreme Allied Commander, South-East Asia, Mountbatten. Working for the *Direction Générale des Etudes et de la Recherche* – the new name of the French secret service – she took part in liaison and intelligence missions, including one to Gen Chiang Kai-shek in Tchungking.

Later she became an administrator for the World Wildlife Fund for France. She had many friends in Britain through her association with the Special Forces Club in London.

Michette Rosenthal was an Officier de la Légion

d'Honneur, was awarded the Croix de Guerre (with palms) and the Médaille de la Résistance, and was vice-president of the Ain Maquisards Association.

She married, in 1948, Capt Serge Borochovitch, a former Free French officer.

May 28 1990

# MAJOR GEOFFREY BURDEN

MAJOR GEOFFREY BURDEN, who has died aged 91, enjoyed adventurous careers both as a soldier and in the Colonial Service, callings which took him to the distant reaches of the Empire.

His career was almost cut short at its beginning. Burden's first commission was in the Gurkha Rifles, and in 1918, as he and his men were packing stores prior to his transfer from the 2/7 to the 4/11 Gurkhas, they were struck by lightning which killed 16 of them and left Burden's hearing permanently impaired.

His next task was dealing with rioting city mobs; on one occasion his company had to occupy a rum factory, where "my main task was to keep the men from getting too drunk to do their jobs".

When his regiment was disbanded at the end of the war Burden transferred to the 130th Baluchis (Jacob's Rifles) and served on the frontier, where the more militant tribes had been liberally supplied with arms by the Germans. In addition to murder, arson, pillage and attacking caravans, they were now raiding into the plains. There were many skirmishes, and Burden twice came within a whisker of being killed.

In 1922 he decided to make a career with the family firm, although he kept in touch by serving with the Royal Engineers as a Territorial. But after three years he abandoned business for the Colonial Service.

His first posting was to Nyasaland. In 1926, with a friend and five carriers, he climbed to the Big Ruo Fall, some 6,000 feet up and said not to have been reached within living memory. "The river cascaded over the edge for the full 900 feet," Burden wrote, "into a black lake with a deafening noise."

Later he had some hair-raising experiences with packs of man-eating lions and marauding elephants, although he had more trouble with such diseases as paratyphoid, malaria and hookworm. Some of his colleagues were mildly eccentric — "I don't keep files because I don't answer letters," said one. But Burden cultivated the acquaintance of every native chief and most of the headmen as well.

In 1936 he joined the King's African Rifles Reserve of Officers, and three years later became director of recruiting in Nyasaland. He also had some secret service duties assigned to him, as it was rumoured that there was German activity in Mozambique; Burden's knowledge of Hindustani enabled him to converse with Indian storekeepers in remote villages.

War service continued with the Rifles in Abyssinia, and later with the blockade of Djibouti. Not the least of the hazards there was the local hospitality. After one dinner he drove his 15-cwt truck into a huge anthill and had to abandon it. His CO put him under open arrest pending an explanation, but when this was given "the proceedings closed with a pink gin".

After a year as assistant chief secretary in Nyasaland Burden was appointed Commissioner of Labour, Gold Coast (Ghana), and then Chief Commissioner of the Northern Territories, Gold Coast. His duties included the organisation and encouragement of soil and water conservation; mass education and community development; training in intensive methods of crop development (rice, groundnuts and millet); and preparing the chiefs and people for self-government.

Burden's final posting was as Nyasaland Government Representative in Southern Rhodesia. After retirement in 1963, he engaged in voluntary service with the Soldiers', Sailors' and Airmen's Families Association in the Farnham and Frensham area.

Geoffrey Noel Burden was born in 1898 and began his military career at the age of 16 when he joined the 7th Devons at the end of the Easter holidays instead of returning to his boarding school in Exeter.

Tall and well-built, he had already been given white feathers by women who had confronted him in the street thinking he was of military age. The Medical Officer turned out to be one of the school doctors who knew his proper age and his history of chest troubles, but gave way to Burden's pleadings with the remark: "It will either kill you or cure you."

One of his earliest duties was to plot the course of Zeppelins with a small compass and a bicycle and then telephone his intelligence to the War Office. But it was soon decided that Burden could stay in the Army only if he sat for the Sandhurst exam.

This meant that he had to return to his school as a

day boy and to attend the Army Class – dressed, much to the envy of the older boys, as a private soldier. Although he just scraped in to Sandhurst he passed out 19th out of 350.

Soon after joining the Gurkha Rifles at Dehra Dun, Burden had a severe attack of jaundice. Interrogated by the CO of the hospital, a Scotsman, he said he had never touched alcohol but only lime juice.

"At once," Burden recalled, "a look of horror spread over his face and he ejaculated: 'Rot gut!' He followed this by telling me that when I recovered I should begin drinking whisky and continue to do so for the rest of my days. I have endeavoured to follow this advice."

Geoffrey Burden had a great zest for life, was hospitable, sociable and could see the humorous side of virtually everything. He made light of the hazards and various unpleasant tropical diseases he encountered during his career, although some left him with serious after-effects.

Burden was appointed MBE in 1938 and CMG in 1952. He is survived by his wife, Nancy, together with a son and a daughter.

May 30 1990

# SQN LDR "TIM" HERVEY

SQUADRON LEADER H. E. "TIM" HERVEY, who has died aged 94, was a gallant airman in both World Wars and a celebrated escaper in the First.

His first escape was from the prisoner-of-war camp at Freiburg. Armed with some wire-cutters which had been smuggled into the camp inside a ham-bone in a Red Cross parcel, Hervey cut his way out of an upper window and lowered himself on a rope improvised from parcel strings. Some way down he was disconcerted to find himself disturbing the halo on a statue of St Peter, but he continued his descent and then walked 80 miles to the Swiss border, only to be caught at the last moment.

This exploit landed Hervey in the "escape-proof" Fort Zorndorf at Custrin, where he met Brian Horrocks. The two were later moved to another camp at Holzminden, run by the irascible commandant Niemeyer, nicknamed "Milwaukee Bill" for his strong American accent.

One day Niemeyer introduced Hervey and Horrocks to his guards: "Look well at these criminals and mark them down. These are not officers and gentlemen, they are criminals!" Shaking his fist in Hervey's face, Niemeyer screamed, "You are very clever? Yes? Well, I make a special study of this escaping. You think I, the commandant, know nothing. You are wrong. I know *damn all*!"

This harangue put Hervey on his mettle, but before he and Horrocks had a chance to escape they were moved again – to a camp run by Niemeyer's equally disobliging brother at Clausthal in the Harz mountains. There Hervey had the idea of simply walking out with the orderlies. Horrocks made a dash for it but was recaptured within sight of the Dutch frontier. Hervey failed even to reach the camp's gates.

A sentry fired on the fleeing Horrocks and then turned his gun on Hervey, who had tripped over a bucket and fallen heavily. The guard pressed the trigger, but had fortunately forgotten to reload.

A civil servant's son, Hamilton Elliott Hervey was

born at Southsea on November 6 1895 and educated at Sedbergh. In 1914 he became an apprentice with the Bristol Aeroplane Co and six months later enlisted in the Royal Flying Corps.

Hervey's service as a gunner and observer was recognised with an MC and Bar. But on April 8 1917 – the day after a duel with the Red Baron, von Richthofen – he was shot down and taken prisoner. He was mentioned in despatches for his escape attempts.

After the war Hervey moved to Australia and flew as a commercial pilot with Shaw-Ross Aviation. He went on to form the Central Aviation Co and was a founder-member of the Gliding Club of Victoria.

A keen student of nature, Hervey was out on a walk one day when his eye was caught by some furry seeds. It occurred to him that these and other oddments might be used to make wildlife pictures.

He had already made a name for himself as a model aircraft designer, but this new hobby soon became a full-time occupation. With flowers, ferns, twigs, pieces of bark and oil paint Hervey created distinctive miniatures of birds and animals against a natural landscape. He later exhibited his work in London and, despite the sneers of the critics, it proved popular with such collectors as Queen Mary and the Dutch Royal Family.

In 1936 Hervey returned to Britain and became the first manager and chief flying instructor of the London Gliding Club. In the Second World War this experience led to his secondment to the newly created Airborne Forces as the first commander of No 1 Glider Training School at Haddenham, Bucks. He also advised MI9, the service set up to encourage and facilitate escape from enemy PoW camps.

In his mid-seventies Hervey took up ballooning, which he continued to enjoy until his 90th year; he was a founder-member of the London Balloon Club.

He is survived by his wife, Constance, and their two daughters.

June 1 1990

# MAJ-GEN VICTOR CAMPBELL

MAJOR-GENERAL VICTOR CAMPBELL, who has died aged 85, was awarded an immediate DSO for his gallantry as Brigade Major of 152 Brigade in the 51st Highland Division in June 1940.

The Division had moved up from Saar (between Colmen and Launstroff) to counter-attack the Germans who were advancing south and west after the last British troops in the north had been evacuated from Dunkirk. After a gruelling march the Brigade was given the task of recapturing the Abbeville bridge which the Germans held in overwhelming strength.

Lacking food, sleep, and air support, they were shelled, mortared, machine-gunned, and dive-bombed when trying to force a way through infantry who vastly outnumbered them – and all in blazing heat. In the course of the fighting the Brigade lost 20 officers and 543 other ranks.

Campbell personally turned a routed battalion around and, armed with a light machine-gun, led it back into action. The remnants of the Division made their way to

St Valéry where they were ordered to surrender. This they refused to do until fog made it impossible for the Navy to reach them; the French had already laid down their arms.

During the next five years Campbell was an inspiration to his fellow prisoners and set an example by his robust and uncompromising attitude to his German captors.

Victor David Graham Campbell was born on March 9 1905, the son of Gen Sir David Campbell, a former Governor of Malta, who had won the Grand National as a subaltern in the 9th Lancers on Soarer in 1896, and his last race at Aldershot as a full General in 1930.

Young Victor was educated at Rugby, where he represented the school at boxing, and at Sandhurst where he was a prize cadet – he passed out first and was awarded the King's Gold Medal and the Anson Memorial Sword. In 1924 he was commissioned into the Queen's Own Cameron Highlanders and became Adjutant in 1933.

Later in the 1930s he was an instructor at Sandhurst, where he founded the Sandhurst Beagles; he had previously hunted and whipped-in to the Aldershot Command Beagles for several seasons.

In 1938 Campbell was a student at the Staff College, Camberley, and in 1939 went to France as a GSO3 with the BEF. He became Brigade Major in 152 Brigade in March 1940.

When freed at the end of the war he refused the extra leave to which he was entitled as a returned PoW. Instead he volunteered for service in the Far East and attended the Senior Officers School at Dehra Dun. Some of his instructing officers at the school were many years his junior, a fact of which they were made to feel uncomfortably aware.

Campbell was then appointed Brigadier and AQMG in 15 Corps in Indonesia but voluntarily reverted to Major to become second-in-command of the 1st Battalion of the Cameron Highlanders in Japan in 1946. From August 1947 to January 1948 he commanded a battalion in Malaya.

His next post was the command of the 1st Battalion of the Gordon Highlanders who were stationed in bomb-threatened Essen. In the strongly tribal Highland Brigade his appointment was not welcomed – and Campbell did little to increase his popularity when he set about "sorting out" a battalion in which morale was low. Nonetheless within a year he had transformed it into one of the best battalions in the Rhine Army.

The writer James Kennaway, then a subaltern in the Battalion, is said to have used Campbell as a model for the character of Col Barlow in his novel *Tunes of Glory*. In the film version, Barlow, a highly strung character who ultimately commits suicide, was played by John Mills. It was pointed out that Campbell would never have committed suicide, though some of those around him might have been tempted to do so – even to commit murder.

In 1950 he was appointed to command 31 Lorried Infantry Brigade in 7th Armoured Division in BAOR, and then became a student at the Imperial Defence College. Later in the 1950s he was Brigadier, General Staff, Western Command, and finally, until his retirement in 1957, Major-General and Chief of Staff HQ, Scottish Command.

In spite of his formidable and well-earned reputation for uncompromising efficiency, Campbell was a compassionate man who would go to great lengths to help soldiers with personal or family problems. His oft-stated philosophy was: "If you are a soldier you must be professional and it must be fun." In a disciplinary interview his voice became ominously quiet but on rare occasions he might conclude with the glimmer of a smile. His inspections were dreaded.

On one occasion he ordered all the "Jocks" to take their boots off. Most were wearing something akin to spats rather than socks. Finally he stopped in front of one old soldier: "Where is your fourth pair of socks?" he demanded. The Jock dived into his kitbag and produced two little balls of wool. To everyone's amazement Campbell smiled – but no one trusted to luck on the inspection the next day, when not even he could find anything wrong.

He was a man totally without vanity or self-interest. Those who served under him came to be grateful for the lessons he taught them and the example he set. After retirement he went to live in Devon where he devoted himself with characteristic energy to local affairs, Civil Defence, hospital management and – for he was a deeply religious man – the Church.

He was chairman of Totnes Petty Sessions Division and of Totnes Rural District Council. He was a Deputy Lieutenant for Devon and served as High Sheriff.

Campbell was appointed OBE in 1946 and CB in 1956. He married, in 1947, Dulcie, widow of one of his best friends, Lt-Col J. A. Goodwin.

June 8 1990

# BRIG ADRIAN GORE

BRIGADIER ADRIAN GORE, a remarkable all-round sportsman and gamesplayer who has died aged 90, won the DSO and Bar for his achievements in North Africa and Italy during the Second World War.

On February 19 1943 Gore, then a colonel, was ordered to take a small composite force – which, in addition to members of his own regiment, the Rifle Brigade, included the Lothian and Border Horse and some Royal Horse Artillery gunners – to block the Thala Road in North Africa.

The Americans holding the Kasserine Pass had been heavily defeated and it was therefore essential to check the advancing German tanks and prevent them from threatening the whole of the rear of the 1st Army. Gore's small force, which was joined by four American tanks, fought the Germans to a standstill in spite of heavy casualties, including the loss of all the RHA officers.

On the night of February 21 Rommel nearly succeeded in penetrating the position by a deception ploy in which he placed a captured British tank at the front of his armoured column. But a British gunner scored a direct hit on a German Panzer III tank and set it on fire.

This gave enough light for another eight German tanks to be knocked out. Although the Valentine tanks used by the Lothians were no match for the German Panzers, they fought doggedly until the last Valentine was destroyed.

Gore remained cool and cheerful throughout, but was nearly killed in the final stage. A shell hit the truck he used for sleeping quarters seconds after he had left it. For his conduct in this decisive battle he was awarded an immediate DSO.

The Bar to his DSO came in Italy, where he commanded 61st Infantry Brigade which was engaged in a number of dour battles, including that for Tossignano in snow and deep mud. He was wounded in the Arno Valley but not as seriously as at first seemed.

At the end of the Italian campaign he was sent to Klagenfort to prevent Tito's partisans establishing themselves there and claiming it as a part of Yugoslavia; Gore arrived there just in time.

A scion of the Gore Baronets of Co Donegal, Adrian Clements Gore was born on May 14 1900. At first it was thought that he had been still-born: he was put on one side; but later one of the nurses looked at him and found he was very much alive.

His father, Col Robert Gore, was killed in action in April 1918 when commanding the Argyll and Sutherland Highlanders. Young Adrian was brought up in Co Kildare where, as he recalled, he "smoked with the butler, played bicycle polo with the groom and gardener, and was taught to shoot by the 'keeper".

He was educated at Eton – where in 1918 he took five wickets for nine runs against Charterhouse – and then at Sandhurst. He was commissioned into the Rifle Brigade in 1920 and in the same year played cricket for the Combined Services against the Australians.

In 1921 he was in Ireland with the regiment and then was sent to Chanak in 1922 when a war with Turkey appeared to be imminent. When the crisis subsided Gore returned to Aldershot and in 1924 was one of a pair to win the Army Racquets Doubles Championship.

In the same year he took seven wickets in the Army *v* Navy match and later played for the Gentlemen *v* Players. The following year he won the Army golf championship. Subsequently he distinguished himself in point-to-points and proved to be a first-class shot and trout and salmon fisherman – he caught a 36lb salmon in the Blackwater in 1929.

In 1933 regimental duties took him to Malta, where he was invited to join Mountbatten on the destroyers during the three-days manoeuvres. "Dickie" Mountbatten's friend Noel Coward, who was also a guest, insisted on sun-bathing naked on the bridge where sailors bringing in signals had to step over his prone body. Gore liked to reminisce how, when the destroyer stopped to enable them to bathe, a sailor contrived to discharge some bilge around Coward just as he came to the surface.

In Malta Gore played polo in a game in which the Army beat the Navy – a feat hitherto deemed impossible. He then returned to England as training officer for the Rifle Brigade; if this had not happened he would almost certainly have been with the 2nd Battalion and been killed or captured at Calais in 1940.

In 1942 Gore was appointed Commander of 10th Battalion of the Rifle Brigade, which landed in North Africa in December 1941. After the North African battles, when he was with the battalion training for the invasion of Italy, he kept a tame rabbit and hedgehog in his tent – earlier in the war he had nurtured an orphaned piglet.

Gore then landed at Anzio where he took over 2nd

Infantry Brigade, before being transferred to 61st Brigade, all of whom were Riflemen. After the war he served for a time in Trieste, and in 1946 took command of the Greenjacket TA Brigade in London.

On his retirement in 1949 he took up farming at Horton Priory in Kent. He was District Commissioner for the East Kent Pony Club.

In a long cricketing career Gore terrified batsmen at Eton, Sandhurst and Lord's. He was still a single handicap golfer in his late seventies and used to go round Littlestone in the equivalent of his age. The redoubtable Brigadier never took a practice shot even on the first tee, and his temperament helped young players in the many school and Army competitions in which he played – particularly the Halford Hewitt.

Gore last shot when he was 88. As his companions worried whether it was safe for him to be out at all, he proceeded, as one put it, "to wipe the eyes of two fellow Guns half his age".

Adrian Gore was loved by all ages – the young especially – for his unselfishness, modesty, integrity and charm. There was always a twinkle in his eye: on his 90th birthday, though a sick man sitting up in bed, he appeared to lose a decade every time a pretty woman walked in to see him.

He was married for 63 years to the former Enid Cairnes, who survives him with a son and a daughter. Mrs Gore was also a keen shot – once when both were in their eighties her husband fell and cut his arm badly. While he was trying to staunch the flow a pack of grouse came over. Instead of rushing to his aid, Enid Gore grabbed his gun and started shooting.

"Get one?" said the Brigadier challengingly as he propped himself up weakly at the bottom of the butt.

June 16 1990

# PEGGY SALAMAN

PEGGY SALAMAN, the aviatrix who has died in Arizona aged 82, achieved fame while still a bright young thing when she beat the London to Cape Town light aeroplane record, picking up a couple of lion cubs on the way.

On October 30 1931 – with a "Cheerio, Mummy, I'm determined to do or die and, believe me, I'm going to do" – Miss Salaman waved her mother goodbye and flew off into the night from the Channel coast airfield at Lympne in Kent.

Peggy Salaman's flight captured the imagination of the press; here was "The Girl With Everything Money Could Buy Who Had Got Bored With It All". Such details as the fact that she had packed an evening gown for Cape Town – and that she had brought along packets of chewing gum to seal any petrol tank leaks – were lovingly chronicled.

Five days, six hours and 40 minutes after she left Lympne she landed in Cape Town – accompanied by Gordon Store, her South African navigator and fellow-pilot. Her time knocked more than a day off the previous record of Lt-Cdr Glen Kidston, who that spring had completed the journey in six days and 10 hours.

But, taking into account the fragility of her little single-engined De Havilland Puss Moth, it was an even greater achievement than the figures indicate. Kidston had flown a heavier and more powerful Lockheed Vega – in effect, a Mini compared with a Rolls.

Indeed the Moth was hardly more than a standard flying club machine, maximum speed 125 mph. There was, however, an additional fuel tank and a metal propeller to add about 5 mph to the speed. Navigation lights were fitted but there was no radio.

The Moth, which she called the *Good Hope*, was a present from her mother. It was dressed in a livery of Navy blue with a pale blue stripe – "Like the perambulator I had for her as a baby," said her mother.

The daughter of a businessman and property developer, Peggy Louise Salaman was born in London in 1907 and educated at Queen's College, Harley Street, and Bentley Priory (which, in 1940, was to become Dowding's HQ during the Battle of Britain).

Finished in Paris, she did a London Season before, in pursuit of her passionate determination to fly, taking lessons at Hanworth with Capt Finley, a former RFC pilot. She obtained an "A" licence, and in July 1931 she entered the Moth in the King's Cup air race, where – accompanied by Lt Geoffrey Rodd as her pilot – she won the prize for the fastest machine.

That October, as she headed for Le Bourget in Paris on the first leg of her epic flight, Miss Salaman's only sartorial concession to aviation was a helmet. The rest of her attire in the cockpit comprised grey flannel trouserings and a white sweater.

A pith helmet and shorts were packed with the ball gown for the tropics. With Store navigating, she flew the old "Red Route" of the British Empire. After Rome and Athens came Juba, where she was much taken by a pair of lion cubs. She duly bought the cuddly young creatures for £25 and named them Juba and Joker; they were bottle-fed on board as the *Good Hope* progressed towards Entebbe.

Then it was on to Bulawayo, but the combination of nightfall and a hilly area urged caution, and she landed in wild bush country between Abercorn and Broken Hill, Northern Rhodesia.

Came the dawn and take-off was found to be impossible until a strip had been prepared. Fortunately Store had armed himself with a machete and she had a revolver with which she felled some young trees. An elephant trench was filled with earth to clear a runway. Airborne again, Store, as she recalled, "threaded his way through Africa as easily as a taxi-man in London".

In the last stages of the adventure Miss Salaman left the 18-day-old cubs at Kimberley to be sent on by train. They had become too much of a handful.

On arriving at Cape Town and hearing that she had broken the record, she trilled: "How perfectly lovely!" She added: "We could have got here much earlier, but we slowed to 90 mph over gorgeous mountains and admired the magnificent scenery."

Afterwards she was told the Moth was now unfit to fly. Store stayed on in South Africa, but she sailed home with the lion cubs in the liner *Warwick Castle*. At sea she heard that the celebrated aviator Jim Mollison, already chasing her record, had crashed in Egypt. She cabled to him: "Hard lines. You missed our luck."

Back in London she returned to the family in Cambridge Square, Bayswater. The cubs resided in the cloakroom, but as they grew the maids complained. Not only were they considered potentially dangerous but there were disagreeable odours – despite unsparing applications of *eau de cologne* – and ineradicable scratches on the parquet floor. Bertram Mills came to the rescue but he was unable to tame them for his circus; eventually the lions, by now renamed Romeo and Juliet, were housed in a private zoo.

Subsequently she gained a commercial licence in America, where she entered a Los Angeles Air Derby and finished 42nd out of 80.

During the Second World War she served in the WAAF, as a plotter, and then in the Wrens. Afterwards she helped to look after displaced children at a camp in Brittany.

Miss Salaman was married briefly to Denis Flanders, the architectural and landscape artist. During a visit to America in the 1950s she met her second husband, Walter Bell, an electrical engineer and airman with two private aircraft.

Flying around America together, they landed one day at Phoenix, Arizona, and were so enchanted with it that they bought a house in the *adobe* style and settled there.

September 12 1990

# Lt-Col Hilary Hook

Lieutenant-Colonel Hilary Hook, who has died aged 72, became a national celebrity overnight in 1987 when he was the subject of an enchanting television film by Molly Dineen about his return to Britain after a lifetime abroad, serving as a soldier and running safaris in Kenya.

The appeal of the programme, *Home from the Hill*, and its larger-than-life central character had echoes of the popular drama series *The Misfit*, starring Ronald Fraser. To television audiences Col Hook appeared a craggy anachronism – the archetypal, and extraordinarily endearing, legacy of Empire struggling to come to terms with the vastly different Britain of the 1980s.

With his monocle and his somewhat affected unfamiliarity with the modern technological world, the retired Cavalry officer undoubtedly relished playing to the gallery; but his old-fashioned decency and sympathy shone through his ostensibly blimpish attitudes. In *Home from the Hill* (also the title of his autobiography) he was shown packing up his rifles and polo sticks – and shooting his chandelier to pieces – before leaving Kenya. He said goodbye to his African butler, whom he movingly described in Kiplingese as "my servant, and a better man".

Back in England after nearly 50 years, Hook moved into modest modern quarters in Wiltshire, where he was seen struggling unavailingly to open a tin of ravioli – cursing colourfully the while – and stocking up with vodka and whisky as he wandered bemused around the local supermarket.

Asked by the director if he was happy at the end of the film, Hook smiled at the unseen Miss Dineen and made a throwaway remark about "divine discontent". It was an irresistible performance which made Hook into something of a star.

The next morning he was on the screen again in a chat show, dealing roguishly with marriage proposals down the telephone from adoring fans, and tactfully with old Sandhurst acquaintances, trying to get in on the act.

He went on to appear on *Wogan* and other programmes, and *Home from the Hill* was repeated to renewed acclaim. While fame bestowed by the box is often transient, Hook made a lasting impression.

Hilary Hook was born on September 26 1917 into an artistic family and brought up in Devon. He spent a seemingly idyllic childhood – in summer catching mackerel and conger eel off Brixham, in winter out with his ferrets or shooting pheasants, in spring collecting birds' eggs on the cliffs.

While still a schoolboy at Canford, in Dorset, he supplied the London Zoo with several specimens of the rare smooth snake, rode to hounds with the Portman, and read widely about big game hunting in Africa and India.

His Army career – which gave Hook, as a friend put it, plenty of scope "for the artful abuse of His Majesty's time" – began in 1938 in India, where he joined the Royal Deccan Horse. When not playing polo, riding in point-to-points, or sticking pigs, Hook was coursing jackals in the Sind desert or shooting bear in Kashmir. While the regiment was undergoing mechanisation during the early stages of the Second World War there was still plenty of time for sport.

In 1943 Hook applied to join the Chindits, but instead he was transferred to the Australian Forces with whom, as a private, he spent an unpleasant time fighting the Japanese in the jungle of New Guinea. Later he resumed his officer's rank and rejoined his regiment for the last months of the Burma campaign. Having returned from India shortly before independence, Hook joined the 7th Hussars and served as a judge in a war crimes trial in Hamburg.

After two seasons hunting with the Zetland, he applied for secondment to the Sudan Defence Force, and spent the next two years, as a company commander, patrolling the vast Equatorial province of southern Sudan – "through the best game country", as instructed. The treks were sometimes arduous, but there were numerous opportunities for game shooting. Signals such as "Reynolds Bey. For information Dixie. Duck are in" would pass between the various posts.

There followed nearly three years in northern Sudan, where Hook was now among Muslim tribesmen, and serving with the Camel Corps and the Western Arab Corps. He left the country two years before the end of the Anglo-Egyptian condominium, but returned in 1962 as military attaché, to find that his old Arabic teacher in Khartoum was now a general and president.

It was a pity that Hook never wrote a book devoted to the Sudan which he knew and understood so well. The six years he spent in the country, both before and after independence, gave him a knowledge of its peoples and problems which few Englishmen could boast.

Before settling in Kenya Hook had also served in Hong Kong – which, except for the sailing, he did not enjoy – and in the Aden Protectorate shortly before independence.

In Kenya Hook ran spectator safaris for 20 years. During 1984 he had two disagreeable surprises. His death was reported at the annual dinner of the Shikar Club in London, and he was evicted from his house at Kiserian. So the hunter decided at last to come home from the hill (though he had stopped hunting many years earlier) to the West Country.

He had two sons: Simon, a painter, and Harry, a

film director whose credits include a remake of *Lord of the Flies* and *The Kitchen Toto*, which was set in Kenya.

**Lt-Col Alec Harper writes**: Nobody could call Hilary Hook a very serious soldier; in fact he used to say that the only reason he joined the Army was because he had read a book called *Bengal Lancer* by Yeats Brown, but he was one of the most amusing and well-read people I have ever known and also a competent naturalist.

Hilary was the last regular officer to join the Royal Deccan Horse before the war and had only been with them about a year when we met in 1940. We were still mounted on horses and did not lose them until June that year, after which we still kept a few of our own. It took us a long time to mechanise and we saw to it that our spare time was enjoyably occupied playing polo or any other sport one does on horseback.

Hilary was attached to Brigade HQ as an intelligence officer and used to alleviate the tedium by studying the polo handicaps and making up rude mottoes for Brigade HQ – such as *Floreat Bovis Excreta* and *Via Virtutis Per Rectum Domini*. The slow progress of mechanisation was not so much due to our stupidity as to lack of equipment. Hilary used to sum up the attitudes of certain senior officers with "See the monkey ride the bicycle."

Hilary and I never soldiered together in the same squadron, or in action, but we shared many sporting moments together and were fortunate to be able to take leave to hunt the wild boar in the Ganges Kadir, having sent our horses on to Meerut by rail.

After the war our paths diverged: Hilary joined the British Army and I became a civilian. But we remained firm friends and saw each other regularly. I always enjoyed his company.

While in the Army he married Jane Budgen, with whom he subsequently ran safaris in Kenya. They made an ideal team for this purpose: Jane being very pretty and an extremely efficient organiser of the camp, while Hilary was an excellent host and knew every animal and bird by heart. They finally parted, being, I suppose, mentally incompatible. I think Hilary was hit very hard by this.

September 15 1990

# LT-COL ALAN PALMER

LIEUTENANT-COLONEL ALAN PALMER, who has died aged 76, was awarded the DSO in 1945 for his service with Special Operations Executive in Albania, where he fought alongside partisan guerrillas in various sabotage operations and became head of the SOE mission in Tirana.

Palmer, who had been parachuted into Albania in 1943, was involved in one of the more bizarre Balkan incidents of the period – the rescue of a party of imperilled American nurses. A Dakota transport had lost its way over Italy and made a forced landing near Berat in southern Albania.

On hearing of their plight, President Roosevelt insisted on an air drop. Palmer helped to retrieve the supplies which included cosmetics and silk stockings.

It was hoped to arrange a pick-up from Gjinokaster airfield but by the time a Wellington bomber and two Dakotas, escorted by 30 Lightning fighters, arrived,

German troops were on the scene. Eventually the nurses were evacuated by sea to Bari in Italy.

Charles Alan Salier Palmer was born on October 23 1913, the only son of Sir Eric Palmer of Shinfield Grange near Reading, who was chairman of Huntley & Palmers. Sir Eric's grandfather was Samuel Palmer, the founder of the biscuit dynasty.

Young Alan was educated at Harrow and Exeter College, Oxford, before entering the family biscuit business. During the early stages of the war he served with the Berkshire Yeomanry. He was Adjutant from 1939 to 1941, GSO3 HQ 6 Division from 1941 to 1942 and GSO2 HQ III Corps from 1942 to 1943. Shortly before landing in Albania in 1943 he took part in an SOE operation in the Dodecanese Islands.

The nature of Palmer's arrival in the Balkan wilderness caused something of a sensation among those who had preceded him. Hardened by the rigours of subversive operations in testing terrain, the understandably scruffy SOE team assembled at the dropping zone to greet him was astonished by both the *personae* of his group and the content of its baggage.

For out of the two RAF Halifax bombers which delivered them, tumbled, among others, a smartly uniformed Major Palmer of the Berkshire Yeomanry, Lt-Col Arthur Nicholls of the Coldstream Guards and their leader, Brig "Trotsky" Davies of the Royal Ulster Rifles. The old sweats of Albania grew ever wider-eyed as tables, chairs, filing cabinet, stationery, as well as an NCO clerk and his typewriter, fell into their midst. The Brigadier (who had been dubbed "Trotsky" at Sandhurst where his report spoke of "disciplined Bolshevism") was a veteran of pre-war North-West Frontier campaigns.

"I have never understood why a soldier need look like a brigand when he is on special operations," pronounced the Brigadier. "We'll have none of that Wingate stuff here." Indeed his batman, equipped with shaving gear, had dropped with him.

In keeping with "Trotsky's" ideas, a mess was established, with cooks, waiters, a barber and shoemaker being culled from Italian camp followers. It was typical of the Brigadier's style to celebrate his wedding anniversary with a slap-up dinner of soup, turkey and pudding, washed down by Italian champagne and liqueurs.

In the event Palmer evaded "Trotsky's" imposition of a Brigade HQ routine on a guerrilla camp in the mountains. He was ordered south from the drop of Biza and joined the 1st Partisan Brigade.

Palmer became particularly friendly with Enver Hoxha, the future Albanian Communist dictator. As civil war threatened between right-wing and left-wing Albanians, Palmer recommended the withdrawal of support from followers of the exiled King Zog and other right-wing elements, and instead urged all-out assistance for Hoxha's National Liberation Committee, which was bearing the brunt of the armed struggle against the German-Italian Axis.

As "Trotsky" Davies disliked moving without 100 mules to transport the impedimenta he felt essential to his mission his presence became rather obvious. In January 1944 he was duly ambushed by a German-led right-wing band, wounded and captured.

After that, Palmer, thanks to good relations with Hoxha, saw to it that his mission in the south and centre of the country adhered to the Left. He suspected that "Trotsky" Davies was possibly the victim of an official

British failure to act upon the Brigadier's advice to withdraw support from right-wing movements.

Palmer, who was mentioned in despatches for his exploits, subsequently headed the SOE mission in Tirana before returning to Reading. He rose to become chairman of Huntley & Palmers in 1963.

When, in 1969, the firm joined with W & R Jacobs and Peek Frean to form Associated Biscuit Manufacturers in order to counter the challenge of United Biscuits, he served as chairman for three years. Together with the rest of the family, he sold his share in Huntley & Palmers when it was bought out by the Nabisco Group in 1983.

Palmer was chairman of the Cake and Biscuit Alliance; a member of the council of the Confederation of British Industry and of the British Productivity Council; and, for 40 years, president of the Reading Conservative Association.

He was appointed CBE in 1969. His recreations were shooting, fishing and tropical agriculture.

He married, in 1939, Auriol, only daughter of Brig-Gen Cyril Harbord.

September 17 1990

# COL SIR DAVID STIRLING

COLONEL SIR DAVID STIRLING, who has died aged 74, was the creator of the Special Air Service, which subsequently became an élite regiment of the British Army and won the admiration of many foreign countries which tried to imitate it.

Stirling won a DSO in 1942 and was appointed OBE

in 1946. Maj-Gen Robert Laycock, head of Combined Operations, said he was one of the most under-decorated soldiers of the Second World War. This was probably because there was no senior officer or other eyewitness of his exploits to recommend him for just reward.

In 1941 Stirling was nicknamed the "Phantom Major" by the Germans for his remarkable exploits far behind their lines in the Western Desert. In the 15 months before he was captured, he and his desert raiders destroyed aircraft, mined roads, derailed trains, fired petrol dumps, blew up ammunition depots, hi-jacked lorries and killed many times their own number. Rommel admitted that Stirling's men caused more damage than any other British unit of equal strength.

In 1942 the SAS was given the status of a full regiment. Montgomery said of its creator: "The boy Stirling is quite mad. However, in war there is a place for mad people." Nevertheless Montgomery refused to allow Stirling to pick recruits at will from his army.

Stirling himself designed the Regiment's cap badge, bearing the words "Who Dares Wins". The motto summed up his philosophy.

The Egyptian appearance of the SAS wings was due to the fact that they were modelled on a fresco in Shepheards Hotel, Cairo, where there was a symbolical ibis with outstretched wings. The ibis was removed and a parachute substituted. The "winged dagger" badge was meant to resemble Excalibur – the sword of freedom.

Archibald David Stirling was born on November 15 1915, the son of Brig-Gen Archibald Stirling of Keir and his wife, Margaret, fourth daughter of the 13th Lord Lovat. David's brother, William Stirling, commanded the 2nd SAS Regiment.

Young David was educated at Ampleforth and Trinity College, Cambridge, but he was sent down after a year and began to study painting. On the outbreak of the Second World War he was in the Rocky Mountains practising climbing with the ultimate object of attempting Everest.

He served with the Scots Guards (the family regiment) for the first six months of the war, and then transferred to No 3 Commando and went to the Middle East as a member of Bob Laycock's "Layforce", which planned to capture Rhodes. When "Layforce" was disbanded, Stirling and a few of his Commando friends decided to teach themselves parachuting with a view to landing behind German lines in the desert and destroying aircraft on the ground.

They "acquired" parachutes and the use of a dangerously unsuitable old Valentia aircraft. Inevitably Stirling was injured, but, in June 1941, while still on crutches, he managed to gate-crash GHQ, Middle East, and gain the approval of the C-in-C, Gen Auchinleck, to enrol 66 of his colleagues for his new enterprise.

In the early days the SAS was known as "L Detachment" of the Special Air Service Brigade, although the latter did not exist. Training was extremely arduous. On one occasion two parachutists were killed owing to faulty static line clips. Stirling identified the fault, made new clips and tested them himself at dawn the next day.

"Were you scared?" he was asked later. "Terrified," he replied, "but what else could I do?"

The first venture by parachute, on November 17 1941, was a total disaster, because of a sudden sandstorm with winds of 90 mph. Of the 66 who set out, only 22 survived.

Undeterred, Stirling continued with his plans, now using trucks and the expertise of the Long Range Desert Group to navigate in the desert. His revised plan for the unit's employment was to travel deep into the desert by truck or jeep, walk several miles to the target airfield, arrive by night, and plant specially timed bombs to explode when all the dispersed German aircraft had been visited.

The bombs were fused by special time-pencils, invented by his colleague, J. S. Lewes, an Australian and former Oxford rowing blue who, with R. B. Mayne (later to win four DSOs), helped to create the unit's think-tank. Stirling had a genius for recruiting suitable people and, among others, John Verney, Fitzroy Maclean, Randolph Churchill and Roy Farran joined him.

The vital achievement of the SAS was that it destroyed on the ground the latest German aircraft, such as Messerschmitt 109Fs (armed with cannon) which in the sky totally outclassed the ageing Hurricanes and Gloster Gauntlets of the scanty Desert Air Force. One of its most spectacular exploits was the raid on Sidi Haneish airfield, when 18 jeeps, each carrying four Vickers K-machine-guns, drove straight down the central runway, destroying Junkers, Heinkels, Messerschmitts and Stukas. They completed their work by driving around the perimeter, destroying no fewer than 40 aircraft.

Soon the SAS was raiding far and wide, taking pressure off Malta by destroying the airfields from which German bombers took off; it also raided Crete several times. In 1942, while his regiment was operating in the restricted area of northern Tunisia, Stirling was captured as 500 Germans surrounded the cave in which he was sleeping. He soon escaped, but he was recaptured.

After being flown to Italy he escaped four more times, but each time his height – 6ft 5in – gave him away. Eventually the Germans interned him in Colditz.

By the time of his final capture, the SAS – which was prepared to reach its targets by parachute, canoe, jeep, submarine or on foot over vast distances – had destroyed 350 German aircraft and numerous hangars, supply dumps, bridges, roads, and vehicles. It had inflicted many casualties and also drawn off many Germans to try to guard their airfields.

While Stirling was a prisoner of war, the regiment and its sub-unit, the Special Boat Squadron, were also ranging from Italy and the Adriatic to the islands in the Aegean and surrounding seas. They played a leading part in disrupting German communications in France.

On his release Stirling went to live in Rhodesia and Kenya, where he founded the Capricorn Africa Society with the objective of promoting racial equality, tolerance and understanding. He was the society's president for 12 years and made more friends among the black than the white community.

In 1959, when he returned to England, he became involved with the syndication of television programmes, and won the franchise for operating Hong Kong's television service. This became Television International Enterprises, of which he was chairman.

Stirling was always careful not to interfere in any way with the SAS which, having been disbanded, was reconstituted to fight in the Malayan emergency. His military expertise, however, and wish to be concerned with projects beneficial to Britain drew him into advising units countering terrorism and subversion in countries where Britain had interests.

In 1967 Stirling and his friends created the Watch-guard Organisation, which, based in Guernsey, employed ex-SAS soldiers to provide bodyguards for Middle Eastern rulers and others. Occasionally, as in Kenya and Dhofar, he was overruled by Whitehall which sent the SAS, with its larger resources, instead.

By 1972 Stirling thought there were too many groups providing similar services, and for reasons of profit rather than patriotism, and he resigned from Watchguard. By this time the highly reputable Control Risks International was operating to frustrate kidnappers, prevent hi-jacks, and negotiate releases.

During the 1970s there were occasional antagonistic probings by the Press as to how far Stirling was involved with mercenary or secret organisations. There were attempts to link his name with Gen Sir Walter Walker's vigilante organisation for civil defence and to imply that he might harbour hostile intentions towards the govern-ment. This was pure slander, as both Walker and Stirling had often made it clear that they were working for the British government of whatever political party, and not against it.

In 1979 Stirling won substantial damages and costs in settlement of a High Court libel action against the magazine *Time Out*, which had published an article implying that Stirling's capture in North Africa in 1943 showed that he was a coward. Since Stirling was a man of legendary bravery, it was difficult to see why such an absurd accusation could have been made.

Extremely courteous, soft-spoken and self-effacing, David Stirling was worshipped by the men of the unit he had created and many more outside it. For a man of his size, he could move extremely swiftly and silently; in his younger days he had been able to stalk a stag and kill it with a knife.

He regarded killing the enemy as an unfortunate necessity. His most memorable characteristics were his creative vision, his cultured outlook, leadership, patience and iron determination – he was always adamant that the SAS soldier must be governed by a self-discipline and never appear to be a heroic figure.

David Stirling had a wide and varied circle of friends, took a lively interest in all games of chance, and was a considerable *bon vivant*.

He was knighted in the New Year Honours list of 1990. He never married.

November 6 1990

# CDR "BIFFY" DUNDERDALE

COMMANDER W. A. "BIFFY" DUNDERDALE, who has died in New York aged 90, was a member of the Secret Service for 38 years and was sometimes spoken of as the prototype of James Bond.

But where Ian Fleming's creation was extrovert and flamboyant, in love with the latest technology, Dunderdale – though one of the ablest agents of his time – really belonged in the *Boys' Own Paper* era of false beards and invisible ink, and was the most reticent of men. To the end of his long life, visitors to his New York apartment could get almost nothing from "Biffy" about his past service.

The son of a Constantinople shipowner, Wilfred Albert Dunderdale was born on Christmas Eve 1899 and educated at the Gymnasium in Nicolaieff on the Black Sea. He was studying to be a naval architect in St Petersburg when the Russian Revolution broke out in 1917.

His father sent him to Vladivostok to take delivery of the first of a new class of Holland-designed submarines, built in America, and deliver it to the Black Sea. To transport a submarine, still in five separate sections, thousands of miles by rail across a country in the throes of a revolution was asking a good deal of a 16-year-old boy – but young Biffy accomplished it.

The submarine was completed too late to serve in the Imperial Navy and was eventually scuttled at Sebastopol in April 1919. By then the political situation in the region was of literally Byzantine complexity. In 1920 British warships operated in the Black Sea and the Sea of Marmara, bombarding shore installations and sending ashore parties of sailors and marines.

With his knowledge of naval engineering – and of Constantinople and the Black Sea ports – his business-like pretext and his fluent Russian, German and French, Biffy Dunderdale made a superb undercover agent for the Navy.

Still only 19, with the honorary rank of sub-lieutenant RNVR and operating under the *nom de guerre* of "Julius", he was twice mentioned in despatches. In 1920 he was promoted honorary lieutenant RNVR and appointed MBE.

Dunderdale joined the Secret Service in 1921 and was at once involved in foiling one of the frequent Turkish plans to infiltrate troops into Constantinople and seize the city from the Allies. This attempt was finally frustrated by "battleship diplomacy" when HMS *Bembow* and attendant destroyers appeared off the city waterfront.

In the autumn of 1922 British and Turkish troops confronted each other at Chanak in the Dardanelles. Fighting was only prevented by the good sense and moral courage of the Army C-in-C, Gen Harington. The end of the crisis brought the exile of Sultan Mohammed VI, who was taken to Malta in the battleship *Malaya*, and the downfall of Lloyd George as Prime Minister.

Dunderdale's part in these events was domestic rather than epic. He was responsible for arranging and paying for the repatriation of ex-members of the Sultan's harem who were not Turkish nationals – including one *houri* from Leamington Spa, packed off home on the Orient Express.

In 1926 he joined the SIS station in Paris, where he worked with the Deuxième Bureau and established good relations with the French – particularly with Col Gustav Bertrand, head of the French Intelligence Service. He was liaison officer in Paris with the Tsarist Supreme Monarchist Council.

Dunderdale was also on good terms with the Poles, which led to a major intelligence coup. The Poles were pioneers in breaking the Enigma machine cyphers which all three German armed forces were using, so it was imperative that British Intelligence obtain an example.

Dunderdale was "the Third Man" at the celebrated meeting under the clock at Victoria Station on August 16 1939 – which might have come straight out of a spy thriller – when "C" himself (head of the British Secret Service) met Bertrand, a member of the Paris embassy staff, and Dunderdale, who had an Enigma machine in his valise. "C" was on his way to a dinner and cut a conspicuous figure as he strode away, in evening dress, with the ribbon of the Legion d'Honneur in his button-hole and the Enigma under his arm.

The day before war was declared Dunderdale was given the rank of Commander RNVR. He was one of the last Englishmen to leave Paris when the Germans entered the city in June 1940.

When he reached Bordeaux an RAF Avro Anson was sent to make sure he escaped. During the war he kept his links with the Poles and was in contact by radio with Bertrand in Vichy France, and with other members of the Deuxième Bureau who had stayed behind.

Dunderdale also had to deal with the notorious prickliness and slack security of the Gaullist Free French in London, and to fight off the attempts of Sir Claude Dansey, "C's" deputy, to dominate both the Free French Intelligence and the Bureau.

His success was shown by the number of different countries who honoured him. He was appointed CMG in 1942. The Poles awarded him the Polonia Restituta in 1943 for services to the Polish Navy; he was made an officer of the American Legion of Merit in 1946 for "Special Services"; he also held the Russian Order of St Anne and the Croix de Guerre, and was an officer of the Legion d'Honneur.

Dunderdale served with the SIS in London after the war until he retired in 1959, but his influence had declined. Perhaps he knew too many secrets, and realised that his life in espionage had been an elaborate game; but he was an excellent host at his apartments in Paris and New York and his house in Surrey.

He was thrice married: first to June Morse, granddaughter of Samuel B. Morse, inventor of the Morse Code; secondly to Dorothy Hyde, who died in 1978; and thirdly to Debbie Jackson, of Boston, Massachusetts.

November 22 1990

# COL "MONTY" WESTROPP

COLONEL "MONTY" WESTROPP, who has died aged 94, had a gallant record in both World Wars, always led his soldiers from the front and had several hairs' breadth escapes from death.

He was selected for staff training but declined the invitation, asserting that his métier was the command of men in action. Westropp had exacting standards and sometimes a terrifying demeanour – which in later life earned him the soubriquet of "The Purple Colonel" – but he inspired intense loyalty among his men.

He had an exemplary regard for his soldiers and their welfare, and during the Second World War was known to have defied higher command when an order to attack was clearly ill-considered and would have resulted in catastrophic losses.

Scion of an Irish Ascendancy family, Lionel Henry Mountifort Westropp was born on February 20 1896, the eldest son of Brig-Gen Henry Westropp and grandson of Sir Michael Westropp, Chief Justice of Bombay.

Educated at Clifton and Sandhurst, young "Monty" was commissioned into the Devonshire Regiment and in

1916 commanded a company in the horrendous Battle of the Somme in which all his senior officers were killed. During this action Westropp was confronted by a major from an adjacent unit who was fleeing, terrified, from the trenches and causing widespread panic. As the man rushed past him 2nd Lieut Westropp drew his pistol and brought him down with a well-aimed shot in the back.

Westropp later recalled how traumatic the occasion had been for a 20-year-old; and that "with the aid of my stick and my good Sergeant-Major, I readdressed the company's attention towards the enemy".

A few days later Westropp was wounded in the head near the notorious Delville Wood, but he returned to the trenches to take part in the Battle of Arras, only to be shot through the leg during an attack on Fresnoy in May 1917. He then survived a seven-hour ordeal, crawling through the mud of No Man's Land, avoiding enemy patrols, to regain the safety of the trenches.

Westropp's conduct might have been formidable when in the line, but it was equally vigorous during periods of relief from the trenches. His favourite form of recreation was to perform Cossack dances on restaurant tables, accompanied by Olga, his Russian girlfriend.

He also found time to write his autobiography, a fascinating and in parts scandalous work, which he published privately – "so that I can say what I like about everyone and not be sued".

In the book, as in life, Westropp's language was pungent and expressive – particularly so in the passages in which he took issue with the official version of the disastrous Battle of Fresnoy.

"I look upon the account in the Official History," he wrote, "as a grave slight on the memory of those, my comrades, who fell in the attack on Fresnoy. They were given an impossible task which they did their utmost to achieve. What more can be asked of soldiers? I, for one, salute them."

Between the wars Westropp spent six years in India and a year in Aden. Powerful and athletic, he excelled in sports during this period, winning the Khud Race in India, shooting tiger and boar, and playing rugby football and polo. On his return to England he also distinguished himself as an Army fencer at successive Royal Tournaments.

From 1933 to 1936 he commanded the anti-gas wing at Winterbourne Gunner, and while there wrote the British Army Manual on gas (chemical) warfare, which was urgently required as British troops in Egypt anticipated the use of gas by Mussolini in Abyssinia.

On the outbreak of the Second World War Westropp was ordered, as a seasoned veteran, to raise and command a new battalion, the 8th King's Own. In this he became both an inspiration and a father figure. He took it to Belgium as part of the BEF and commanded it with distinction in the evacuation from Dunkirk.

Before going down to the beach he assembled the officers and reminded them that they wore the badge of one of the oldest regiments of the line. "We will therefore represent the regiment as we march down to the beach this afternoon," he said. "We must not let it down and we must set an example to the rabble on the beach."

The battalion set off in perfect step, arms swinging in unison, rifles correctly slung, officers and NCOs properly spaced. The "rabble on the beach", reported the Canadian historian Walter Lord, "were suitably impressed".

Subsequently, when taking the battalion to Malta aboard HMS *Manchester*, Westropp was torpedoed and also attacked from the air. Again he survived, despite the destruction of his cabin and the death of five of his officers. His battalion, by then known as "Westropp's Own", served throughout the siege of Malta, when the island was under constant enemy attack and on starvation rations.

In 1943 Westropp was promoted Colonel and Area Military Commander for Jerusalem, before taking part in the invasion of Sicily and Italy at the Area Headquarters.

After the war he was appointed Colonel of the Devonshire Regiment and Deputy Lieutenant of the county. He became involved in local affairs as a councillor, and was active on behalf of the Conservative party.

Westropp married, in 1937, Muriel Jorgensen; they had two sons.

February 2 1991

# ELSIE GRISCTI

ELSIE GRISCTI, who has died aged 70, showed remarkable courage in Nazi-occupied Holland during the Second World War when, quite independently of MI9's established escape system, she hid and fed Allied airmen and arranged for their return.

Born Elsie Elizabeth Agnes Stokes on January 21 1921, she had begun life in the Netherlands, where her English father and German mother ran a Berlitz language school. But her father died when she was seven, and she was brought up by maternal relations in Germany.

She then returned to Holland where, when the Germans overran the country in 1940, she was a nurse in a hospital at Weert. Her British origins became known, and on Christmas Eve 1940 she was arrested by the Nazis.

She was interned in a camp but contrived her release through the drastic means of sticking a rusty needle into her thigh. As she intended the wound became infected – so badly that the Germans sent her home to die.

This she notably failed to do, to the benefit of several Allied airmen shot down in Holland. Her bravery and resolution were exemplified in the story of Gerry Lorne, a bomb-aimer in 218 Squadron, whose aircraft was brought down by a Ju88 night-fighter at the end of August 1943.

Having extricated himself from his parachute, entangled in a tree, Lorne, leg and ankle broken, hobbled to a farmhouse, where he was interrogated by a Roman Catholic priest sent to learn if he were a German intelligence stooge. His *bona fides* established, Lorne lived at first in a chicken run, from which Miss Stokes conveyed him by wheelbarrow to a hiding-place in a wood. There she nursed him for 10 days, feeding him with apples and milk, until he was well enough to attempt an escape.

Miss Stokes persuaded a Dutch doctor to drive him into Belgium, where a more regular escape and evasion organisation took over. Through this and other exploits she became recognised by the RAF Escaping Society as one of their most valuable helpers.

After the Liberation Miss Stokes nursed in a Canadian field hospital. In 1948 she moved to London and three years later married Joseph Griscti, a Maltese businessman.

Mrs Griscti worked for Barclays Bank and helped at a home for elderly Jewish refugees in Bath before joining British Airways, where she was for many years a translator and interpreter. She retired in 1979, subsequently devoting herself to charitable causes and to the RAF Escaping Society.

February 12 1991

# ADML SIR FREDERICK PARHAM

ADMIRAL SIR FREDERICK PARHAM, who has died aged 90, commanded the heavy cruiser *Belfast* during the dramatic chase and destruction of the German battle cruiser *Scharnhorst* by ships of the Home Fleet off the North Cape of Norway on December 26 1943.

*Scharnhorst* had sailed from a Norwegian fjord on Christmas Day to attack convoy JW55B on its way to Murmansk and the next morning encountered *Belfast*, wearing the flag of Rear-Adml Bob Burnett, commanding the 10th Cruiser Squadron, and two other cruisers, *Norfolk* and *Sheffield*.

It was *Belfast* which first detected the enemy by radar at 8.40 am at a range of 16 miles; and some 30 minutes later *Belfast*'s star shell bursting overhead caught *Scharnhorst* completely by surprise. After a brief gun action, *Scharnhorst* broke away.

Burnett decided not to try to follow but to fall on the convoy – a decision which was later criticised. At the time Burnett was greatly distressed to receive a somewhat sharp signal from his C-in-C, Adml Sir Bruce Fraser, flying his flag in the battleship *Duke of York*, some distance away.

Burnett asked Parham if he'd done the right thing. "Poor old Bob," said Parham later, "he was a terribly emotional chap, he was jolly near in tears about it. I was able to reassure him and tell him he had done *exactly* the right thing."

Both men were vindicated when *Scharnhorst* threatened the convoy again and *Belfast* had another radar contact just after midday. For the second time the cruisers caught *Scharnhorst* by surprise.

After another gun action, in which *Norfolk* was hit, *Scharnhorst* turned to run for home, closely followed by the cruisers and Home Fleet destroyers. But *Norfolk* dropped back to put out a fire, and *Sheffield* suffered a main engine defect, so *Belfast* was soon alone.

In what Fraser called an exemplary piece of shadowing, *Belfast* broadcast her own position, course and speed, and *Scharnhorst*'s range, course and speed, every 15 minutes for the next three and a half hours. Throughout that time Parham marvelled that *Belfast* was never attacked.

"*Scharnhorst* was a much bigger ship than us," he said. "She'd only got to turn round for 10 minutes and she could have blown us clean out of the water."

So accurate was *Belfast*'s reporting that Fraser was able to ponder whether he should have the battle before or after his tea and to decide on the latter option. It was forecast that *Scharnhorst* would appear on the flagship's radar screen at 4.15 pm: the actual time was 4.17.

*Duke of York*'s star shell caught *Scharnhorst* by surprise for the third and last time, and in the final act of the drama the enemy was brought to bay and sunk by gunfire and by torpedoes from the destroyers, with only 36 survivors from her total complement of over 2,000. Parham was awarded the DSO.

*Belfast* had covered several Arctic convoys in 1943, and in October sailed with the Home Fleet to accompany the American carrier *Ranger* for an air strike on the Norwegian port of Bodo. In April 1944 *Belfast* was in the Home Fleet covering force for the Fleet Air Arm carrier aircraft strike on the German battleship *Tirpitz* in Altenfjord. At 5.30 am on D-Day (June 6) she was off Juno beach, Normandy, carrying out a two-hour bombardment of a German howitzer battery.

When the Green Howards overran that battery later they found the guns out of action and the crews sheltering in concrete bunkers. For the rest of that day and the next week *Belfast* supported the 3rd Canadian Division and by June 14 had fired 1,996 six-inch shells. When she left to reload with ammunition, Parham was delighted to receive an appreciative signal from the Force commander, praising *Belfast*'s gunnery in verse.

On June 25 *Belfast* was back to bombard railways and bridges near Caen, and on July 8 she supported the Royal Marines at Port-en-Bassein and the assault on Caen the next day. Parham was mentioned in despatches.

Frederick Robertson Parham was born on January 9 1901 and joined the Navy as a cadet in 1914, going to

Osborne and Dartmouth. His first posting as a midshipman was to the battleship *Malaya*, which he joined in the Grand Fleet in 1917.

From 1925 he specialised in gunnery and after early promotion was appointed Experimental Commander at HMS *Excellent*, the gunnery establishment at Whale Island, Portsmouth, in 1934. Three years later he commanded the destroyer *Shikari*, which controlled by radio the movements of the old battleship *Centurion*, used as a gunnery and bombing target ship by the Mediterranean Fleet.

While *Centurion* kept a steady course, bombing results were good, but as soon as Parham varied course and speed accuracy fell off markedly. As a result the Fleet Air Arm largely abandoned high-level bombing of ships and concentrated on torpedo and dive bombing.

In 1938 Parham took command of the brand new Tribal class destroyer *Gurkha* and commanded her for the first months of the war – until February 1940, when he went to the Admiralty, first as assistant and then as deputy director of Naval Ordnance. He was closely involved with the application of radar to surface fire control – techniques which were to prove so effective against *Scharnhorst*.

After *Belfast* he went to the Admiralty again, as director of the Operations Division (Foreign) and then as director of the whole division. His last seagoing command was *Vanguard* – arguably the most beautiful battleship ever built for the Navy.

He took her over in May 1947, after she had returned from the royal tour of South Africa, and commanded her at home and in the Mediterranean until July 1949. He was Deputy Chief of Personnel from 1949 until 1951, when he was Flag Officer Flotillas and second-in-command Mediterranean Fleet.

Parham would have been Second Sea Lord in 1953 but was prevented by illness. In 1954 he presided over an investigation into the deployment of warships. Prewar foreign commissions of two years and more were no longer acceptable.

Parham arrived at a solution, generally welcomed in the Service, of splitting a ship's time between foreign and home stations, with no ship having to spend more than nine months on average abroad.

He was Fourth Sea Lord and Chief of Supplies and Transport from 1954 to 1955; and his last appointment was C-in-C The Nore from 1955 until his retirement in 1959.

Parham was vice-chairman of the British Waterways Board from 1963 to 1967. He was appointed CBE in 1949 and CB in 1951, and promoted to KCB in 1955 and GBE in 1959. He also received Portuguese, Iraqi and Italian orders while acting as host to visiting heads of State as C-in-C The Nore. He was naval ADC to King George VI in 1949.

Parham married first, in 1926, Kathleen Dobrée Carey, who died in 1973; they had a son. He married secondly, in 1978, Mrs Joan Saunders (*née* Charig).

**John Winton writes**: "Freddie" Parham was never tested as a fleet commander but as a wartime sea captain he was second to none.

In *Belfast* he had "a very green lot of sailors". Many of her company of 900 had never been to sea before, and some of her RNVR officers were at sea as officers for the first time, but Parham welded them all together into a most efficient fighting unit.

As a man, he was a most agreeable shipmate, generous with praise, sparing with criticism and intensely loyal to those above and below him. He never set out to attract attention to himself but rose steadily through the Navy by sheer merit.

As the senior survivor of the Battle of North Cape he was always ready to give information and interviews. He would recall with humour that long and anxious day of battle, the bitter cold and very bad weather with only pale daylight for a short time around noon. "The best way to get the feel of that day," he said, "would be to read the despatches in a refrigerator, being heavily rocked, by the light of a single candle, with occasionally someone banging on the outside with a very large hammer."

March 27 1991

# LT-COL CHARLES "THE BOSS" TRIPP

LIEUTENANT-COLONEL CHARLES "THE BOSS" TRIPP, who has died aged 89, achieved notable successes in command of the 1st Commando Fiji Guerrillas when operating behind Japanese lines in the southern island group between late 1942 and late 1943.

When the unit was eventually disbanded in May 1944, 40 per cent of the officers and 30 per cent of the sergeants had been killed in action behind enemy lines.

In December 1942, although Japanese expansion to

the south and the immediate threat to Australia had been checked by the Battle of the Coral Sea, the Japanese still occupied every island of tactical value in the south-west Pacific. Gen MacArthur's strategy was to recapture key bases in a series of hopping movements until he reached Iwo Jima and Okinawa – and an invasion on Japan itself became practical.

But the Japanese were building an airfield on Guadalcanal and a seaplane base at Tulagi. They would put up a determined opposition to any Allied invasion force as they had massed their troops for the further attempt on Australia.

In order to operate in the Japanese rear areas and acquire intelligence, a 200-strong Commando force was raised; it contained New Zealanders, English, Americans, and a mixture of Fijians, Tongans and Solomon Islanders. Although already 40, Tripp was the toughest and most enduring man in the unit, as well as being an inspired leader who earned the affectionate sobriquet of "The Boss".

A New Zealander, Charles William Howard Tripp was born on February 22 1902, and educated at Christ's College, Christchurch, New Zealand, and Trinity Hall, Cambridge. On coming down from the university he returned to New Zealand and began farming on land settled by his grandfather in 1856.

When he volunteered for the Army at the start of the Second World War he was graded as being too old; in an attempt to keep him out of harm, he was posted to Fiji.

When the Commando unit was formed, missionaries, who had spent 40 years damping down the Fijians' warlike instincts, were now called on for advice on rekindling it, which they supplied. Recruiting was carried out with regard to native customs, which included quaffing numerous bowls of *Kava* and the presentation of whale's teeth to the officers.

By the time the Commandos were ready for action, rigorous training schedules had made them expert in bushcraft, camouflage, jungle warfare and silent killing. Their first successful operation was on Guadalcanal, where they dislocated Japanese plans, inflicted numerous casualties and acquired valuable intelligence on enemy movements and equipment. Up until this time they were known as the Southern Independent Commando, but now Tripp was told to raise a special force to be known as the 1st Commando Fiji Guerrillas.

This outfit reached unprecedented heights of marksmanship and jungle warfare endurance. It was said: "When the Fiji Commandos raid at night, death wears velvet gloves."

Communication with the Fijians was in pidgin English; an aircraft was "schooner-belong-Jesus-Christ", but they soon learned to recognise various types, such as B17 and P38.

Initially they used Thompson sub-machine guns, but then found the Australian Owen guns more effective. Much of their work consisted of eliminating the groups of spies that the Japanese had left behind.

Their most important achievement was assisting in the capture of Munda Airfield on New Georgia, around which there were known to be 5,000 Japanese. Tripp's guerrillas arrived after an 11-hour voyage on an American destroyer which was chased by, but escaped from, three Japanese warships. Then they cleared the smaller islands of Japanese before moving inland.

The ensuing conflict included numerous close-quarter fights at night. It was described as "very personal".

On one occasion, a Japanese machine-gunner opened up on Tripp, who was leading a patrol, at 10 yards range. Tripp's carbine jammed as he tried to return the fire so he threw the weapon at the gunner and raced off into the undergrowth at what he described as world record-breaking speed.

The Japanese threw grenades after him but as he looked for a hiding place he saw another party of a dozen Japanese approaching. He shot the leader with his automatic, and in the confusion managed to slip away and rejoin his patrol.

They settled down for the night only to find they were in the middle of a strongly held enemy position. Inevitably they were discovered, but again managed to escape into the jungle after a brisk fight in the dark.

Tripp had a lucky escape when a Japanese bullet was deflected by his cigarette-lighter – subsequently a Tripp family treasure. When the moon came up, American artillery began shelling the area and Tripp, realising that he could easily be mistaken in the dark for a Japanese, decided to walk around the position while the soldiers were all securely in their foxholes.

In doing so he found various telephone lines to mortar posts, which he cut; their exhausted crews were asleep and he was undetected. He then headed south through a swamp, reached an American regimental HQ and gave them the information he had gathered. In consequence the Americans were able to push on to the coast and secure the beach-head at Laiana.

After the capture of Munda, Tripp took a force of 50

guerrillas to Vella Lavelle, where they acquired maps from dead Japanese and identified various targets for American artillery. This prevented the Japanese from turning the island into a strongpoint.

At the conclusion of these exploits, Tripp was awarded the DSO and the American Silver Star. Thirty-five other members of his guerrillas received gallantry awards.

Tripp's citation mentioned that "the 1st Commando Fiji Guerrillas furnished distant reconnaissance patrols which worked well into enemy territory often at great hazard and furnished battle guides, and in some instances actually led front-line units in combat and assaults on enemy positions. Tripp himself engaged in much patrolling in addition to planning, supervising and conducting the activities of the entire detachment in a most capable fashion".

He later described his guerrilla work as "the best three years' holiday I ever had, and I got paid for it too". After the war he was involved in the rehabilitation of ex-Servicemen and land allocations.

Tripp was noted for his pioneering spirit and his readiness to embrace all the technological advances in agriculture. Both Baden-Powell and Shackleton stayed with the family and from these visits Tripp became extremely interested in pioneering and Antarctica; he eventually assembled one of the largest collections of Antarctic memorabilia in the Southern Hemisphere.

At Cambridge he had been a respectable oarsman and a good boxer and rugby footballer, as well as acquiring a lifelong passion for Kipling which he could recite for hours on end.

Back in New Zealand he became a world-renowned

cattle breeder and exported many Poll Herefords to Canada and Britain where they won prizes and record prices. "The Boss" was a tall, taciturn, raw-boned figure who believed in leading from the front and trusting his men. Very few failed him.

An altogether exceptional man, Charles Tripp had sailed round Cape Horn twice before he was 10 and was still getting up at 5 am in the month he died in his 90th year.

His wife, Myra, predeceased him. They had two sons and two daughters.

April 1 1991

# HARRY RÉE

HARRY RÉE, who has died aged 76, had two distinguished careers – first in the Special Operations Executive during the Second World War, and then as Professor of Education at York University, after which he went back to school as a classroom teacher, an almost unheard-of self-demotion.

Rée – like Francis Cammaerts, another of SOE's best agents – had begun the war as a conscientious objector, before a change of heart led him to sign up as a gunner. In 1942, after a spell in Intelligence, Rée was recruited by Major Peter Lee, who had created SOE's No 2 Field Section, and commissioned with the rank of captain as a field security conducting officer.

This entailed keeping an eye on radio operators. Among Rée's duties was to assess the operators' reliability on a booze-up, as well as their ability to resist temptation by women. In London this test was taken a stage further when the men were given the addresses of enthusiastic amateurs, who took them to bed and reported their susceptibility to seduction by female Gestapo agents.

All this whetted Rée's appetite to operate in the field himself and he badgered Lee to let him train as an agent. Lee was horrified, telling him: "You know far too much about the system to risk capture, torture and interrogation."

When Lee was posted to North Africa, however, Rée was able to persuade SOE's "F" Section to parachute him into France. His arrival, in April 1943, was disconcerting. A container accompanying him was caught on a pylon; his first safe address turned out to be a hotel the Gestapo had occupied two weeks earlier.

Moreover, the agent whom Rée had been told to contact at Clermont-Ferrand, on hearing Rée's French, advised him to pack it in: the SOE had hoped that Rée's Mancunian accent might pass for Alsatian. Nevertheless he remained in France for most of 1943, training and operating with the *maquis* in the Jura mountains.

Operating under the codename "César" and the assumed identity of "Henri Rehman", itinerant watch-maker, Rée was a brilliant saboteur. His invention of what became known as blackmail sabotage at the Peugeot works at Sochaux, near Montbeliard, has assumed text-book status in the literature of subversion.

The peacetime car factory was busily engaged producing arms for the Luftwaffe and Wehrmacht. Rée went to see Roger Peugeot, who ran the works, and suggested he co-operate with internal sabotage in return for an agreement with the RAF to call off attacks on the plant – attacks which were costing civilian lives.

The subsequent explosions within the factory destroyed a 600-ton press vital in the construction of tank turrets. Later, when the Germans sought to replace it with a press delivered by canal, Rée sank the barge.

Eventually rumbled, Rée hit the German military policeman sent to arrest him over the head with a bottle of Armagnac, but was shot in the process: one bullet penetrated a lung, another grazed his heart. After a 20-minute struggle during which he bit off the German's nose, Rée escaped. He managed to cross a river and crawl several miles through the countryside to the Swiss border.

Harry Alfred Rée was born at Manchester on October 15 1914, the youngest of eight children. His grandfather had emigrated from Germany in the 1870s; his mother was French.

Young Harry was educated at Shrewsbury and St John's College, Cambridge, where he read economics and modern languages. His first job was as a French master at Penge Grammar School, and after the war Rée returned to teaching.

In 1947 he went to Bradford Grammar School as French master; four years later he became headmaster of Watford Grammar School; and in 1961 he co-founded the seminal "Agreement to Broaden the Curriculum", a movement against "the undesirable degree of specialisation" in the public and grammar schools.

In the same year Lord James of Rusholme, the first Vice-Chancellor of York University, invited Rée to become Professor of Education. He took up the post when the university opened its doors to students in 1963.

At York, Rée established himself as a leading contributor to national debates about the role of education:

he was no respecter of received wisdom, of pedants, or of teachers and academics unduly preoccupied with their own prestige. When the Bachelor of Education degree was launched, for instance, he spoke of trainee teachers suffering from "unwanted and indigestible academic teaching which they mistake for scholarship."

In 1965 Rée announced the creation of SASSD, the Society for the Abolition of School Speech Days. Four years later he was the moving spirit behind SPERTTT, the Society for the Promotion of Educational Reform Through Teacher Training – which pressed, among other things, for a regular interchange of functions between teachers and college lecturers. "We teachers," he declared, "must come off our pedestals."

Before he went to York Rée had been a militant supporter of the grammar school and wrote a well-argued book on the subject, *The Essential Grammar School*. He later underwent an almost Pauline conversion and became an equally vigorous advocate of comprehensives.

Thenceforward Rée was firmly aligned with the progressives. The rallying cry among them was "relevance", and Rée's thinking was undoubtedly influential in disseminating that hard-to-define concept. But he gradually began to realise that he had had no experience of meeting the real challenge of secondary school teaching – educating the large majority who had no motivation to go on to higher education.

He therefore left York in 1974 to become the lowest grade of language teacher at Woodberry Down Comprehensive School, London, arguing: "People who've been in the teacher training business *should* go back into the schools."

Rée was rising 60. The crowd-control aspect of teaching in a comprehensive came as a surprise to him, and later he frankly admitted that his attempts to teach French to unacademic, unmotivated pupils with wildly varying levels of ability were a failure; but his zest was undiminished. He remained at the school for six years until finally retiring in 1980.

Rée then took up the cause of "Community Education" – "raising the school leaving age to 90", as he put it – and for seven years edited the Community Education Development Centre Monthly Bulletin, *Network*. He greatly admired and was much influenced by the educational eccentric Henry Morris, who pioneered the pre-war "Village Colleges" in Cambridgeshire.

In 1973 Rée published a notable book about Morris, *Educator Extraordinary*, in furtherance of his strong belief that schools should not shut themselves off from the rest of the community, and should "consciously encourage the formation of an educated public opinion, without which democracy cannot survive the cultural pollution by which it is increasingly threatened."

Rée, who had a house at Ingleborough, grew to love the dales and moorlands of Yorkshire: he wrote *Three Peaks of Yorkshire* (1983), with photographs by Caroline Forbes, as a tribute to the landscape of Ingleborough, Penyghent and Whernside.

For his work with the Resistance Rée was appointed OBE in 1945 and awarded the DSO and the Croix de Guerre.

Shortly before his death he spoke at Valencay at the unveiling, by Queen Elizabeth the Queen Mother, of a memorial to members of the SOE's French section.

Rée married, in 1943, Hetty Vine, who predeceased him; they had two sons and a daughter. He married secondly, in 1965, Peta Garrett.

May 20 1991

# Lt-Col Richard Broad

LIEUTENANT-COLONEL RICHARD BROAD, who has died aged 81, led seven fellow Seaforth Highlanders in a prolonged and exciting escape from France in 1940, and subsequently led clandestine operations for Special Operations Executive.

The Seaforths were surrounded by German tanks at St Valery in June 1940; most of the HQ staff were dead or wounded. The majority of the eight surviving officers spoke of fighting to the death with their 100 men, but Broad, though only a subaltern, argued that their first duty was towards those under their command.

The men were exhausted, hungry and lacking sleep; and there were many wounded in urgent need of medical attention. But Broad insisted that those who were able should make a break for it.

Major Murray Grant, the acting CO, agreed. The Germans were informed of the surrender and asked to collect the wounded. Meanwhile Broad, together with a sergeant and five privates – a sixth soon joined them – dashed through the cordon under the nose of a tank and disappeared into a cornfield.

They headed south for the Seine, which they reached after six days and nights near Duclair. The river is about

250 yards wide at this point, but the Seaforths, having chanced upon a timber yard, built a raft.

The crossing miscarried. Much equipment was left on the bottom of the Seine; Broad and his men, soaked, struggled back to the north bank. They struck towards the Channel, and after 12 days and nights reached Honfleur, where they learnt that France had capitulated, but that part of the south had been left unoccupied.

Broad abandoned any idea of escaping across the Channel and began to set his sights on the far distant Riviera. Meanwhile his party was valiantly assisted by the mother superior of a convent who adopted Broad as her "war son", and by a local police commissioner.

The men were also indebted to the eccentric pipe-smoking Mlle Marie-Thérèse Burgis, whose shaggy and ferocious Briard dogs frightened Germans away from Le Manoir du Parc, the château in which she accommodated some of the Seaforths. In the New Year of 1941 Mme Nicole Bouchet de Fareins, one of two sisters who daily risked their lives for Broad and his men, visited Paris on their behalf.

Through Comte Pierre d'Harcourt of French Intelligence she arranged for Broad to stay in Paris with Princesse Jacqueline de Broglie. Broad was given the codename "Marguerite" in his contacts with the nascent Resistance; he and his group were also referred to as "Snow White and the Seven Dwarfs".

It helped that Broad spoke good French: the problem of financing the escape was solved after he was introduced to d'Harcourt's uncle, Prince Jean de Caraman Chimay, head of Veuve Clicquot. The night before Broad returned to Honfleur he dined at Maxim's with Princesse

Jacqueline. They had hardly unfolded their napkins before Hermann Goering and his party sat down at a nearby table. The *Reichsmarschall* beamed contentedly in Broad's direction.

Back in Honfleur, Broad organised the passage of his "Dwarfs" to Paris, where the American journalist Steele Powers provided him with a letter which stated that he was an American citizen and a Red Cross ambulance driver. But it was by rail that Broad and his men reached the demarcation line, which they managed to cross into unoccupied France. Nevertheless the Dwarfs had to endure a series of difficult prison and internment camp experiences, until Broad encountered Capt Ian Garrow at Marseille. Garrow was a fellow Seaforth, and the progenitor of the "Pat" escape line which Pat O'Leary (*qv*) eventually established for MI9.

When Broad's group crossed into Spain they suffered further hardships at the hands of Spanish officials who, convinced that Hitler had won the war, cast them into prison. But after frustrating delays the British consulate secured their release, and the long adventure ended with their repatriation from Gibraltar.

Richard Lowther Broad was born on April 10 1910. His education was dogged by asthma which later almost kept him out of the Army, and which plagued him during his escape from France. By 1938 he was a partner in a City stockbroking firm. With war clearly imminent, he was accepted by the Supplementary Reserve and commissioned into the Seaforth Highlanders.

In June 1941, after his escape and debriefing by MI9, Broad was still only a second lieutenant. Promotion had passed him by because he had been "missing believed killed".

He was awarded the MC – which he received reluctantly, feeling that the courage of his Dwarfs had gone unrecognised – and invited to join SOE with the rank of captain.

Broad was swiftly promoted to major and took part in the seizure of Madagascar from the Vichy French. He helped to secure the port of Diego Suarez and then entered the capital Tananarive posing as an American Caltex Oil representative.

Broad returned home for a parachute course and was then transferred to Combined Operations. For much of 1943 he was involved in raids undertaken to gain experience for the invasion of Normandy.

His responsibilities required him to work closely with Lord Louis Mountbatten, who was head of Combined Operations. But he still kept in touch with SOE, for whom he recruited Nancy Wake ("the White Mouse"), who had helped him in France.

Broad was next appointed to the command of No 10 Commando's "Crossbow Force", set up to destroy V1 flying-bomb sites – though the operation was eventually cancelled in favour of pinpoint attacks from the air. In the summer of 1944 Broad transferred to Airborne Forces, and that September he was dropped into France to reinforce the *Maquis*. Another mission was to deliver a large sum of money to Gen Granval at Nancy.

After the relief of Paris Gen de Gaulle personally decorated Broad with the Legion d'Honneur and Croix de Guerre avec Palme; a second Croix de Guerre avec Palme followed a month later.

Broad was an assistant military attaché in Paris until the summer of 1945, when he transferred to Berlin as second-in-command of a liaison group.

After the war he worked as a businessman in South Africa, eventually settling in Devon to farm. But the French people who had helped save his life were never forgotten. He both visited them in France and entertained them at his own home. It was largely to preserve their memory that he collaborated with the author Rex Woods to produce an autobiography, *A Talent to Survive* (1982).

He is survived by his wife Joan, and by a son and a daughter.

May 21 1991

# BRIG LORNE CAMPBELL OF AIRDS, VC

BRIGADIER LORNE CAMPBELL OF AIRDS, who has died aged 88, had an outstanding record in the Second World War, in which he won the DSO at Dunkirk, a Bar at El Alamein and the Victoria Cross in Tunisia.

Then a lieutenant-colonel, Campbell was leading an attack by his battalion of the Argyll and Sutherland Highlanders when it was counter-attacked by the Germans and he was wounded in the neck by a mortar burst.

"On April 6, 1943", read the citation for his VC, "in the attack upon the Wadi Akarit position, the task of breaking through the enemy minefield and anti-tank ditch to the east of the Roumana feature and of forming the initial bridgehead for a brigade of the 51st Highland Division was allotted to the battalion of the Argyll and Sutherland Highlanders commanded by Lt-Col Campbell."

The attack had to form up in complete darkness and had to traverse the main off-shoot of the Wadi Akarit at an angle to the line of advance. In spite of heavy machine-gun and shell fire in the early stages of the attack, Campbell successfully accomplished this difficult operation, captured at least 600 prisoners and led his battalion to its objective, having to cross an unswept portion of the enemy minefield in doing so.

Later, upon reaching his objective he found that a gap which had been blown by the Royal Engineers in the anti-tank ditch did not correspond with the vehicle lane which had been cleared in the minefield. Realising the vital necessity of quickly establishing a gap for the passage of anti-tank guns, he took personal charge of this operation.

It was now broad daylight and under very heavy machine-gun fire and shell fire, he succeeded in making a personal reconnaissance and in conducting operations which led to the establishing of a vehicle gap.

Throughout the day Campbell held his position with his battalion in the face of extremely heavy and constant shell fire, which the enemy was able to bring to bear by direct observation. At about 4.30 in the afternoon determined enemy counter-attack began to develop accompanied by tanks. In this phase of the fighting Campbell's personality dominated the battlefield by a "display of valour and utter disregard for personal safety, which could not have been excelled", as the citation noted.

Realising that it was imperative for the future success of the Army plan to hold the bridgehead his battalion had captured, he inspired his men by his presence in the forefront of the battle, cheering them on and rallying them as he moved to those points where the fighting was heaviest.

When his left forward company was forced to give

ground he went forward alone, into a hail of fire and personally reorganised their position, remaining with the company until the attack at this point was held.

As reinforcements arrived upon the scene he was seen standing in the open directing the fight under close-range fire of enemy infantry and he continued to do so although already painfully wounded in the neck by shell fire. It was not until the battle died down that he allowed his wound to be dressed. Even then, although in great pain, he refused to be evacuated, remaining with his battalion and continuing to inspire them by his presence on the field. Darkness fell with the Argylls still holding their positions, though many of its officers and men had become casualties.

Earlier in the war, Campbell had won a DSO in France where he was second-in-command of the 8th Argyll and Sutherland Highlanders. Although the remainder of the 51st Highland Division was captured at St Valery, Campbell managed to make his way through the German lines to see what had happened to the two leading companies of his battalion.

He found they had reached the coast and were sheltering in a lighthouse. Here they were attacked by men from Rommel's division but, led by Campbell, they fought their way out and, after marching for three nights, got out via Le Havre. They returned to take part in the abortive attempt to launch a second British Expeditionary Force via Cherbourg.

Back in Britain Campbell was hailed in newspaper headlines for his Dunkirk exploits as "THE MAN WHO SAVED 200". One of the 200 said: "The Argylls will follow him anywhere."

A colonel's son, Lorne Maclaine Campbell was born on July 22 1902 into a distinguished Highland family.

His uncle, Vice-Adml Gordon Campbell, an expert on Q ships, had won a VC in the First World War but refused a Bar to it in favour of another nominee; he also won the DSO and two Bars.

Young Lorne was educated at Dulwich and was a postmaster (scholar) at Merton College, Oxford. On coming down from the university, Campbell worked in his father's wine shipping business.

In 1921 he joined his father's regiment, the 8th Argyll and Sutherland Highlanders, as a Territorial officer and gave up much of his free time to soldiering.

In the Second World War, after the fall of France, Campbell was transferred to command the 7th Battalion of the Argylls in the re-raised 51st Highland Division for the North African campaign. He won a Bar to his DSO by leading his battalion in a successful attack at a critical moment in the Alamein battle in 1942.

Following the desert battles, Campbell was given command of 13th Infantry Brigade in 5th Division and at times commanded the division itself in the campaign through Sicily and Italy. One of its more notable actions was at the crossing of the Senio river.

When he returned on leave in October 1944 Campbell was given a hero's welcome at Auchendarroch, Argyll, the home of his wife's family. He arrived in the steamer *Loch Fyne*, which was decked with flowers, and the pipes began to play as soon as he set foot on land. Then cheer after cheer rang across the loch as a battalion of the Argylls marched past.

From 1944 to 1945, he was Brigadier, General Staff, in the military mission in Washington; subsequently he served in Germany, where he investigated the possibility of restarting the Boy Scout movement, which had been abolished by Hitler and replaced by his infamous youth organisations. Campbell had always been an enthusiastic supporter of the Boy Scout movement and, at one stage, was in the running for appointment to Chief Scout.

After the war, he returned to the family business – which had been badly blitzed – and rebuilt it. He went on to be elected Master of the Vintners Company. He was also a Vice-Lieutenant for the City of London.

Six foot three inches tall, Campbell cut an impressive figure. In his younger days he had been a good all-round athlete: he won a half-Blue for athletics and played rugby football for the Oxford Greyhounds. A damaged cartilage prevented him from winning a Blue.

He was also a good club cricketer, turning out for I Zingari, and was keen on all field sports, particularly fishing, and he was an enthusiastic gardener.

In battle, Campbell was very controlled and won widespread admiration for his coolheadedness in crises. He had outstanding gifts of leadership. It was typical of the man that, on being awarded the VC, he was at pains to transfer the honour to his men. "From El Alamein to Tunis every man of my battalion was simply magnificent," he said. "They never failed me, though sometimes I was almost apologetic when asking them to make attack after attack."

Besides the VC, DSO and Bar, Campbell was mentioned four times in despatches; received the Territorial Decoration in 1941; was appointed OBE in 1968; and was an Officer of the American Legion of Merit.

He married, in 1935, Muriel, only daughter of Alastair Campbell of Auchendarroch. She died in 1950. They had two sons.

May 28 1991

# XAN FIELDING

XAN FIELDING, the author, translator, journalist and adventurous traveller, who has died in Paris aged 72, lived a charmed life as a Special Operations Executive agent in Crete, France and the Far East during the Second World War.

Short, dark, athletic and a brilliant linguist, he was God's gift to operations in rugged mountainous regions and wherever his languages were needed.

Major Fielding was awarded the DSO in September 1942, "for going into a town", as he said later with a typical modesty.

He had a boyish, slightly rebellious spirit which he shared with many of his contemporaries in SOE. His self-confessed, or self-proclaimed, amateurishness certainly belied a tough professionalism, great resourcefulness and bravery in action. Fielding was the sort of man one would be happy to go into the jungle with.

While still in his early twenties he was responsible for clandestine and subversive activities in large areas of enemy-occupied Crete. He survived numerous encounters with German forces, only to be rumbled by the Gestapo in France towards the end of hostilities in Europe.

Even then his luck held. Locked in a death cell at Digne in 1944, he was "sprung" in an audacious move by Christine Granville (*née* Krystyna Skarbeck) whose SOE exploits matched his.

Alexander Wallace Fielding was born at Ootacamund, India, on November 26 1918. His family had long links with the Raj and his father was a major in the 50th Sikhs.

Xan's mother died at his birth and he was largely brought up at Nice, where his grandmother's family had considerable property. Fluent in French, he subsequently became a proficient classicist at Charterhouse and then studied briefly at Bonn, Munich and Freiburg Universities in Germany. He saw what was happening in that country and was so shocked at the attitude of the Chamberlain government that he came close to joining the Communist party.

At the end of the 1930s Fielding – who had recently been sacked as a sub-editor on the *Cyprus Times* and was by now unsuccessfully running a bar – found himself a misfit in the Mediterranean colony. Colonial officials abhorred his refusal to adopt their disdainful description of Cypriots as "Cyps". That he was also reasonably fluent in Greek rendered him suspect to district commissioners, who could not speak the language of the people they administered.

At the outbreak of the Second World War, haunted by the thought that he might find himself trapped in Cyprus for the duration, he fled to Greece and found asylum on St Nicholas, an island owned by the anthropologist, Francis Turville Petre. Fielding dreaded not so much the battlefield as joining the conventional officers' mess. But eventually news of the fall of France, the Dunkirk evacuation and the Battle of Britain induced a "stab of guilt".

He returned to the colony and was commissioned as an intelligence officer into the Cyprus Regiment, which appealed to him on account of its perverse refusal to have any regimental pride.

On hearing in Cairo that Cretans had taken up arms against the Germans, he yearned, as he wrote later, to help lead "this concerted uprising of the technically non-combatant".

When Crete fell, Fielding was interviewed in Egypt by SOE. He was asked: "Have you any personal objection to committing a murder?" His response being deemed acceptable, Fielding was put ashore in Crete with a load of weapons and explosives by Cdr "Crap" Miers, VC, skipper of the submarine *Torbay*.

Fielding, who had adopted the style and dress of a Greek highland peasant, was accompanied by a First World War veteran, who was inseparable from his solar topee and unrecognisable as the village schoolmaster he was supposed to impersonate.

Fortunately it was not long before he teamed up with the far more kindred spirit of Patrick Leigh Fermor. Sporting a royal blue waistcoat, lined with scarlet shot silk and embroidered with black arabesques – and singing folk songs in several languages – "Paddy" Leigh Fermor enlivened their meetings in desolate mountain hide-outs.

Fielding understood the need for reliable intelligence and communications, and he daringly set up his head-quarters near Crete's northern coastal road in the prox-imity of German units. He experienced, as he put it, a childish excitement in "brushing shoulders with the *Wehrmacht*" in the corridors of the town hall when calling on the mayor of Crete's capital, Canea. And he found it entertaining to attend parties given for the Germans by Cretan associates feigning fraternisation.

Operationally, Crete had become a massive transit camp to reinforce the Afrika Korps. Among his intelligence successes Fielding signalled the timetable of transports taking off from the airfield at Maleme, enabling the RAF to intercept them.

After six months he was picked up by a Greek submarine and given a breather in Cairo. This gave him a chance to niggle about the inaccuracy of RAF air drops.

As a result Fielding was invited to observe, from the front turret of a Wellington, a drop arranged for Leigh Fermor high up in the White Mountains. Considerably shaken by the experience – not least the anti-aircraft fire – he returned to the island by Greek submarine at the end of 1942 and never complained again.

Following the Crete mission, he parachuted into the south of France in the summer of 1944. Bearing papers announcing him as Armand Pont-Leve, a young clerk in the Electric Company of Nimes – but codenamed "Cathedrale" – Fielding was received by Francis Cammaerts (*alias* "Roger") and also by Christine Granville.

Fielding found them "an imposing pair". Still in uniform, he felt "rather like a novice in the presence of a prior and prioress". The canister containing his civilian clothes, with poison pill sewn into the jacket, was missing and he felt something of a freak in the baggy Charlie Chaplin trouserings produced by "Roger".

Shortly afterwards he was in Cammaerts's car when it was stopped at a road block near Digne. Questions revealed that SOE staff in Algiers had failed to stamp a current date on his otherwise impeccable papers. Worse, Fielding had split a large sum of French money between "Roger" and himself, and the enemy twigged that the notes were all in the same series.

Christine Granville was not with them and news of their arrests reached her on the Italian border. Earlier she had been arrested, but had managed to convince her German interrogators that she was a local peasant girl.

She arrived at Digne prison and passed herself off as "Roger's" wife – and, for good measure, as a niece of Gen Montgomery. She persuaded an Alsatian named Albert Schenck, a liaison officer between the French prefecture and the German *Siecherheitsdienst*, to co-operate by reminding him that the Allies had already landed on the Riviera.

Schenck put Christine on to a Belgian, Max Waem, who agreed to help, though his price was two million francs. SOE in Algiers dropped the money in. As a result Fielding and "Roger" were led out of prison. Believing themselves on the way to be shot, they were astonished to be welcomed by Christine who was waiting with a car.

Fielding was awarded the Croix de Guerre in France in 1944. Before the war in Europe ended, he returned to Crete; he was one of the first into liberated Athens.

During the war Fielding would often pass through Cairo, which became a sort of SOE headquarters for the Mediterranean and Middle East, and meet up with kindred spirits such as David Smiley, "Billy" McLean (*qv*), Peter Kemp (*qv*) and Alan Hare. In 1945 they decided that the place to be was the Far East. As Fielding put it: "I was at a loose end and wanted to see what was going on out there."

He spent some months in Cambodia, with a Japanese driver fighting the Vietminh. Then came a six-month stint with the Special Intelligence Service in Germany, and an appointment as United Nations observer in the Balkans.

Peacetime, though, brought disillusionment and a

disturbing sense of misgiving. But in 1948 an encounter with the Marchioness of Bath at what she described as an "hilarious lunch" predestined the course of much of the rest of his life. She had recently taken up photography in place of painting; he was planning a book on Crete. The upshot was that Daphne Bath accompanied his return to the White Mountains to illustrate the book. They married in 1953.

Soon there was another and more welcome distraction. Michael Powell was filming *Ill Met by Moonlight* – the story of Paddy Leigh Fermor's wartime abduction of Gen Kreipe, the German commander in Crete – and Fielding was hired as technical adviser. Dirk Bogarde played Leigh Fermor and Fielding lent him his Cretan guerrilla's cloak and coached him in the part.


**Patrick Leigh Fermor writes:** After an early essay at painting, Xan Fielding wandered to Greece and the islands, added Greek to his list of languages and acquired a lasting attachment to the Greeks.

His life took on an adventurous and peripatetic turn. Early in 1942 he was landed in plain clothes and by submarine in German-occupied Crete. Germany was in full advance on all fronts and Crete was a strongly galvanised Luftwaffe base for the Desert War. The mountains were full of stray British and Commonwealth soldiers who had broken out of PoW camps or been left behind after the Battle, a mortal danger to the Cretans who hid and fed them.

Gathering and evacuating them from remote caves was among Xan's first tasks. Establishing a network of agents and signalling information back to Cairo came next, followed by directing parachute drops to the growing guerrilla bands and the organisation of sabotage, and propaganda while maintaining liaison with the island Resistance leaders.

Light and fine-boned when suitably cloaked and daggered, Xan could be taken for a Cretan. With his determination, humour and intuitive sympathy and his quick mastery of dialect and songs, he made countless friends, and worked there precariously for two years.

In 1944, the war moving west, he was dropped in the Vercors region to the French *maquis*. He returned to Crete for a final two months before the liberation, then headed for Cambodia on further SOE missions and spent some time on the Tibet border before returning to the West Bank in Greece.

Xan commanded a mixed Allied unit supervising the 1946 elections, and during prolonged leave in Rhodes, his friend Lawrence Durrell – who was press officer there – insisted on printing a set of Fielding's poems, which make one wish he had written many more. Chafing at Oxford life as a demobilised undergraduate, he worked for a spell with the Beaverbrook Press and found it even less congenial.

These years were perplexed by tangled Dickensian lawsuits in Nice: family property had been unrecoverably misappropriated in the occupation. During that harassing time he wrote *Hide and Seek*, an exciting account of his experiences in Crete.

Soon after he married Daphne Bath, and they travelled all over the island for his long book *The Stronghold*, a combination of travel and history.

They first settled in Portugal. Then a long sojourn in the Kasbah of Tangier – perhaps inspired by the film

*Pepe le Moko* – gave rise to his book *Corsair Country*, the history of the pirates of the Barbary Coast.

Near Uzèz in Languedoc, their next long halt, his excellent French suggested translation as a profession and he put more than 30 books into English, including many by Lartéguy and Chevalier, and Malraux's *Les Noyers d' Altenbourg*.

After a friendly separation from Daphne he married Agnes ("Magouche") Phillips, daughter of Adml John II Magruder, of the United States Navy. They were extremely happy.

Xan and Magouche took root in the Serrania de Ronda, which looks across Andalusian ilex-woods to the Atlas. There he edited the correspondence of his friend and neighbour, Gerald Brenan, with Ralph Partridge, and continued his translations.

Xan's own book, *The Money Spinner*, about the Monaco casino – the hazards of gambling had always fascinated him – came out in 1977. Later, *Winds of the World* gave free rein to his interest in atmospheric commotions and their mythology.

In the winter of 1990 *One Man and his Time* appeared; it described the life, and the Asian, Ethiopian and Arabian travels, of his old friend "Billy" McLean (*qv*), the wartime commander of the SOE mission in Albania.

At almost the same time Xan was smitten by cancer and he and Magouche moved to Paris for therapy. Though fatally stricken for the last eight months, he was suddenly, three months ago, granted a respite which exactly coincided with the ceremonies for the 50th anniversary of the Battle of Crete and the Resistance.

At a special parade of the Greek navy at Souda, he and six Allied officers were decorated with the commemorative medal of the Resistance, and for 10 days he visited scores of mountain friends from 50 years before. His return was everywhere greeted with feasting and songs.

Xan Fielding was a gifted, many-sided, courageous and romantic figure, deeply committed to his friends, civilised and bohemian at the same time, with a thoughtful style leavened by spontaneous gaiety and a dash of recklessness. He was altogether outstanding.

*August 20 1991*

# "DODO" LEES

DOLORES "DODO" LEES, who has died aged 71, gave gallant service as the only British nurse in the French army in the Second World War – she was twice awarded the Croix de Guerre – and went on to fight three parliamentary elections as a Labour candidate.

That she failed to secure a seat had more to do with the entrenched Conservatism of the constituencies in which she stood, than any weakness in her platform performances. Indeed, as Sir Fitzroy Maclean, who won a narrow victory over her at Lancaster in 1951, later admitted, she put him in fear of losing.

By a curious coincidence, Maclean's powers of persuasion had earlier triumphed over those of Dodo's equally audacious brother, Capt Michael Lees. Lees had been dropped into Axis-occupied Yugoslavia by the Special Operations Executive to help Gen Mihailovich's resistance fighters, while Maclean had liaised with Marshal Tito. In the event Maclean's reports to the Prime

Minister, Winston Churchill, helped to sway Allied support away from Mihailovich and in favour of Tito.

"Dodo" Lees seemed predestined for adventure from the outset of her career, which she began as a young journalist working for Lord Beaverbrook. As a stringer for the *Daily Express* in Germany in the 1930s, she excited the interest of Hitler, who admired her long legs and her oratorial skills. They shared the same birthday, which led the Führer to predict that the young British journalist was destined for a grand career in British politics.

His admiration was not reciprocated by Lees. When German troops invaded Czechoslovakia in March 1939, she lent her passport to a Jewish woman in Prague to enable her to escape.

Lees then enrolled as a VAD nurse and spent the next four years working in military hospitals. She enjoyed nursing, but disliked much of the routine of hospital life, and in 1944 persuaded Ernest Bevin, then Minister of Labour, to mark her card for employment as an ambulance driver in the French Red Cross.

Lees was one of the first women to cross the Channel after D-Day. She served with the 6th Colonial Infantry Regiment of Gen de Gaulle's Free French forces, and then, in the winter of 1944–45, crossed the German lines, disguised as a civilian, to bring medical succour to the Resistance fighters in the Vosges mountains.

She gained the two Croix de Guerre awards during the Rhine and Danube campaigns, when she showed great courage in rescuing wounded men under fire.

Dolores Lees was born on April 20 1920, the daughter of Capt Bernard Lees of the Dorset Yeomanry and Nigerian Police. Her paternal grandfather was Sir

Elliott Lees, 1st Bt, of South Lychet Manor in Dorset and formerly MP for Oldham and Birkenhead. Her maternal grandmother was a Weld of Chideock, a branch of the eminent Roman Catholic dynasty.

Her father died tragically from a gunshot wound, when Dodo was a child, and at 14, after education by governesses in the country, she was sent to school on the Continent. She returned home fluent in French and German, and in the early part of 1939 was one of the most vivacious debutantes of the Season.

After the war Lees was commissioned into the French army as a lieutenant and was appointed personal staff officer to Marchal Leclerc.

In November 1947 she was due to accompany him to French Indo-China, when he was killed in an air crash in Algeria. She was seconded instead to the French Foreign Office, and sent to America to deliver a series of lectures to express French support for the Marshall Plan.

Lees then left the French army and, on her return home to Dorset, joined the Labour party. In 1949 she fought Brendan Bracken unsuccessfully at Bournemouth East and two years later almost unseated Sir Fitzroy Maclean in Lancaster.

She was offered a safe Labour seat in 1953, but she was now engaged to a naval officer, Cdr "Chipps" Selby Bennett, and she opted to follow her husband on his foreign postings instead.

In 1955 they went to live in Malta, where her cousins, the Strickland family, helped her to find outlets for her enthusiasm for public service. Dom Mintoff, the mercurial Prime Minister, was much taken by her, and Mrs Selby Bennett, as she now was, was soon laying the foundations of the island's tourist trade. She maintained a close friendship with Mintoff, and later played a vital role in restraining some of his wilder anti-British actions.

In 1966 her husband was appointed defence attaché in Venezuela, Colombia, Panama and the Dominican Republic, and during the next three years she travelled all over Latin America, then under threat from Cuba.

Although she remained a committed Labour supporter to the end of her life, Lees was a vehement defender of foxhunting. In 1989 she canvassed, unsuccessfully, against her husband, when he stood as a Conservative member of Dorset County Council.

She is survived by her husband and their two sons.

August 30 1991

# ELVIRE DE GREEF

ELVIRE DE GREEF, who has died in Brussels aged 94, was a key figure in the hugely successful Comet Line, which arranged the escapes of Allied airmen and others from occupied France during the Second World War.

"Tante Go", as she was generally known, was personally credited with the escapes of some 337 aircrew members. At the end of the war she was awarded the George Medal.

De Greef was greatly admired by MI9, which financed and assisted the escape lines from London, and was an especial favourite of Airey Neave, the future Conservative minister who had joined the secret organisation after his escape from Colditz. Neave later described her as "slight, with a round face and high cheekbones.

Her eyes were prominent, grey tinged with green, and she had short dark hair . . . she was ruthless."

Tante Go, so named because of her dog Go Go, worked in close conjunction with her family. She ran the "safe house" at Anglet, near Bayonne, where her husband, Fernand de Greef, had a job as an interpreter with the German Kommandatur. Her son, Freddy, acted as a courier, and her daughter, Janine, as an escort.

The de Greefs' most daring exploit involved the escape of one Florentino Goicoechea, a giant Basque smuggler, whom Tante Go had earlier enlisted to guide parties of airmen across the rugged mountain terrain between France and Spain. Goicoechea was returning to France in the summer of 1943, when he was fired on by a German patrol. He was hit in the leg in three places, and rolled down a mountainside, just managing to hide the papers he was carrying before being arrested.

He owned up to being a smuggler – but to nothing more – and was taken to a hospital staffed by nuns. But the Gestapo had its suspicions, and Tante Go decided to spring him from the hospital before he could be removed for interrogation.

Because of his job at the German Kommandatur, her husband had access to blank identity cards, rubber stamps and other bureaucratic paraphernalia, and was thus able to forge an entry pass to the hospital for Tante Go. With the pass – which looked as if it had been issued by the local Gestapo at Hendaye, on the Franco-Spanish border – Tante Go made several visits to a friend who was in a bed next to Goicoechea, whom she pretended not to recognise.

On the day before the planned escape she dropped a

handkerchief by his bed and, while stopping to pick it up, whispered the time he would be collected. The next day Fernand de Greef donned a Gestapo uniform and drove into the hospital courtyard in an ambulance, driven by the concierge of the Anglet town hall and containing two Resistance men, disguised as stretcher-bearers.

As de Greef barked orders in German, Goicoechea was carried out to the ambulance. The operation was so realistic that when the Bayonne Gestapo arrived to investigate, they were easily persuaded that their colleagues at Hendaye had taken the case over.

Goicoechea went on to resume his vital role in assisting escape parties. He died in 1980 and his grave at Giboure is marked by a plaque which records the gratitude of members of the RAF Escaping Society.

Elvire Berlemont was born in Brussels on June 29 1897 and married Fernand de Greef some time before the outbreak of the Second World War.

In 1940, when the Low Countries and France were invaded, the de Greefs tried to escape to Britain from Bordeaux, but this proved impossible. They stayed behind and rented a villa at Anglet. There Tante Go teamed up with Dédée de Jongh, the remarkable young founder of the Comet Line.

While frequenting the bistros of Bayonne and St Jean de Luz and generally familiarising herself with the seedy side of life in the south, Tante Go acquired information about the German officers' black market activities, which enabled her to blackmail them.

Indeed there was very little which eluded Tante Go in the area. When one of her agents, Jean Dassié, the supervisor of the telephone exchange, was betrayed, she bicycled furiously around Bayonne, warning her network of aides that they were in peril. She also managed to despatch her two main agents to safety at MI9 in London.

Unhappily Dédée de Jongh had also been betrayed – though she survived her ordeal in a German concentration camp, and was hailed after the war as one of MI9's greatest heroines. Subsequently Tante Go was herself arrested, but she was not detained for long, for by now she knew far too much about her captors' illegal activities.

Tante Go resumed her work on the Comet Line. She passed her last airman, Flt Sgt Emeny, out to Spain two days before D-Day.

After the war the de Greefs returned to live in Brussels.

Elvire de Greef is survived by her daughter.

September 3 1991

# BRIG "SPEEDY" BREDIN

BRIG "SPEEDY" BREDIN, who has died aged 80, won an MC in Normandy and a DSO in Holland, both in 1944, and was mentioned in despatches in Malaya in 1956.

A soldier who led from the front, "Speedy" was always particularly careful to preserve an immaculate appearance – for the sake of regimental morale. In Normandy in 1944, when moving forward with his radio operator, he was caught in the open in the middle of an enemy artillery barrage. Observers felt that this must be the end of him and, when the barrage lifted, went in to bury the remains. To their considerable surprise they found "Speedy" not only standing up but demanding of his radio operator: "Brush me down, brush me down!"

Ten years later, commanding the 1/6th Gurkhas at Ipoh, Malaya, Bredin wore the starched shirting and shorts so characteristic of the period. As he was the CO, the *dhobi wallah* starched and creased his shorts to such perfection that when he sat in his office he would take them off and stand them up in the corner: none of his visitors was the wiser.

Before emerging to inspect the lines, "Speedy" would step into the crisp shorts, giving no sign that he had been working at his desk in a temperature of more than 90°F, with accompanying humidity.

Scion of an Anglo-Irish military family, Alexander Edward Craven Bredin was born in 1911 in Rangoon; his father was a colonel in the Indian Army. He was educated at King's, Canterbury, and Sandhurst. Commissioned into the Dorsetshire Regiment in 1931, he soon acquired the nickname "Speedy" for his ability to arrive on parade just on time.

In 1936 the regiment moved to Palestine, where the Arab rebellion had begun; but after a year restoring order, a draft commanded by Bredin sailed for India, where it joined the 1st Battalion in the Khyber Pass. The valleys were stiflingly hot and the peaks bitingly cold. Fighting was as natural as breathing to the tribesmen, who were expert marksmen, and a careless move could offer a target which a sniper was unlikely to miss.

When the battalion moved to Nowshera, Bredin became the brigade intelligence officer under the future Field Marshal Alexander; and in 1939 Bredin served as air liaison officer during the Waziristan operation. While on the North-West Frontier he travelled through Afghanistan to Bamian, and through Chitral and Gilgit to Kashmir; much of the country he traversed had peaks which ranged up to 20,000 ft.

On the outbreak of the Second World War the regiment was withdrawn and stationed at Malta, but as there was no imminent threat from Italy, Bredin and others were sent back to Dorset.

In the autumn of 1940 Bredin was sent to Gibraltar, where he found himself on the staff. He managed to reach a more active area by travelling on a Halifax bomber through enemy-infested airspace to 18th Indian Brigade.

Next he went to the 10th Indian Division, before returning to the 1st Dorsets, brigaded with the 2nd Devons and 1st Hampshires in 231 (Malta) Brigade.

After training in amphibious landing techniques on the Suez Canal, Bredin, now a company commander, landed in Sicily. Later in the battle for the island he became second-in-command of the 1st York and Lancaster Regiment, with which he landed and fought in Italy.

He was then permitted to rejoin the 1st Dorsets; they trained in the West Country before landing in Normandy on D-Day and capturing Arromanches. From then on it was heavy fighting, first through the Normandy Bocage and then up to the "island" between Nijmegen and Arnhem.

Although the 50th Division (of which the 1st Dorsets were a part) was returned to England after nearly two years of continuous action, Bredin was soon back in the thick of the North-West Europe campaign, in command of the 5th Dorsets. He led them in the Rhine crossing and into Germany.

After the war Bredin was on the staff of Western Command; AQ in the Middle East; and OC, Company Commanders' Division, at the School of Infantry, Warminster. Then, in 1954, he was selected by Field Marshal Sir John Harding, Colonel of the Regiment, to command 1/6th Gurkhas in Malaya, which he did for two years.

From 1956 to 1959 Bredin commanded 156 (Lowland) Infantry Brigade (TA) – a singular appointment for a Sassenach of Irish extraction. Later he became Inspector of Physical Training at the War Office and Commandant of the APTC. From 1967 to 1977 Bredin was Colonel of the Devonshire and Dorset Regiments, and made four visits to Northern Ireland.

He became president of the Dorset Regimental Association in 1962, and was the first president of the D-Day and Normandy Fellowship. On his visit to Normandy in 1978 the grateful villagers of Hottot renamed the square "*Place du Dorset Regiment – A E C Bredin Commanding Officer*".

He was the author of several books, including *Three Assault Landings: the 1st Dorsets 1939–45*; *The Happy Warriors: The Gurkhas*; *The History of the Devonshire and Dorset Regiment 1958–83*; and *The History of the Irish Soldier Throughout the Ages*.

"Speedy" Bredin was above all a fighting soldier who took a great pleasure in the fact that most of his service was with the troops and little of it spent in the War Office. In his younger days he was an excellent athlete and cricketer, and rode to hounds with the Cattistock.

In retirement he was active in local affairs and a faithful contributor to the correspondence columns of *The Daily Telegraph*, where he expounded on the virtues of the infantry and the old county regiments, while excoriating politicians bent on defence cuts. "I am sure I speak for many," he declared in 1964, "if I say I would rather pay for British infantrymen than for 'false teeth for foreigners' and other luxurious trappings which go towards making us an effete as well as an affluent nation."

Bredin was a Deputy Lieutenant for Devon.

He married Desiree Mills. They had a son, now serving in the Guards, and a daughter, who predeceased him.

November 8 1991

# "BROOKIE" BROOKE-SMITH

TOM "BROOKIE" BROOKE-SMITH, who has died aged 73, exemplified the popular image of a test pilot.

He was a jovial, larger-than-life figure, and his exploits spanned the pre-war period of flying for fun and the jet age.

One of the leading experimental fliers of his time, Brooke-Smith was the first pilot to make a jet-powered vertical take-off in a fixed-wing aircraft, then translate into aerodynamic flight, and return to the hover for the vertical landing.

As chief test pilot for Short Brothers of Belfast he was told that the company had received contracts for two SC 1 delta wing experimental vertical take-off and landing aircraft. It struck him that he was, as he put it, "on a collision course with Sir Isaac Newton".

His initial step was to learn to fly a helicopter; he had gone solo by teatime on the first day. Eventually, on April 6 1960 – after four years' experimental work with his team – Brooke-Smith fired the lift engines which lit, he noted, "like the top of a gas cooker".

He had, in short, pioneered VTOL flight and that year the aviation world paid tribute to him when he demonstrated it at the Farnborough Air Show.

A Fenland farmer's son, Thomas William Brooke-Smith was born on August 14 1918. His grandfather had introduced the King Edward potato.

At the age of four young Tom was much impressed by the sight of a helmeted pilot, who had landed in one of his father's fields in order to ask the way. Later, as a pupil at Bedford School, he would eagerly bicycle to watch the flying at the airship station at Cardington and at RAF Henlow.

He began to learn to fly at Brooklands in his teens, and at 16 left Bedford to study aeronautical engineering at Chelsea College. The day after his 17th birthday he went solo.

After logging 250 hours, he joined the Hope air taxi company at Croydon and subsequently moved on to Air Dispatch, the enterprise owned by the pioneer aviatrix, Mrs Victor Bruce (see *The Daily Telegraph Book of Obituaries: A Celebration of Eccentric Lives*).

On the outbreak of the Second World War in 1939 civil airlines were directed to war tasks, and Brooke-Smith spent that winter flying equipment to France in De Havilland Dragons.

When the Battle of Britain began in 1940, he was recruited by Air Transport Auxiliary. Within two days he had flown deliveries of a Miles Master, Lysander,

Spitfire and Hurricane, although he had never been in any of their cockpits before.

Brooke-Smith's "big break" as a test pilot came in 1941 after he had ferried Stirling bombers from the Short factory in Belfast. Shorts snapped him up to test Stirlings and Sunderland flying-boats as they came off the production line.

By the age of 23 "Brookie" had flown 83 aircraft types. He also had a runabout of his own, a Short 31, a half-scale four-engined Stirling.

Brooke-Smith did not formally qualify as a test pilot until after the war in 1947, when he passed the arduous course at the Empire Test Pilots School. The next year he returned to Shorts as chief test pilot.

Soon he was facing up to the challenge of the SB 1. This was a tail-less glider, built in 1951 to experiment with a crescent-shaped isoclinic wing design, and with moving wing-tip controls – characteristics considered helpful at the time – towards producing a future V-bomber design.

Brooke-Smith was also much involved with the Sperrin, a bomber developed in case the Valiant, Vulcan and Victor V-bombers failed. Many of his ideas were taken into the design and he was greatly disappointed when the Valiant was selected as the RAF's first V-bomber, and only two Sperrins were built.

But it was the tail-less glider which dealt "Brookie" the greatest blow of his career. He was testing it when the machine went out of control, hit the runway at Aldergrove, near Belfast, at more than 100 mph and smashed to pieces. Brooke-Smith suffered severe spinal injuries and spent months in hospital.

From his bed he recommended rebuilding the

machine, and suggested that this time it should be powered with two mini-jets. It was called the Sherpa and handled well, but the isoclinic experiment was abandoned.

Then came the vertical take-off and landing break-through. After his triumphant demonstration at Farn-borough in 1960, he intended to retire and was not even planning to fly the aircraft away from the air show.

In the event, however, he was the only experienced pilot available. After the aircraft had been refuelled at Boscombe Down, three tyres burst simultaneously on take-off, and only Brooke-Smith's exceptional skill and experience averted disaster. At the Air League Ball that year he was presented by the Duke of Hamilton with a pair of numberplates for his motor-car bearing the proud legend "1 VTO".

Next "Brookie" transferred his presentational skills to the world of public relations. He ran his own company and was also group public relations executive for Flight Refuelling.

He was elected a Fellow of the Royal Aeronautical Society in 1961; held the Derry and Richards Memorial Medal for experimental test flying, the Britannia Trophy, the Segrave Trophy, and the Founder's Medal of the Air League of the British Empire; and was a former master of the Guild of Air Pilots and Navigators.

Brooke-Smith is survived by his wife, Joey, a son and two daughters.

November 14 1991

# COL "RAN" DAVIDSON

COLONEL "RAN" DAVIDSON, who has died aged 89, was one of the most admired and popular of all Gurkha officers.

His survival to a great age was all the more extraordinary in view of his appalling treatment by the Japanese when they interrogated him in 1942. When serving as Brigade Major of 22 Indian Brigade he was captured at Kluang, Malaya, on February 1. As he refused to give any of the information his captors demanded he was tied to a tree and flogged mercilessly with steel-corded dog whips; he was then left hanging in the tree throughout the night in his ropes.

A fortnight later the Japanese captured Singapore, and Davidson and his fellows were kept in squalor. Eventually the prisoners who were able to walk were sent up to Thailand. For the four-day journey they were crammed into steel railway trucks, baking hot by day and freezing cold at night. Food was barely at subsistence level.

On arrival at the working camp in Thailand, Davidson was elected camp adjutant and as such had to try to do his best for the men who were being sent out to work while dying of malnutrition and dysentery. He helped to organise a system by which news from clandestine radios, operated at great risk to the users, was circulated without jeopardising the source.

This was an enormous boost to morale. Subsequently he was appointed MBE for what were described as "special services". Not least of his satisfactions sub-

215

sequently was to learn that one of his brothers had slipped into Singapore harbour in 1943 with a few companions and sunk 36,000 tons of Japanese shipping. This raid was excitingly depicted in an Australian-made film.

Randolph Alan Noel Davidson – known as "Ran" or "David" – was born on June 9 1902 and educated at Cheltenham and Sandhurst. He joined the 1st Battalion of the 4th Prince of Wales's Own Gurkha Rifles in 1923.

By 1930 he had risen to become adjutant and the next year he accompanied the regimental deputation to Kathmandu. He attended the Staff College from 1936 to 1937.

After his release from captivity Davidson took command of the 2nd Battalion of his regiment. In 1947, after the end of the Raj, he was invited to become adviser to the regimental centre, with the task of handing over the regiment to the newly appointed Indian officers and establishing goodwill between the old and the new.

He was so successful that close liaison exists to this day. He then transferred to the British Brigade of Gurkhas, becoming Colonel, Brigade of Gurkhas, the first holder of a new appointment carrying great influence.

From 1949 to 1954 he was chief recruiting officer in Darjeeling, where he became a favourite of the tea-planters. They still recall his *Pun Nautch* (a Nepalese dance) performed on a table top at the New Year ball.

Before finally retiring, Davidson served with the Malayan police until the end of the emergency in an Intelligence role. It was said that somewhere he must have discovered the secret of eternal youth for he never seemed to show his age.

He spoke flawless Gurkhali, and on a visit to India in 1986 was requested at short notice to address his old regiment. He did so apparently effortlessly, with memorable effect.

Although kind and gentle in manner, with a boyish sense of humour, "Ran" was known to have courage of the highest quality and possessed an unswerving devotion to the Gurkhas.

When the first newsletter of his former regiment was published in India the then colonel, Rajbir Chopra, wrote in the preface: "He is like a man which built a house and digged deep, and laid the foundation on a rock; and when the flood arose, and the stream beat vehemently upon that house, it could not shake it."

November 14 1991

# CAPT J. S. "STEVE" STEVENS

CAPTAIN J. S. "STEVE" STEVENS, who has died aged 75, was one of the select band of captains of the 10th Submarine Flotilla, based in Malta during the Second World War.

The flotilla carried out a sustained and successful onslaught against enemy ships in the Mediterranean which had a major effect on the Allies' land campaign in North Africa.

"Steve" Stevens commanded the small "U" Class *P46* (later renamed *Unruffled* after Winston Churchill decreed that all submarines should have names instead of numbers) from June 1942 until October 1943 and sank 35,000 tons of enemy shipping, including 12 supply ships and a tanker of 10,000 tons.

*Unruffled* also sank numerous smaller targets by gunfire; shot up trains on Italian coastal railways; launched two-man "chariots" for Operation Principal, an attack on shipping in Palermo harbour in January 1943; and acted as an offshore navigational beacon for the landings in Sicily in July.

Stevens was awarded the DSO in May 1943, and a Bar in September.

In November 1942 *Unruffled* was in a patrol line of submarines, guarding the Torch landings in North Africa from a possible sortie by the main Italian fleet.

Forewarned by Ultra Special Intelligence, *Unruffled* lay in wait off the north coast of Sicily for the Italian cruiser *Atillo Regolo*. Attacking through a destroyer screen, Stevens hit the cruiser with one torpedo and blew off her bow.

Stevens's friends pulled his leg after Gen Eisenhower called him "the maddest submarine captain in the Royal Navy" because he had no torpedoes left after his attack and so could not finish *Regolo* off. "Ike" was using the word in its American sense, meaning angry. In fact, "Unruffled" was the perfect description of the temperament of Stevens.

It was customary for submarine COs to stand down occasionally, while a spare CO took over for one or more patrols. Stevens refused to be relieved and carried out 23 consecutive war patrols.

His sailors found him the kindest and most considerate of men. He was a shrewd judge of their psychology, and regularly had a large postbag of letters from wives and girlfriends appreciative of the care and concern he showed towards their menfolk.

*Unruffled* had acquired a cat at Gibraltar called Timoshenko, after the Russian general. The animal settled down on board so quickly that Stevens and his sailors were convinced that it must have been a submariner in a previous existence. Stevens recognised that the cat had become the submarine's talisman and when one day it went missing, he would not sail for a patrol until it was found and brought back on board.

John Samuel Stevens was born on March 19 1916, and joined the Navy as a cadet at Dartmouth in May 1929. He served as a midshipman in the battleship *Revenge* and in the Mediterranean in the cruiser *Devonshire* at the time of the Abyssinian crisis in 1935.

Two years later he joined the Submarine Service and in 1938 was posted to *Triumph* as torpedo officer. On Boxing Day 1939, on patrol off Heligoland, *Triumph* hit a drifting mine which blew off 18 ft of her bows and cracked or removed all her forward torpedo tube bow caps.

Fortunately none of the torpedoes in the tubes exploded. While *Triumph* was being repaired, Stevens was appointed to the French submarine *Circe* as liaison officer.

Although he had only schoolboy French, he hit it off well with French submariners who, on account of his appetite and luxurious red beard, dubbed him "*Henri Huit*". His next submarine was *Thunderbolt*, which, as *Thetis*, had sunk during her acceptance trials in Liverpool Bay in June 1939 but, after salvage, had been renamed and recommissioned.

Stevens was not the man to worry about the ghosts

of the past and they were in any case all exorcised on *Thunderbolt*'s first patrol, when she sank the Italian U-boat *Capitano Tarantini* in the Bay of Biscay on December 15 1940. Stevens was awarded the DSC.

His first command in 1941 had been the old training boat *H50*. After *Unruffled* he commissioned the larger "T" Class *Turpin*.

On a patrol off Norway in April 1945, *Turpin* was detected and chased by a sister boat *Tapir*, whose captain was one of Stevens's greatest friends. *Tapir*'s captain was sure he had a U-boat until Stevens challenged him and signalled: "Don't shoot, Steve here!"

Stevens took *Turpin* out to the Far East where she was about to sail on her first patrol when the war ended.

Stevens retained his sense of humour under stress; he once misjudged an approach to the depot ship, so that *Turpin*'s sharp stem punctured the depot-ship's side and a torrent of oil poured out of a ruptured fuel tank. Unabashed, Stevens looked up at the row of senior faces on the depot ship's upper deck and shouted: "What ho! A gusher!"

After the war Stevens commanded two more submarines, *Tantalus* and *Tudor*, and then went to Oslo on the Nato staff. In 1957 he went to Halifax, Nova Scotia, to command the 6th Submarine Division.

This was not a promotion job: Stevens was no intriguer and abhorred office politics. Had he schemed more and laughed less, he might have reached flag rank.

"Steve" had a sharp eye for pretentiousness. As flag captain to the C-in-C Home Fleet in the depot ship *Tyne*, he once had to read an expression of "Their Lordships' official displeasure" to a young would-be naval novelist who had offended against the letter, though not the spirit, of the regulations governing the submission of manuscripts to publishers. Stevens did his duty, before observing "Bloody bumbledom!" and taking the budding author off to the cuddy for large gins.

After another Nato appointment on the staff of SHAPE at Versailles, he went to HMS *Dolphin*, the submariners' *alma mater* at Gosport. There, he is still remembered by submariners as one of the best of men.

In retirement he served as a schools liaison officer, encouraging teenage boys to consider the Royal Navy as a possible career.

In 1971 he published his hilarious memoirs, *Never Volunteer: A Submariner's Scrapbook*.

He is survived by his wife, Sybil, and a daughter.

November 20 1991

# TOM BAKER

TOM BAKER, a singular Suffolk character, who has died aged 96, looked after the celebrated duck decoy on the Pretyman estate of Orwell near Ipswich.

When the late Sir Peter Scott took over the decoy he held out his hand, with what he hoped was a modest smile, and said: "Is this the man who knows more about duck than I do?" Baker replied in his direct Suffolk way: "I reckon I do." After this exchange the *rapport* between the two men was never quite what it might have been.

Baker had begun work as decoyman on the Orwell estate after serving throughout the First World War in the Suffolk Regiment. In one year, 1925/26, he caught 9,500 ducks.

When the late Mrs Pretyman (elder daughter of the 2nd Lord Cranworth, KG, a shooting companion of King George V) was first married in the early 1930s, she watched a catch and said:

"Oh Tom, how can you? The poor things. And they're so pretty." To which Baker responded: "You'll be lucky, madam, when your time comes, if you go as quick."

A gamekeeper's son, Thomas Baker was born in 1895 and volunteered for the Suffolks in 1914.

While training at Colchester he defeated the British Army champion at the rifle range. In France he became a renowned sniper.

On one occasion he stayed up for a week, watching for a German sniper who had killed many men. At last he saw a slight movement in a haystack; he fired at it and out toppled the German sniper.

When Col Maxse took over the Suffolks he complained of their scruffiness: "I wouldn't mind in the line, but here it looks dreadful." At this point Baker put his hand up and the sergeant-major gestured fiercely. "No," said the Colonel, "let that young man speak. I want to hear what the men think."

Baker spoke out: "We'd be a sight cleaner, Sir, if we had any soap or cleaning materials. We ran out a year ago, and you know you can't always afford 'em and you can't always steal 'em."

The Colonel was silent for a while, and then said quietly: "I'll see you get them." The men took it for the usual easy promise, but ample cleaning materials arrived next day and the Suffolks became so smart that other regiments copied them.

Baker would also recall how the Suffolks trained for

Gallipoli, brought amphibious warfare to a fine art and were then sent back to France while untrained men were sent to take their place. "And when we heard what happened to them poor boys, we wept."

He had total recall of everything he had ever seen, so to talk to him was to be on the Somme. His account of the First World War was exact, dramatic and fascinating – except in one particular: he would never tell how he won his Military Medal.

He celebrated his 91st birthday by going pigeon shooting, and brought down three high birds. At 94 he was still digging and scything, and always took a walk every day; his notion of a walk was seldom less than a mile and often about five.

Tom Baker was a good Christian but preferred not to talk about it.

He is survived by a son and three daughters.

December 2 1991

# Lt-Col "Skinny" Laugher

Lieutenant-Colonel F. F. "Skinny" Laugher, who has died aged 81, began his military career with the 1st Dorset Regiment on the North-West Frontier.

Later he was second-in-command of an anti-aircraft regiment in the North African campaign; then he commanded a battalion of the Royal Welch Fusiliers for 18 months; and finally he raised and commanded the 6th Battalion of the Malay Regiment.

A noted character, "Skinny" Laugher (pronounced *Law*) was invariably accompanied by his dog, Bonzo. "My name's Laugher," he would announce on first meeting, "and this is Bonzo." Bonzo – "as doggy as Skinny was bloody infantry", as an acquaintance put it – was of indeterminate ancestry but extremely loyal.

Skinny himself was a brisk, outspoken but kindly man in a sound Dorset tradition. Although actually born outside the county – in Bristol – he always considered himself a true son of Dorset.

Francis Fletcher Laugher was born on October 16 1910 and educated at Cheltenham and Sandhurst (where he was a contemporary of David Niven). He was commissioned into the Dorset Regiment in 1930 and departed for India the next year.

In 1936 he was sent on a Signal course at Poona, where they wanted to retain him as an instructor, but this was not allowed as his battalion was then at the important post of Landi Kotal at the top of the Khyber Pass. Signalling was by Morse Code, flag or heliograph, which reflected the sun's rays and had a range of 90 miles. Transport was by mule, and the Afridis were always on the watch for any opportunity to inflict casualties on convoys or even training exercises. Laugher was considered outstanding as a soldier, but he also availed himself of the other activities available in the area, such as polo and duck-shooting.

In November 1942 he took part in "Operation Torch", the 1st Army's landing in Algeria, designed to trap Rommel, who was retreating from the 8th Army. Here Laugher was second-in-command of 105 Light Anti-Aircraft Regiment, which had been converted to the artillery from the infantry role as 8th Dorset.

At the conclusion of the campaign Laugher attended the Staff College, Camberley, then for a short period served as deputy assistant adjutant-general in HQ 45 Division. During the North-West Europe campaign he served again with the 1st Battalion and was awarded an MC in Holland.

In 1945 he took command of the 6th Battalion of the Royal Welch Fusiliers for 18 months in Germany. During this time he also received the Freedom of Caernarvon on behalf of the battalion in 1946, while his battalion had the distinction of being the only British infantry in the Paris Victory Parade.

Later that year Laugher was posted to Greece as GSO1 in the British Military Mission. Although officially a staff officer, he took part in the fighting in the 9th Greek Division against the Communists in the Grammos Mountains.

At the end of the campaign he was appointed OBE. His next posting was to Austria in the Allied Quadripartite Occupation, and then on to Malaya.

From 1953 to 1955, under his command, the 6th Battalion of the Malay Regiment killed more bandits than any other battalion and was the first to receive its Colour from the High Commissioner. It was also the first to have been "Malayanised".

At the end of the period Laugher was mentioned in despatches. His last appointment was GSO1 Training at the War Office. On retirement he bought a 90-acre farm in Dorset with a herd of pedigree Ayrshires. "Very hard work," he used to say, "but most interesting."

Skinny Laugher was a first-class rifle shot and a golfer with a handicap of two. He ran the Army Golfing Society matched against the Navy for 10 years, and played for Dorset and for the Old Cheltonians in the Halford-Hewitt.

Laugher is survived by his wife, Alison, a son and two daughters.

January 16 1992

# PAMELA SCOTT

PAMELA SCOTT, who has died aged 75, hailed from the pinnacle of the aristocracy as a granddaughter of the 6th Duke of Buccleuch, but whereas her remote ancestors had expended their energies upon cattle thieving in the Borders, she brought her native toughness and resilience to bear upon running the family estate in Kenya.

It was in 1934, when she was only 18, and fresh from the London Season, that her father, Lord Francis Scott, who wanted to devote himself to Kenyan politics, made her manager of the 3,500-acre property at Rongai. The family house, Deloraine, was vast, but the conditions of life were primitive. Water for the farm had to be carried over two miles, while the railway was some 20 miles away.

Pamela Scott, entirely without expert help, perforce relied on trial and error to learn the arcane arts of animal husbandry — castration, dehorning, branding, calving and rearing. All work on the farm came within her ambit: she studied accounting, undertook building and fencing, put down metalled roads, constructed dams — even on occasions acted as midwife.

The struggles and hardships of the life were strangely at odds with her pedigree. Miss Scott was often at the end of her financial tether; yet after her cousin, Lady Alice, married the Duke of Gloucester in 1935, the indigent farmer received clothes that had been used for state occasions.

Pamela Scott's resource never failed. When one of her workers began to wither away after being put under the witchdoctor's spell, she concocted an antidote – consisting largely of kerosene, scent, and Eno's fruit salts – which proved entirely successful, if somewhat violent, in ejecting the evil spirits.

Her family had never encouraged sentimentality. "You're a damn fool, woman", her crippled father would yell, while lunging at her with a stick – yet she judged him "the kindest of men".

She admitted some nervousness when attending London dinner parties as a girl, but in the real world nothing daunted her. Informed on one occasion that a drug-crazed native was coming up to the house with the intention of butchering her, she stood her ground and trapped him in the cellar.

During the Mau Mau terror in the 1950s, when so many Europeans barricaded themselves in their houses, Miss Scott left Deloraine open as usual. Her precautions consisted of arming herself with a Beretta pistol and putting a Masai on the veranda, so that his shrieks might give warning in case of attack.

In the last analysis her best security lay in her work for the Africans. Over 45 years her management of the farm yielded extraordinary achievements. She started with only 17 cows; in 1979 there were 1,700 cattle. By the time she retired, the farm was run entirely by Africans.

The estate had become a flourishing community of

more than a thousand people. Miss Scott had established a school on the farm which grew to take 300 children, some of whom went on to further education. A few of them even reached universities in Europe and America: the *alumni* of Deloraine included an architect, civil servants, nurses and journalists.

It was no wonder that Miss Scott showed impatience at the image of decadence among white Kenyans purveyed in James Fox's book *White Mischief* (1982). She would point out that the Happy Valley set represented perhaps a dozen people out of 40,000 settlers. She herself strove to develop the land for everyone and played her part in ensuring that after independence Kenya was in the vanguard of the new African countries.

Pamela Violet Montagu-Douglas-Scott was born in July 1916. Her father was the youngest of six sons of the 6th Duke of Buccleuch and 8th Duke of Queensberry, the greatest territorial magnate in the British Isles and a descendant of Charles II through the Duke of Monmouth.

Pamela Scott's maternal grandfather was Viscount Melgund, a dashing horseman (he rode four times in the Grand National) who, as the 4th Earl of Minto, became Governor-General of Canada and Curzon's successor as Viceroy of India.

Lord Francis Scott, Pamela's father, had emigrated to Kenya after the First World War. For all the rigours of the pioneering life, the Scotts remained a magnet for visiting dignitaries.

In 1924 the Duke and Duchess of York (later King George VI and Queen Elizabeth) came to stay, and Pamela Scott remembered being upset at having temporarily to forfeit her pony to the Duchess. Four years later the visit of the Prince of Wales caused her fewer problems, even if the Prince distinguished himself in Nairobi by rolling about on the floor of the Muthaiga Club with Lady Delamere.

Pamela's education was a sketchy affair, as her parents took the view that examinations made a child narrow-minded. Few of the governesses who came to Deloraine lasted the pace.

Her childhood was interspersed by visits to England, during which she would make the rounds of the Buccleuch seats. When Queen Mary invited Pamela to tea the girl inquired whether she had diamonds on her sponge. The Queen, always severely practical, replied that she had not; they would be very scratchy.

At 15, Pamela was sent to boarding school at Downe House, near Newbury, which she loathed. Subsequent skirmishes with learning occurred in Paris and Devon.

But her heart was always in Africa. Her father had taught her to ride on the principle that no one could be any good until they had fallen off 50 times; as a result she became a fine horsewoman, and an enthusiast of the Turf.

For all her educational deficiencies, Miss Scott possessed a stern capacity for self-control — she was, for example, a rigorous teetotaller — which enabled her to succeed in all that she attempted. But she inherited to the full her family's suspicion of intellectuals.

When Cyril Connolly went to stay at Deloraine she introduced him as "John O'Connor", and did not conceal her exasperation when that literary luminary sulked. "He might as well not have been there," she complained.

The kind of man that Pamela Scott admired was one who could break a horse, calve a cow, or overhaul a tractor. Even so, when dancing with farm managers in

Nairobi, her mind would turn to more primitive entertainment, to the Masai warriors leaping up and down to a slow chant under the stars.

She was interested in African history, customs and languages, though she berated herself for talking Kiswahili "like an uneducated yokel". The phrase reflected her aristocratic disdain for distinctions of race or education.

It was natural for her to find an English equivalent to the Masai initiation ceremonies (including female circumcision) which she witnessed. "I suppose all this business . . . gave them confidence and made them self-reliant, which was very much what my season in London had been meant to do for me."

Equally, while other whites went on about the horror of Mau Mau atrocities, she would reflect that only about 30 Europeans had been killed, whereas some 10,000 Kikuyu had perished.

In 1962, when so many settlers, fearful of black rule, were leaving Kenya, Miss Scott expanded her landholding by purchasing the farm next door. After independence, which came the next year, she was one of the first Europeans to take citizenship of the new country.

She actually preferred the African regime to colonial society. Her work on agricultural committees continued; she became a member of the board of governors of Egerton Agricultural College; and she helped to raise funds for a secondary school.

In 1979 she sold her farm to the Rift Valley College of Science and Technology, although she stayed on in the house and rented back some 60 acres for cattle. Perhaps her best epitaph was spoken by Daniel arap Moi, the President of Kenya: "This one looks white, but she is black at heart."

Pamela Scott's memoirs, *A Nice Place To Live*, offer many fascinating insights on life in Kenya and on her own admirable character.

"I remember her as a strikingly beautiful young woman," said one of her male contemporaries, "but it was not advisable to take liberties."

She never married.

February 10 1992

# GP CAPT RON HOCKEY

GROUP CAPTAIN RON HOCKEY, one of the RAF's most outstanding pilots, who has died aged 80, flew clandestine missions for the Special Operations Executive during the Second World War – notably, in 1941, a perilous round trip to Czechoslovakia, where he dropped the assassins of the Nazi *gauleiter* Reinhard Heydrich.

Already experienced in the task of dropping agents into German-occupied Europe, Hockey took off from Tangmere in Sussex at 2200 hrs on December 28 1941. On board his four-engined Halifax bomber of No 138 Special Duties Squadron were seven agents – or "Joes", as SOE aircrew called their passengers – comprising two communications and training teams and "Anthropoid", the codename for the Czech assassins, Jozef Gabcik and Jan Kubis.

Despite a signal from the Czech resistance which cast doubt on the value of killing Heydrich (Himmler's deputy) and spoke of dire consequences, Dr Eduard Benes, head of the Czech government-in-exile, insisted on the murder. Mass arrests were to follow, and many thousands of Czechs died – including, in a direct reprisal, the entire populations of the villages of Lidice and Lezaky.

But Hockey, renowned for his imperturbability, would have known nothing of this. He was, in his own modest opinion, "just the bus driver".

This sortie, like so many others, required locating three separate dropping zones ("DZs") in snow and ever-decreasing visibility, defying flak and night fighters. But Hockey was unfazed.

In the event, when over Czechoslovakia, he was forced lower and lower by the weather, and obliged to make blind drops. It was remarkable that none turned out to be further than 10 miles from the DZ.

Nor did the nightmarish conditions abate on the return journey. As he crossed the French coast, his aircraft battered by flak, the escape hatch section of the canopy blew open and jammed. His second pilot, standing beside him, managed to hang on to it.

When Hockey finally landed at Tangmere at 0819 hrs the next morning he had been airborne for more than 10 hours.

In 1991 Hockey unveiled a 138 Squadron plaque in the crypt of St Cyril and Methodius church in Prague to mark the spot where the two hunted Czech agents, holed up with five other resistance fighters, had turned their guns on themselves after holding off 600 enemy troops for many hours.

Latterly Hockey also helped with arrangements for an exhibition to be staged at the Imperial War Museum to commemorate the 50th anniversary of Heydrich's assassination in May 1942.

A Devonian, Ronald Clifton Hockey was born on

August 4 1911 and educated at Heles School, Exeter, and Imperial College, London, where he was a Kitchener Scholar and obtained an engineering degree.

He later joined the Royal Aircraft Establishment at Farnborough as a technical officer, and, in 1937, became an inspector of accidents at the Air Ministry. He also flew as a sergeant and instructor in the RAF Volunteer Reserve and by the outbreak of the war in 1939 he was a pilot officer in No 24, a communications squadron, flying an odd assortment of aircraft.

Shortly before and after the fall of France in the spring and early summer of 1940 this duty introduced him to the business of flying in and out of all manner of fields. He piloted Churchill to France and back on at least one occasion in 1940 and, during the Dunkirk period, picked up French VIPs and stragglers from the British Expeditionary Force.

In November 1940 Hockey joined a flight of two Whitley bombers and a Lysander light Army co-operation aircraft, which was committed to supporting Churchill's directive to SOE "to set Europe ablaze". Through carrying out a number of drops over France and Belgium, Hockey began to establish himself as one of the leading pilots in this moonlight speciality.

Initially he was based on the heath at Newmarket, where he lived in a hayloft and flew from the hallowed turf; the racecourse grandstand and its cellars provided the Flight's headquarters. In May 1941 the Flight grew into 138 and 161 Squadrons, and Hockey, by now a flying officer, flew 138's first operation, accompanied by Sqn Ldr Charles Pickard, celebrated for the film *Target for Tonight*.

It was typical of Hockey to learn to parachute at the

SOE's jump school at Ringway so that as a pilot despatching "Joes" he could know something of their problems. One of the pilots there, bored with circuiting to train parachutists, was a certain Sqn Ldr Romanoff.

Hockey, shortly to command 138 Squadron as a wing commander, sympathised with Romanoff. After taking him unofficially on several sorties as second pilot in early 1942, he arranged his transfer to the squadron as a flight commander. But as he took off on his first trip as captain, Romanoff crashed. Hockey, in the tower, dashed for a van and then ran across ploughed fields to the burning wreckage, only to arrive as ammunition grenades and other explosives went up.

Thrown some 40 yards, he returned to the blaze and managed to extract the rear gunner, who was the sole survivor. Hockey recovered, although he carried splinters all over his body for the rest of his life.

He experienced another close call shortly afterwards when he was despatched to Egypt with urgent supplies. He stopped over at Malta, where his Halifax was badly holed on the ground during enemy air attacks.

After this hazardous introduction to the Mediterranean theatre, Hockey was posted there in June 1943 to build up air support for SOE operations. He formed No 334 Wing for this purpose.

In early 1944 he returned to 38 Group, charged with assisting SOE's preparations for D-Day. He trained with 6th Airborne Division's tug-towing pilots.

In 1946 Hockey, by then a group captain, completed a test pilot's course at the Empire Test Pilots School. He remained in the reserve and maintained close links with aviation.

He was successively a departmental head at the

Cranfield College of Aeronautics; divisional engineer with Smiths Aircraft Instruments; general manager of Blackburns (where he tested the Beverley transport); managing director of Arthur Low & Sons, engineers; and chief of mission at the International Labour Office in first Sudan and then Ghana.

Ron Hockey was a dedicated yachtsman and ocean racer; in his youth he had boxed as a heavyweight and played rugby for Wasps. He was a Fellow of the Royal Aeronautical and Royal Geographical Societies.

He was awarded the DFC in 1942, DSO in 1943 and was mentioned in despatches in 1945. He also held the Czech Military Cross and Cross of Valour, and received the Air Efficiency award in 1942 and clasp in 1951. He was a Deputy Lieutenant for Dunbartonshire.

Hockey married Winifred Holt; they had a son and a daughter.

February 25 1992

# DAVID BELL

DAVID BELL, who has died aged 71, lost both his hands and his eyes while serving in the Second World War, and went on to show remarkable courage and enterprise in setting up his own business, taking two university degrees and working for disabled people.

While serving with the Royal Engineers in the desert, he was wounded before the "Battle of Knightsbridge" in June 1942. He had volunteered to clear a minefield and a booby-trap blew up in his face.

Bell was injured so badly his comrades thought he

would not survive. But he managed to tell his rescuers how to put a stone in the crook of each elbow and bind up his arms to staunch the blood. He then led them back the way he had come, before lapsing into unconsciousness. He remained in a coma until August.

Bell was taken out of Tobruk by the last ship and evacuated to South Africa, where surgeons fashioned a pair of "tweezers" out of the remnants of the thumb and forefinger of his left hand – although he was unable to read Braille. Field Marshal Smuts, who visited Bell in hospital, was so impressed with his character that he presented him with his Victory pin.

David Bell was born in Edinburgh on February 6 1921 and began his career as a draughtsman with SMT Edinburgh, the omnibus company. After Munich he found he was unable to enlist in the Services because he was in a reserved occupation. But eventually he wangled his way into the Royal Engineers and was sent out to North Africa with the 1st Field Squadron.

In June 1943 he returned from South Africa to the St Dunstan's Rehabilitation Unit in Church Stretton, Shropshire. "Give me 10 years," he said, "and I'll show what I can do."

During his time at St Dunstan's he became a proficient typist and intended to make his living as an interpreter or translator – he spoke fluent French, German and Afrikaans.

In 1943 he became engaged to Sibyl Page, a voluntary worker, and they were married in 1945. He then decided to go into business as a tobacconist and confectioner.

St Dunstan's built equipment which took change and delivered goods; he worked these with his "tweezers" with astonishing precision. His business was supported by St Dunstan's and it soon thrived. In 1950 he went up to Edinburgh University. His fellow undergraduates established a group which would recite lecture notes and read set books to him. Thanks to his amazing memory, he graduated with an MA in 1952 and a BComm in 1955.

Bell kept in touch with the university as honorary president of the Commerce Graduates and as a member of the Council's business committee in the 1980s. He was also a member of the Edinburgh Merchant Company and Edinburgh Senior Chamber of Commerce.

He sat on the BBC Scotland Appeals Committee, hospital boards and was a vice-president of the National Federation of the Blind. In 1962 he became founder chairman of the Edinburgh Ex-Tablers' 41 Club, and was elected president in 1983.

In 1957 he was the subject of BBC Television's *This is Your Life*. In 1972 he was appointed MBE for his work for disabled people.

He is survived by his wife, a son and a daughter.

March 11 1992

# WILLIAM STAFFORD

WILLIAM STAFFORD, who has died aged 85, earned his nickname of "the Iron Broom" for his stalwart service in tracking down criminals and terrorists in Malaya in the 1940s and 1950s.

He was also known as "Two-Gun" Stafford for his habit of carrying two automatics whenever a gun-battle was pending. Though still a captain in the Army, Stafford was appointed chief of the CID and Detective Branch of the Malayan Police in January 1946.

He faced a particularly difficult task in the post, since many of his opponents turned out to have been his former colleagues in Force 136, the anti-Japanese guerrilla force established by Special Operations Executive in the Burma and Malaya jungles during the Second World War.

As soon as the Japanese had surrendered, many of the guerrillas, armed with SOE-supplied weapons, had embarked on a life of murder and pillage, or become Communists dedicated to driving out the British and establishing a Soviet-backed Malaya. The guerrillas (mainly Chinese) were offered a $600 bonus if they returned their arms, but many claimed to have "lost" them. There were those among the criminal riff-raff, though, who resented being dragooned into the Malayan Communist party, and from these Stafford set up a network of informers and agents.

Naturally the dissidents refused to be seen in daylight talking to a European, so Stafford would meet them in a dark cinema in Kuala Lumpur. Sometimes he learned of huge dumps of arms buried in the jungle – one cache contained 257 handguns, 350 grenades and 30,000 rounds of ammunition.

Armed gangs, such as the Green Dragons, were highly organised for their trade of robbery, murder and kidnapping, and Stafford had many close encounters with them – including gunfights to the death.

One especially testing experience was his arrest of a man who had run amok with a *kris* (a wavy Malay sword), killing more than 20 complete strangers and wounding many more, including some British Servicemen. After

Stafford captured the man, he was hanged at Puda Jail, Kuala Lumpur.

Danger did not just come from the local terrorist population, though. On one occasion Stafford found his jeep being chased by a wild elephant along a jungle path. "Elephants can move very quickly and this was no exception," he recalled gruffly, but he narrowly outpaced it.

When the "Emergency" was at its peak, Stafford enlisted the help of the Aborigines in capturing bandits. One morning a young Sakai appeared in his office with a large sack, explaining that he had come for his reward. He opened up the sack and three Chinese heads rolled out, complete with hats. The bearer was overjoyed to be rewarded with a sack of rice and three cartons of cigarettes.

William Frederick Stafford was born at Margate on September 15 1906. His great-grandfather had fought in the Battle of Trafalgar and then served as town crier of Margate for 46 years; his father served in the Navy, and was drowned at sea soon after young William was born.

After education at local schools the boy worked as an assistant cellarman in the mornings and assistant billiards marker in the afternoons. He then joined the Navy as a stoker, serving in Hong Kong and China.

In spite of the typhoons and floods, Stafford loved the station. During one flood he went to Hankow, 800 miles up the Yangtse, where, in a motor boat, he rescued Charles Lindbergh and his wife who had come to China in a sea-plane to drop supplies to beleaguered villages. Their sea-plane had been turned over by the strong current.

Having bought himself out of the Navy, Stafford

joined the Admiralty Police. He learned Chinese and some dialects, and was transferred to Singapore, where well-deserved promotion rapidly followed.

By way of recreation there, Stafford would go crocodile-hunting. He learned how to catch the reptiles with his bare hands – "not as dangerous as it sounded if you knew how to do it". Crocodiles, as he would explain, can only move forwards, albeit rather quickly, so the trick was to make them bite on a stick and then secure their jaws. The hunters sold their catch to the Chinese in Singapore for $1 per ft, to be used for handbags and medicines.

Stafford himself also received $1 a ft for boa-constrictors, "which are not really dangerous unless they can secure a purchase round a tree. The first thing you should do therefore is to grasp the tail and put it in a bag; this then enables you to club it on the head."

Stafford was in Singapore when the Japanese invaded. He survived the thunderous chaos of the initial assault by taking shelter in a large iron pipe; he then managed to board what must have been the very last ship to leave Singapore.

After a hazardous journey he reached Ceylon, where he joined the Army. He was gazetted as a captain, but was soon asked to volunteer for SOE.

For his first assignment he had to acquire a deep sun tan and dress up as a native in order to take a sloop with a Burmese crew and land 10 agents in Burma.

Next, he was sent with his section to Poona to be trained in sabotage, explosives and silent killing. The visit was cut short, though, when the men put too much plastic explosive under a railway line and blew up a large section which landed on the colonel's office.

No one was hurt, but Stafford and his colleagues were promptly returned to Britain for further training. They also had to test various forms of experimental equipment; these included midget submarines, in one of which he was nearly drowned at the bottom of Fishguard Harbour.

Afterwards Stafford went to India to complete a course in parachuting, ready for dropping into the Malayan jungle. But peace intervened.

He and his wife arrived in Kuala Lumpur by train in 1946, and were rather alarmed to be allotted a house which had no less than 38 lightning conductors. It seemed there was something in the soil in the area which attracted lightning, but the house, though often struck, was never seriously damaged.

That the potentially explosive situation in Malaya was cleared up undoubtedly owed much to Stafford's cool, quick-witted approach.

"The Iron Broom" earned the respect both of those whom he protected and those he pursued, some of whom even shielded him from the Communists, having decided that he was preferable to the tyranny of their own regime.

Stafford also developed a rapport with members of the local wildlife population. The Raub police district to which he was assigned was as large as Sussex, and had 90 per cent virgin jungle.

On one occasion, *en route* to an isolated police station, his party encountered a tigress. Everyone opened fire at once and, after the kill, discovered three week-old cubs.

Stafford took them home, where he and his wife nursed them and his children took them for walks on leads like dogs. When they grew too big and expensive to look after, he sent them to London: one is now at Whipsnade, one at Dublin and the third in Edinburgh.

Stafford retired from the Malayan Police in 1957 and then worked for 17 years, in absolute secrecy, as a field investigating officer in Britain.

He was awarded the King's Police Medal and the Colonial Police Medal for Gallantry.

Stafford is survived by his wife, Margaret, a son and a daughter.

March 27 1992

# COL FRANK "MONOCLE" MORGAN

COLONEL FRANK "MONOCLE" MORGAN, who has died aged 99, served with the Imperial Camel Corps in the campaigns against the Turks in the First World War, and with the Royal Corps of Signals in the Second.

Morgan – variously known as "Monocle" and "Pinpoint" – was chief air formation signals officer in France in 1940 and in the Middle East and Italy from 1943 to 1945. Between the wars, and after the second, he farmed in west Wales. When blindness compelled him to give up farming in 1966 he learned Braille and carried on with his public duties, being much in demand as a witty public speaker.

Morgan had a broad range of knowledge which included literature, history, law, mathematics, agriculture and science; he contributed articles to newspapers and magazines and throughout his life wrote light verse.

Frank Stanley Morgan was born in 1893 at Seoul in Korea, where his father, a commissioner of the Imperial Chinese Customs, was on a tour of duty. His mother was a niece of his father, and young Frank claimed this relationship made him his own great-uncle.

He spent much of his childhood in China but returned home to school at Marlborough. He then read law at Christ Church, Oxford.

In 1914 he enlisted in the Pembroke Yeomanry but two years later was seconded to Signals, then a branch of the Royal Engineers. He subsequently served as signals officer with the Imperial Camel Corps, taking part in cavalry battles against the Turks in Egypt and Palestine.

Of the Imperial Camel Corps he would say that it comprised an aristocratic element among its officers and complete ruffians in the ranks; all they had in common was a disdain for danger.

When he asked once for a volunteer bugler, a particularly blackguardly fellow stepped forward. "Can you blow the bugle?" asked Morgan. "Oh, no," replied the man. "I thought you said *burglar*. I am very good at that."

When the major objectives of the Palestine campaign had been achieved Morgan was transferred back to France to serve in the trenches as an expert on telephone communications. Hundreds of miles of telephone cables were laid in France, sometimes by horses, sometimes by men and sometimes by dogs with small drums on their backs. Lines were often cut by shell fire, and in repairing them it was not easy to know whether one was joining one's own line or one of the enemy's.

Morgan was the first to learn of the Armistice in the trenches, where he intercepted instructions from the

German GHQ ordering the generals to lay down their arms.

After the war he returned to farm his estate in Wales. In 1920 he joined the newly formed Royal Signals (TA), and then transferred to the Supplementary Reserve in 1925.

During this period he was active in public service in the Principality, and devoted himself to the development of scouting, and became a friend of Sir Robert Baden-Powell, the founder of the Boy Scout movement. He was awarded the Order of the Silver Wolf for his services to scouting.

In 1939 Morgan went to France at OC2 Air Formation Signals and played a key role in organising telecommunications between the French and British forces: for this he was appointed CBE. Just before leaving France in 1940 he had given a final dinner party at the Ritz in Paris to members of his unit, but had inadvertently left without paying the bill. When dining there again in 1945, after the Liberation, he found the old bill laid respectfully beside the new bill by his plate, without comment.

After the fall of France he had become chief signals officer, Aldershot Command. He was deputy chief signals officer, Western Command, from 1941 to 1942; and then CSO Air Formation Signals, Home Forces, in 1943.

Next Morgan was posted to the Middle East and from 1944 to 1945 was CSO, Air Formation Signals, Middle East. During the period he had also taken part in the invasion of Italy.

He retired from the Army in 1948 and returned once more to his estate at Bishopton, where he devoted himself to farm improvements. He became a county councillor, sat on the Gower Bench, served on innumerable committees (including the governing body of the Church of Wales) and was appointed a Deputy Lieutenant for Glamorgan in 1948.

A volume of his light verse, appropriately called *Lines of Communication*, was published on his 80th birthday. At the age of 98 he contributed a preface to the biography of Col De Lancey Forth, of the Imperial Camel Corps.

Morgan was honorary Colonel of 50 and 80 Air Formation Signal Regiments from 1952 to 1960 and was awarded the ERD.

Frank Morgan was a tall, hawk-like figure, noted for certain eccentricities. He had lost an eye as a child and wore an eyeglass in the remaining one. He could eject this by jerking his head upwards, and then catch it again in the socket. He said he found this a useful trick when addressing restive or sleepy audiences.

Perhaps the most remarkable feature of "Monocle" Morgan was his adaptability. Brought up at a time when military aircraft would have seemed a fantasy, he later became an expert on one of the most complicated of signal functions, air-land co-operation. Yet he never forgot that when the Pembroke Yeomanry had been mustered in 1914 the occasion had all the marks of a medieval call to arms.

He married first, in 1918, Gladys Joan Warde, who died in 1953; and secondly, in 1956, Lt-Col Helen Pine, WRAC.

April 6 1992

# COL MAURICE
# BUCKMASTER

COLONEL MAURICE BUCKMASTER, who has died aged 90, led the French section of the Special Operations Executive for most of the Second World War.

After the Dunkirk evacuation in the early summer of 1940 Churchill's directive to SOE "to set Europe ablaze" was hardly more than an act of faith. Even a year later, as Buckmaster contemplated empty "in" and "out" trays at SOE's Baker Street headquarters, sabotage and subversion across the Channel seemed almost an impossibility.

"The fact is," Buckmaster was told when he first reported to Baker Street as information officer, "everything's highly embryonic here." So he busied himself with self-imposed duties; initially it seemed sensible for him to remember what he could about French factories which he had visited while working as the manager of the Ford Motor Co in France before the war.

Then, late one night when Buckmaster was responsible for security of the building, he challenged a dimly lit figure in a doorway. "My name's Hambro," the shadow said. "I happen to be the No 2 in this SOE set-up."

And so Sir Charles Hambro, the banker, settled down to question Buckmaster. The upshot was that, in July 1941, Hambro was instrumental in Buckmaster receiving temporary control of the Belgian section.

That September Buckmaster was promoted to head the French section, almost certainly the hottest seat in

SOE. For the next three years he masterminded the training and dispatch of agents to France.

Buckmaster faced a formidable task in their selection. Not the least of the crosses he had to bear was the abiding suspicion of Gen de Gaulle, who insisted that SOE would not be allowed to recruit French nationals but only French speakers with British passports, Quebecois – whose accent was usually unmistakable – and Mauritians. So, for the most part, he picked and trained half-French men and women or others with a good knowledge of the language and the country.

Buckmaster's agents were to provide a roll of honour second to none in the story of British wartime undercover operations. Their stories inspired a host of books, films and television series. Some agents, such as Violette Szabo, were tortured and shot. Others, like Odette Churchill, suffered at the hands of the Gestapo, but survived.

The high losses of the men and women whom Buckmaster sent to France have since raised questions about his methods. In retrospect, and with hindsight, Buckmaster has been unfairly criticised for running an "amateurish" organisation and incurring unnecessary loss of life.

But this was emphatically not how it seemed in the years when Europe was occupied by a ruthless Nazi regime – and when sabotaging railways and communications, attacking road convoys, supporting and arming the Resistance were considered paramount.

As M. R. D. Foot, the least partisan of SOE's historians, has observed in connection with Buckmaster: "Was it not Turenne who said, the general who made no mistakes has commanded in remarkably few battles?"

Charges of amateurism were particularly misplaced coming from the Secret Intelligence Service, which was not averse to obstructing Buckmaster's section. For his part Buckmaster did his best to turn such rivalries to good purpose and looked upon the competitive element in such relations as encouraging each group to seek to outdo the other. He described such liaison as existed with de Gaulle as owing everything to the tact and charm of SOE officers – "the only weapon against jealousy and intransigence."

Amid such arrows, it comforted Buckmaster that, when it was all over, Eisenhower credited his French section with contributing significantly to shortening the war by six months. "It was," Ike said, "the equivalent of 15 divisions."

Perhaps the most telling tribute of all came from Hitler, whom Buckmaster quoted as saying: "When I get to London I am not sure who I shall hang first – Churchill or that man Buckmaster."

Early in life Buckmaster had been steeled by the vicissitudes of fate: home life was precarious as his father's business fluctuated between prosperity and decline.

Maurice James Buckmaster was born on January 11 1902. He went to Eton, but it was touch and go in his last year whether the fees could be found. When his father was made bankrupt the school recognised his prowess by giving young Maurice a scholarship.

He had already demonstrated a remarkable facility for speaking French and was particularly influenced by a master named Robert Larsonnier whom he used, in later years, to describe as "a wonderful man". The verdict was characteristic, for Buckmaster tended to divide the world into three categories: "Wonderful men", "Splendid girls" and "Not my cup of tea".

After school he was sent to France where he perfected his command of the language working as a journalist on *Le Matin*. There followed six years with the merchant bank, J. Henry Schroder & Co.

Then, in 1929, he joined Ford, first as assistant to the chairman and thereafter as their manager in France and then the whole of Europe. Buckmaster's European contacts and linguistic abilities inevitably led, on the outbreak of the Second World War, to a job in the Intelligence Corps. He claimed, aged 37, to be the oldest second lieutenant in the Army.

His task was to arrange suitable French billets for 50 Division, a job which led to a lifelong friendship with Paul Krug, head of the celebrated champagne house.

At Dunkirk in 1940 Buckmaster was ordered by the future Field Marshal Templer to stay behind with the rear-guard on the grounds that when the Germans arrived Buckmaster would have only to divest himself of his uniform to pass himself off as a native Frenchman for the duration. In the event, he managed a spectacular escape, and was reunited with his division and his batman, who had inadvertently made off with his puttees.

"Thank God, Sir," Buckmaster used to recall the man saying. "You're safe, Sir. Your puttees, Sir!"

In the autumn of 1940 Buckmaster's fluency in French secured attachment to "Operation Menace", an ill-fated Anglo-French enterprise designed to wrest Dakar, capital of French West Africa, from the Vichy government and hand the port over to the Free French under de Gaulle. Buckmaster recalled this fiasco as "sitting in the Bay of Rifisque and being bombarded and dive-bombed for 24 hours, and torpedoed." In 1941 50 Division was posted to North Africa, where Buckmaster reasoned that his French would be of little use, so he presented himself at the War Office, hoping to find more relevant employment. There he bumped into Templer again.

"Ah, Buckmaster," he said, "you speak French. Got a job for you. Start this afternoon. No 64 Baker Street."

Once in the hot seat – after succeeding H. A. R. Marriott, a director of Courtauld's French company – Buckmaster, ably assisted by Vera Atkins, worked up to 18 hours a day. He would occasionally give himself a break by bicycling home to Chelsea for an early dinner before returning at 8 pm to Baker Street, where he would remain until 4 am.

Buckmaster was acutely aware of the loneliness of his agents and of their doubts about those such as himself understanding or even caring about their problems. So he made a point of presenting them, as they were leaving for France, with personal gifts – for instance, gold cufflinks or cigarette cases for the men, powder compacts for the women – carefully manufactured to disguise their origin. "You can always hock it," he used to say, "if you run out of money."

By the end of the war Buckmaster had been responsible for the training and dispatch of some 500 people. He was devastated by the loss of men and women whom he regarded as close personal friends and felt keenly the responsibility of sending them, however unwittingly, to their deaths.

He was always fiercely loyal to his operatives, who

included men like Richard Heslop, codenamed "Xavier", who sent a fusillade of boulders on to a Panzer division on the Route Hannibal, delaying its arrival in Normandy until a crucial 17 days after D-Day. Then there were the two schoolmasters, Francis Cammaerts and Harry Rée (*qv*). By the summer of 1944 Cammaerts had been so successful in the South of France that Buckmaster could claim that he had 10,000 men under his orders – at least half of whom had been armed by his efforts.

Rée immobilised the tank turret production factory at the Peugeot works at Sochaux. It was his demolition exploit which gave Buckmaster the satisfaction of calling on "Bomber" Harris at Bomber Command HQ with photographic evidence. Harris had hitherto been sceptical of SOE's ability to blow up targets which, he maintained, were better left to his air crew.

Buckmaster found it intensely frustrating that he himself was not allowed to go into enemy territory. Nonetheless, this did not prevent him on one occasion – so the story went – from flying to France in a Lysander in order to make essential voice to voice contact with George Starr, one of his agents in the Gers.

As they approached the rendezvous Buckmaster's pilot remarked crisply: "Look at those bloody awful lights."

At which Starr's inimitable Staffordshire voice cut in over the plane's radio: "Your lights would be bloody awful too, if you had the Gestapo less than a mile away." Starr merged into occupied France so successfully that he became mayor of his local village.

Perhaps the most characteristic story of Buckmaster was his reaction to Gen de Gaulle's postwar attempt to expel Starr on the grounds that he did not hold a French passport. Starr replied that he only answered to his Colonel and asked Buckmaster for orders. Buckmaster cabled: "*Tu y es, tu y reste*", which he himself translated gruffly as "Don't budge an inch". This rather impressed de Gaulle who relented at once and gave Starr the Légion d'Honneur instead.

Although SOE was wound up after the war Buckmaster worked resolutely to ensure that the French section's connections with the Resistance lived on through an old comrades' association, the Amicale Libre de Résistance – more popularly known as the "Amicale Buck".

In 1945 Buckmaster returned to Ford, first in his old job as head of Europe and subsequently as director of public relations. Then, in 1960, he went freelance.

He was best known in the field of public relations as an appropriately effervescent PRO for the wines of Champagne. Certainly this account was his first love and consumed most of his time, enabling him to retain his close links with his beloved France and with men like Krug.

A trip to Champagne with Buckmaster was a privileged opportunity to see a rare example of the *Entente Cordiale* in action – as well as being an intoxicating and stylish *caves*-crawl, in which the various houses vied with each other in doing honour to the legendary Col Buckmaster and his friends.

Buckmaster divided his later years between a small flat in Chelsea and a country hotel in Sussex. Although he became increasingly frail, his spirit was always indomitable and his speech forthright.

France honoured Buckmaster as a Chevalier de la

Légion d'Honneur in 1945 and raised him in 1978 to the rank of Officier. He was also awarded the Croix de Guerre avec palmes and the Medaille de la Résistance, as well as the American Legion of Merit. Britain appointed him an OBE in 1943, which many felt to be less than generous.

He wrote two volumes of autobiography, *Specially Employed* and *They Fought Alone*.

Buckmaster, who described his recreation as "family life", married first, in 1927, May Dorothy Steed; they had a son and two daughters. He married secondly, in 1941, Anna Cecilia Reinstein, who died in 1988.

April 20 1992

# CDR JOHN BROMAGE

COMMANDER JOHN BROMAGE, one of the most successful submarine captains of the Second World War, who has died aged 86, was best known for his outstanding record in command of *P212*, which he commissioned early in 1942.

Known to her sailors as the "steamboat", because her number was the degree Fahrenheit at which water boils – and later renamed *Sahib* at Churchill's behest – *P212* went out to the Mediterranean in August 1942 to carry out war patrols from Algiers and then Malta.

On the night of November 14, Bromage brought an enemy transport to a halt with gunfire and then sank it with one torpedo. Closing the spot, Bromage was astonished to find what seemed to be hundreds of swimmers in the water, and voices calling out in English.

"Any Englishmen in the water?" Bromage shouted. Back came the reply: "Nae, but there's a Scotsman!"

Some of the survivors were indeed British, and Bromage was impressed by the orderly manner in which they waited their turn to be rescued. In half-an-hour 26 British and 35 Italians were brought on board, before the approach of an enemy vessel was detected and Bromage was forced to abandon the remaining survivors.

It transpired that the transport, the 1,580-ton *Scillin*, had been carrying 810 British prisoners of war and 200 Italian troops. The torpedo had actually exploded in the hold where the PoWs had been confined.

Bromage and his sailors were deeply upset by this "friendly fire" incident, but he was absolved of any blame. The target had been darkened and was carrying enemy war material on a recognised enemy route between Tripoli and Sicily.

The survivors were landed next day in Malta, where the submarine had to be specially cleaned and fumigated because so many of the British PoWs were suffering from dysentery.

On patrol along the north coast of Sicily in January 1943, Bromage made a daring daylight penetration of Milazzo harbour to torpedo a ship alongside, going so close to the shore that the entire periscope view was filled by a fruit seller's donkey.

Early on January 21, west of Corsica, he sighted *U301* on the surface and sank it with one torpedo from a salvo of three fired at long range. A midshipman, the sole survivor, was picked up. The young man had been a lookout, and his only concern was whether Bromage had attacked from "his" sector. For that and other sinkings, Bromage was awarded the DSO.

On April 24, Bromage attacked and sank a ship from a convoy off the north coast of Sicily. The escort, of two corvettes and a torpedo boat, counter-attacked with an accurate pattern of depth charges which badly damaged *Sahib*. With rapid flooding aft, the submarine went out of control.

Bromage decided to surface, where the main engines were started and *Sahib* was soon making 13 knots, eagerly pursued and fired on by the Italian escort. Bromage later thanked an Italian captain for deliberately aiming to miss, only to be told he had been aiming to hit.

*Sahib*'s stern was well under water, and it was clear she was sinking. Bromage gave orders to scuttle and abandon ship. He was going down to check everyone was clear when he met a stoker coming up the ladder with a laundry bag full of dhobeying.

He told him to drop it at once and get over the side. Bromage himself went into the water as *Sahib*'s hull tipped up vertically and slid stern first out of sight.

*Sahib*'s survivors were machine-gunned in the water by a passing Ju 88 and one man was killed, but the rest – six officers and 40 ratings – were picked up and became PoWs. Of these 23 later escaped from PoW camp, and 12 made "home runs".

Bromage himself escaped but was recaptured and taken to Germany, where he kept his composure and sense of humour in captivity even when he and other PoWs were marched away from the approaching Allied armies. He was finally freed in April 1945, when Allied troops reached his PoW camp.

John Henry Bromage was born on August 18 1915, and went to Dartmouth as a cadet in 1928. He joined the submarine service in 1936, and his first boat was *Snapper* in the Mediterranean.

He served as her navigating officer until the war, when he had several hectic patrols off the Dutch and Norwegian coasts. In 1940 he joined *Sealion*, which was rammed off Christiansund.

The next year he passed the CO's qualifying course (the "Perisher") and was given his first command, the training boat *H33* at Rothesay.

He was awarded the DSC in May 1940 for his service in *Snapper*, and a Bar for his last patrols in *Sahib* after he returned from PoW camp in 1945.

John Bromage had been a superb wartime CO, but he never really settled in the postwar Navy. Perhaps peacetime was too tame for him. He was much tougher than he looked and could be ruthless. Asked how the inspection of one submarine in his flotilla had gone, he said simply: "Oh, I sacked the engineer officer."

His last submarine command was *Thule* in 1949. He was commander (submarines) in Londonderry and in Australia. He was as witty and autocratic as ever, and never lost his knack of spotting ability in a young officer.

But none of his appointments seemed likely to lead to promotion – the title of his last, Boom Defence Officer, Clyde, seemed to have the syllables of finality. He retired in 1965 and worked for the Ministry of Defence, "positive vetting" security applicants.

He is survived by his second wife, Barbara, and by a son and three daughters of his first marriage.

June 3 1992

# COL "BINKS" FIRBANK

COLONEL L. T. "BINKS" FIRBANK, late of the Indian Army cavalry, who has died aged 91, enjoyed a long and varied military career.

After serving on the North-West Frontier in the 1920s and 1930s, he became an adviser to the Indian Army; in the 1940s he commanded the Sunderbund Flotilla on the Arakan coast before going to Singapore as civil defence officer.

"Binks" Firbank was an all-round sportsman – he excelled at polo, hunting, racing and pig-sticking and was also Army fencing and squash rackets champion. He was selected for the British Olympics modern pentathlon in 1939 but the outbreak of war prevented the 1940 Games taking place.

Leslie Telford Firbank was born in Ceylon on June 5 1901, the son of a district engineer on the East Indian Railway. He was educated at Cheltenham and Woolwich (for which he rode and fenced) and was commissioned to the Royal Artillery in 1921.

He was soon posted to India, served in various small frontier wars and held an independent command between Bannu and Razmak. Firbank passed out Grade I from the equitation course at the Cavalry School at Saugor, then returned to the Frontier Province in 100th 4.5 Howitzer Battery.

In 1927 he "got his jacket" (that is to say, he was selected for the Royal Horse Artillery) and served with Mercer's Troop in Meerut. His next career move was prompted by love.

When the father of Firbank's sweetheart made it known that he would not hear of his daughter marrying a "poor Horse Gunner", he transferred to the better-paid Indian Army, joining Sam Browne's Cavalry (12th Frontier Force). Soon afterwards the girl changed her mind and said she did not wish to marry him after all.

Not long after Firbank joined, the regiment moved to Jubbultore and he was appointed to train young Indian soldiers to prepare for entry to the Indian Military Academy. In 1936, however, Sam Browne's became a training regiment and all the British officers were required to find other units.

Firbank joined the 8th King George V's Own Light Cavalry, which at that time was marching from Kohat to Bannu to fight the Fakir of Ipi in Waziristan, who had united squabbling tribes and raised a force of many thousands.

The tribesmen regarded fighting as a most agreeable way of life – they were well armed and were experts at rapid movement, fieldcraft, camouflage, marksmanship and ambushes.

Firbank was given command of B Squadron in his new regiment. It consisted mostly of Awans, Punjabi Mussulmans who claimed to be descendants from Alexander the Great's invasion of India in 326 BC – they were tall, wore bobbed hair and were, in Firbank's estimation, "splendid chaps".

Having reached Bannu and pitched camp, he was suddenly informed that a raid was taking place on the village of Khairu Kel. He deployed the squadron, sited two machine-guns, and led a foot party into the attack. After a brisk fight the enemy fled.

Firbank was appointed OBE for this swift and

decisive action, which denied the Fakir urgently needed food supplies.

In 1939 he became adjutant of Kitchener College at Nowgong; he was then military adviser, and organised a training school for Indian State Forces. His next posting enabled him to use his sailing experience in the Indian Water Transport Service.

From 1944 to 1945 Firbank commanded the 7th Rajput Regiment in the Arakan. Two years later he was appointed to train cadets at the Indian Military Academy at Dehra Dun.

Then, in 1951, having retired from the army, Firbank became commander of the Singapore Civil Defence Corps, grooming them for special roles in the "Emergency".

In 1958 he took a "retired officer's" appointment as a staff captain administering the multi-racial civilian labour force working on the military bases, with its active trade unions.

"Binks" Firbank was the ideal Edwardian gentleman – modest, courageous, cultured, impeccably mannered and sporting. He wrote long letters in elegant script, was a connoisseur of books, pictures and prints, and loved music and the ballet. He was unfailingly good tempered.

He married, in 1932, Cynthia Prince; they had two daughters – Anne, an actress, and Elizabeth, a musician. He married secondly, Lee.

July 31 1992

# AIR VICE-MARSHAL
# BRIAN YOUNG

AIR VICE-MARSHAL BRIAN YOUNG, who has died aged 74, was a fighter pilot during the Second World War and completed his career as Commandant-General of the RAF Regiment, the Air Force's ground defence and ceremonial "soldiers".

At the outbreak of the war Young was stationed at Biggin Hill as adjutant of No 31, a Gloster Gauntlet biplane squadron. "There was a sort of carnival feeling," Young recalled. "601 Squadron of the Royal Auxiliary Air Force came to Biggin and used to play polo on motor-bikes."

When No 615 ("Churchill's Own") was ordered to France with the British Expeditionary Force, Young arranged for a transfer. No 615 was also an auxiliary squadron and he had to accommodate his Cranwell-trained sense of discipline to the squadron's more rumbustious ways as it settled in at Merville with obsolescent Gloster Gladiators.

The squadron was partially re-equipped with Hawker Hurricane 8-gun monoplane fighters. Young and his fellow pilots were learning to fly them when, on May 10 1940, Hitler launched the *blitzkrieg* which swept the BEF out of the Low Countries and France.

The first pilot up took a Gladiator because he had not yet flown a Hurricane. Shortly afterwards, Young's Hurricane was shot down in flames by an Me109, which dived past him as he baled out. As Young neared the ground British troops opened fire at him and he could hear them shouting "Bloody swine!"

"Then there was a tremendous explosion," recalled Young, "this was a hand grenade which was chucked at me. I looked up and British soldiers had their bayonets an inch from my nose. All my clothes had burnt off. I said rather hysterically: 'Who the bloody hell do you think I am? *A Hun dressed up as a chorus girl?*'"

"What have we done?" said a soldier. "We have shot an Englishman!"

"I am not a bloody Englishman," yelled Young. "I'm South African."

Then somebody close at hand answered in Afrikaans. This was too much for the British troops who rounded on them both as a "couple of bloody Huns". The Afrikaans-speaker had to do some fast talking in order to persuade the troops he was an RAMC corporal from South Africa who happened to be passing in an ambulance. The corporal dressed Young's burns, the gaping hole the British grenade had left in his side and the bullet wounds.

Brian Pashley Young was born in Zululand on May 5 1918. At the time his father, a solicitor by profession, was farming cotton. Young Brian was educated at Michaelhouse School. As a boy he helped to deliver newspapers to remote places by aircraft.

Infected by the flying bug, he won a cadet scholarship at RAF College, Cranwell, where he was commissioned in 1938. As a cadet he composed a poem, *Flight*, which has subsequently inspired generations of young fliers:

> *How can they know the joy to be alive*
> *Who have not flown?*

> *To loop and spin, and roll and climb and dive*
> *The very sky one's own.*
> *The surge of power as engines race,*
> *The sting of speed,*
> *The rude wind – buffet on one's face,*
> *To live indeed!*

After his adventures in France, Young had his burns repaired by the plastic surgeon Sir Harold Gillies. Because of eye scarring he was no longer fit enough to fly fighters, so he switched to flying sorties in the Battle of the Atlantic from 1942 to 1943 with Nos 246 and 422 Sunderland flying-boat squadrons.

In 1944 he was appointed station commander on Masirah Island in the Gulf and subsequently held Middle East and Air Ministry staff appointments until 1950 when he was posted to Bomber Command. As CO of No 232 Operational Conversion Unit in the mid-1950s Young played a key role in introducing the Vickers Valiant.

In the early 1960s he was Assistant Chief of Staff, Intelligence, at Nato's Fontainebleau HQ and was closely involved with the Cuban missile crisis nuclear alert.

In 1964 he was appointed to command the Central Reconnaissance Establishment and four years later moved to the RAF Regiment. On his retirement from the Service in 1973 Young joined the Department of the Environment as a planning inspector.

Brian Young ran for the RAF before the war and played on the wing in the rugby XV afterwards. He also captained the Wasps.

He was appointed OBE in 1944, CBE in 1960 and

CB in 1972. He married, in 1942, Pat Cole; they had three sons and two daughters.

August 4 1992

# KATTALIN AGUIRRE

KATTALIN AGUIRRE, who has died aged 94, helped hundreds of Allied aircrew to evade capture during the Second World War and escape from France to fight again.

A diminutive and resourceful widow, Mme Aguirre earned her living as a cleaner in an hotel billeting German officers. There, while engaged in such duties as polishing jackboots (the heels of which she took pride in sabotaging), this indomitable Basque woman picked up snippets of information which proved helpful to her clandestine activities.

These included smuggling parts of radio equipment and working for Resistance groups in the area. Mme Aguirre was a key figure at the end of the celebrated Comet Line (based in Brussels), which passed escaping Allied airmen from Paris and elsewhere in France and the Low Countries to the Bayonne area in the south and then on to the last stage of their 1,000-mile journeys.

Mme Aguirre won the love and respect of the airmen she protected, as they awaited the arduous walk across the Pyrenees to Spain. But, as the priest pointed out at her funeral, she was not without a hint of malice when confounding the enemy. Indeed, she was reputed to have decapitated one German soldier who presumed to obstruct her.

She was born Kattalin Lamothe at Ciboure near Bayonne in 1897. She married a local fisherman called Aguirre, who died from the effects of gassing suffered in the First World War. They had a daughter.

During the Second World War Mme Aguirre would nanny the Allied airmen before entrusting them to Florentino Goicoechea, the giant guide whose knowledge of the Pyrenees maintained the remarkable escaping record of Countess "Dedée" de Jongh's Comet Line.

One of Mme Aguirre's former charges, George Duffy (a 78 Squadron Halifax bomber sergeant pilot shot down over Holland in June 1943), recalled her as "motherly but tough". She insisted Duffy "ate a good meal before setting off on the 14-hour climb through the Pyrenees".

Duffy, later a flight lieutenant and a BOAC captain, was one of several aircrew who visited her regularly over the years and who, through membership of the RAF Escaping Society, helped to ensure for her a carefree old age.

Mme Aguirre herself seldom spoke of her wartime service, which had been of such great value to MI9, the London-based escape and evasion organisation. In her old age she attended a reception in a Royal Navy frigate visiting the South of France. The presence of this little old lady in black puzzled those present until she happened to open her handbag in search of a handkerchief – affording the guests a glimpse of a string of medals.

Kattalin Aguirre was a Chevalier of the Legion of Honour, and held the Medaille Militaire, both the French and the Belgian Croix de Guerre, the French and Belgian

Medailles de la Résistance and King George VI's Medal
for Freedom.

*August 6 1992*

# WING CDR WILLIE FRY

WING COMMANDER WILLIE FRY, who has died aged
95, was an air ace of the First World War, when he flew
as deputy flight commander to the legendary Canadian
Billy Bishop, VC, in the Royal Flying Corps.

Fry won the MC in 1917, and achieved 11 "kills",
among them Walter von Bulow, of the German hunter-
fighter squadron known as *Jasta Boelcke* (with 28 victories
to his name). In January 1918 Fry's Sopwith Dolphin
sent von Bulow's aircraft spinning into the shelled area
south of Passchendaele.

It was a lucky addition to his score. Fry, prone to
extravagance on his leaves, had returned to his squadron
early and was on offensive patrol when he encountered "a
tremendous battle between a large number of British and
German scouts".

"I dived," he recalled, "on one of a formation of five
Albatros scouts. The aircraft rolled and went down in a
steep spiral."

Fry did not know at the time that his opponent was
von Bulow, but the German may well have recognised
him, as Fry was celebrated for his leopard-skin flying
helmet, purchased from Rowland Hill's taxidermist's
emporium in Piccadilly. Once, after a forced landing, Fry
caught the eye of an official Australian war artist, who
was so taken by the leopard-skin helmet that he asked

Fry to pose for him – an impromptu sitting was duly granted.

Besides serving as deputy flight leader to Billy Bishop in No 60 Squadron in the Battle of Arras in the summer of 1917, Fry flew at various times with such aces as Albert Ball and J. B. McCudden.

At Arras Maj-Gen Hugh Trenchard, commanding the Royal Flying Corps, threw everything in to break the temporary enemy air superiority. Between April 23 and June 21 Fry flew his Nieuport on 118 sorties – more than 170 hours.

That May, acting as flight leader in Bishop's absence, Fry took off to investigate an Albatros 1,000ft over the aerodrome and forced its pilot down. On landing alongside, he shook hands with the enemy pilot, Georg North, and invited him for luncheon in the mess. After plying the German with drink, Fry discovered that the Albatros was an improved and previously unknown type. Trenchard dropped by to take a look, and the aircraft was shipped across the Channel for inspection.

On another occasion in that hectic summer of 1917 Fry was lunching with Bishop when they received a message that a two-seater was spotting artillery over British lines. They left the table and took off into the air, where they discovered there were, in fact, two enemy aircraft. In the combat report Bishop recorded that, "With Lieut Fry following me I dived at two two-seaters. I fired 20 rounds at one and turned off, Lieut Fry diving on it and firing. I dived again as he stopped firing and fired about 40 rounds, in the course of which the enemy observer stopped firing. The machine did two turns of a spin and then nose-dived to earth where we saw it crash."

What Bishop did not report was that after an hour

he returned with Fry to finish the luncheon, which had been kept hot for them.

By the autumn of 1917 Fry had moved to No 23 Squadron, equipped with SPAD single-seater scouts. That November Fry broke a cardinal rule by failing to fly straight back to his airfield after a fight, in case of unseen damage. Over the Poperinghe-Ypres main road his engine seized, but he managed to nose-dive into a gap between two huts used as field hospital wards.

William Mayes Fry was born on November 14 1896 into an Exmoor farming family. He was educated at King's College, Taunton, and Brighton College.

Young Willie was working as a junior bank clerk when the outbreak of war in August 1914 offered an escape from the drudgery of the ledgers. By November he was in France with the London Rifle Brigade, thereby qualifying as one of the "Old Contemptibles". But the Army discovered that Fry had been under age when he arrived in France.

He was sent home, after observing the remarkable Christmas truce of 1914. "It was entirely a soldiers' truce," Fry recalled, "quite spontaneous on both sides. At the time the ordinary soldier saw nothing incongruous in it. It occurred and was welcomed as a temporary relief from the continuous hostilities of the previous weeks. Somehow no one seemed to have given a thought that fraternisation with the enemy was an offence punishable by death – an extraordinary thing when nearly every participant was a regular soldier.

"It was a strange feeling to stand on that still day between the trenches and look along the line on both flanks and see irregular groups of both sides standing quietly about – their alignment showing roughly the line of the front trenches which we had never seen before, because to look above the trench in daylight would have been suicide."

Back home Fry was almost immediately commissioned into the Somerset Light Infantry, from which he volunteered for the RFC. After serving in Nos 11, 12, 56, 60, 23 and 79 Squadrons, Fry flew in the Middle East with No 25 Squadron of the new Royal Air Force until he was released in 1919 to study forestry at Brasenose College, Oxford.

Fry's plan was to join the woods and forests department of the Indian Civil Service. Within 18 months, however, he had rejoined the RAF as a flying officer and returned to the Middle East, where he flew Sopwith Snipes with No 1 Squadron in Iraq.

He remained in the Service until 1934, when he was placed on the Reserve. He then established himself as a corn merchant, selling malting barley to brewers.

On the outbreak of the Second World War in 1939 Fry was recalled to the RAF. He received command of the Kent coast fighter station at Hawkinge in 1941 and was mentioned in despatches in 1943.

Later Fry filled a succession of administrative posts, before retiring in 1945 as a wing commander. He then resumed his activities in the corn trade, and became renowned in East Anglia as a good judge of barley. In the 1960s he sold the business and retired to Somerset, but he missed Norfolk and eventually moved back there.

Willie Fry was a brave, if obstinate man, with a talent for friendship and a capacity for having fun. His recreations were shooting, fishing and the Turf.

He married, in 1926, Katherine, daughter of Maj-

Gen Sir Frederick Carrington. She died in 1985. They had a son and a daughter.

August 13 1992

# VICTORIA LIDIARD

VICTORIA LIDIARD, who has died aged 102, was imprisoned in 1912 for her activities as a member of the women's suffrage movement.

In response to Mrs Pankhurst's call to march at the Liberal Government's refusal to give women the vote, Lidiard travelled to London from her home in Bristol, and took part with 200 other women in a window-smashing protest down the length of Oxford Street. Afterwards Lidiard walked to Whitehall, where she threw a stone through a window of the War Office. A policeman standing nearby later declared that he could hardly believe his eyes, for Miss Lidiard, with her rolled hair and high-necked lace blousing, had looked the picture of innocence.

Surrounded by phalanxes of policemen, the accused was led to Bow Street. On the way she contrived to dispose of the other stones that she had in her pocket. On arrival she was dismayed to find that the policeman bringing up the rear had picked up each stone, one by one. "I thought that was particularly mean," she recalled.

Lidiard was sentenced to two months' hard labour at Holloway Prison, and was kept in solitary confinement in a cell containing nothing but a straw mattress on a board. The prisoner was undaunted, however. She kept her spirits up by singing at the top of her voice through the high cell window.

An antique dealer's daughter, she was born Victoria Simmons on December 23 1889 at Windsor, although the family moved to Bristol when she was a child. She owed much of her pioneering spirit to her mother, who sent all her four daughters to book-keeping classes, and encouraged them to think for themselves.

Young Victoria joined the Women's Social and Political Union, before becoming a suffragette in 1907. She campaigned tirelessly for the movement, selling its weekly paper, *Votes for Women*, and speaking at street-corner meetings – being spat on the while.

During the First World War she moved to London and helped run a guesthouse in Kensington, and at weekends worked in a Battersea munitions factory. In 1918, when women won the vote, she married Alexander Lidiard, a major in the 5th Manchester Rifles and an active member of the Men's Political Union for Women's Enfranchisement.

After the war the couple trained in ophthalmology, and she became the first woman staff refractionist at the London Refraction Hospital.

Lidiard remained a member of the National Council for Women for most of her life. Latterly, from her flat at Hove, she championed a wide selection of animal charities.

Her last campaign was in support of the ordination of women, a cause she likened to the one for which she had fought so many years before. "I don't mind people giving reasons," she would say, "but not stupid prejudices."

October 13 1992

# CHARLES FRASER-SMITH

CHARLES FRASER-SMITH, who has died aged 88, was the Secret Services gadgets wizard during the Second World War, a role which made him the model for "Q" in the James Bond books.

His professional pride, however, was offended by Ian Fleming's amateurism. He had sent golf balls with compasses inside to prisoners in Germany; the tricked-up golf balls in *Diamonds Are Forever*, by contrast, would not even have bounced.

Much of Fraser-Smith's work was directed towards helping prisoners of the Reich, or agents in Nazi Germany. There were metal saws sewn into regulation-issue military shoe laces – sometimes used for cutting off frost-bitten fingers. There was a briar pipe with asbestos lining which allowed maps to be concealed in the bowl.

Maps were also hidden in hairbrushes which could be opened by the tugging of particular bristles, or printed on silk in invisible ink, which, Fraser-Smith explained, "you could develop in your own Jimmy Riddle". (After the war the silk was sold as scarves to unsuspecting debutantes.)

Agents were given cigarette lighters that contained cameras, and shaving brushes that opened (by unscrewing a special left-hand thread) to provide space for film. It was thus possible to send back ground-level pictures of the damage wrought by Bomber Command, and to pinpoint the V-1 launching pads.

Fountain pens, fake cigarettes and even false teeth were all useful receptacles, whether for mini-telescopes, compasses or other miniature tools. Particularly valuable to agents in the field was a magnet which Fraser-Smith invented to immobilise the house electricity meter during transmission, leaving the enemy direction-finding teams with no surge to track down.

He was also concerned with concentrated rations for the Chindits behind Japanese lines in Burma, experimenting with cubes of potato powder. Chivers produced the powder; Coty, the cosmetics firm, made it into cubes. The results were less than delicious; it was rumoured that after the war the surplus stock was fed to prisoners at Dartmoor.

In 1943 Fraser-Smith was asked to provide a special watertight container measuring 6ft 3in by 3ft, complete with valve, vacuum pump and a Mae West life jacket. As he later discovered, it was required by that master of deception Lt-Cdr Montagu for his plan to wash up a corpse carrying documents designed to put the enemy off the scent about the Allies' invasion of Sicily. This exploit was subsequently celebrated in the book and film *The Man Who Never Was*.

In 1941, after Rudolf Hess had landed in Scotland, Fraser-Smith was ordered to take advantage of the heaven-sent opportunity to make an exact copy of the Deputy Führer's uniform. He was never convinced, however, that the man who had flown to Britain was the real Hess.

Officially, Fraser-Smith was attached to the clothing and textile department of the Ministry of Supply, in a building opposite St James's Park underground station. Neither his colleagues nor even his secretary were *au fait* with the true nature of his work: orders would come over the telephone.

Fraser-Smith did not meet his contact until one day the unknown voice invited him to the opera. When he arrived, the man in the next seat hardly spoke to him at all, and it was only years later that Fraser-Smith realised that his neighbour had been Sir Claude Dansey, a key figure in wartime intelligence.

Since he had little official clout, Fraser-Smith perforce adopted an impressive manner when soliciting help from companies. "I always spoke as if I were Churchill himself," he recalled.

For all the excitements of his work, and the ingenuity with which he discharged it, Fraser-Smith took a resolutely realistic view. "Only fools and barbarians glorify war. Aggressive war is a beastly and depraved business, and fighting an aggressor is a sad and an uncomfortable job ... but it has to be done when there is no alternative." It was the comment of a deeply religious man who had been led by chance to his strange occupation.

One of four children of a solicitor who owned a wholesale grocery business, Charles Fraser-Smith was born in 1904. Orphaned at the age of seven, he was brought up by a missionary family in Hertfordshire.

After a spell at Watford Grammar School he went to Brighton College where he proved "scholastically useless except for woodwork and science and making things". He then became a prep-school master at Portsmouth. Later, drawn to agriculture, he paid £1 a week for the privilege of working from dawn to dusk on a farm.

In the hope of weaning him from this life, his family sent him to France to learn the language. Having mastered French, Fraser-Smith moved on to Morocco, where he bought a farm between Marrakesh and the Atlas mountains.

Here he proved a quick learner and an inspired improviser, introducing new ploughs, irrigation schemes and proper fertilisation. Before long he was running estates for the chief religious judge and the Moroccan royal family.

At the same time, inspired by two aunts who had died of typhoid while working as missionaries in Tangier, Fraser-Smith managed to build up two orphanages, one near Marrakesh, the other near Tangier.

On his return to England in 1939, he could only find a job as a motor-bicycle dispatch rider. Later he worked at the Avro aircraft factory, until the day that he went to deliver a sermon at the Open Brethren Evangelical Church at Leeds.

As luck had it, George Rice, head of the Ministry of Supply in Leeds, was in the congregation with Sir George Oliver, from the same Ministry in Whitehall. Fraser-Smith described his Moroccan experience in some detail, unwittingly giving a compelling picture of his inventiveness and self-reliance. Afterwards the men from the Ministry approached him with the offer of "a funny job in London".

When the war was over, he stayed on to discharge more mundane tasks at the Ministry of Supply, until he suffered a breakdown in health, doubtless brought on by his long period of secret work without any break for holidays. Fraser-Smith contemplated a return to Morocco, but settled instead for Devon, where he bought a derelict dairy farm, which he restored to prosperity.

His wartime exploits remained largely unknown until, egged on by his son-in-law and liberated by the expiry of the 30 years' silence required by the Official Secrets Act, he produced *The Secret War of Charles Fraser-Smith*.

He was a member of the Gideons and a life governor of the British and Foreign Bible Society.

Fraser-Smith married first, in 1934, Blanche Ellis; they had a son and a daughter. After her death he married secondly, Selina Richardson.

*November 12 1992*

# LT-COL "TITUS" OATTS

LIEUTENANT-COLONEL L. B. "TITUS" OATTS, who has died aged 90, won a DSO while commanding the Chin Levies in Burma in the Second World War.

His first assignment in 1940 was to penetrate the Naga Hills, in areas previously unexplored, and put them under the administration of the Government of Burma. This was the only way by which the war-like Nagas could be prevented from raiding such adjoining areas as Assam to obtain slaves and victims for human sacrifices.

"Titus" Oatts's first experience of these jungle people gave little indication of what valuable allies they would later become. They had curious conventions of chivalry and would not fight invaders without a preliminary parley.

On a remote jungle path Oatts would come upon a pile of branches with plantains laid on top; he would then wait with an interpreter, leaving his soldiers 200 yards behind. The Nagas, as he recalled, would then "suddenly materialise as if they had shot up out of trap doors". At the end of the parley they disappeared just as quickly: "One moment they were there, the next they were gone, without even a trembling of a leaf to mark their passage. They went into battle naked apart from spears, bows and an implement like an elongated meat chopper with which they were adept at removing people's heads. They also coated their bodies with lime from head to foot, giving them an extremely ghoulish appearance.

"Against this grey-white background their teeth and lips stood out in crimson paint, making it look as if they had been sucking someone's blood. Fixed to each man's temples, so skilfully that they seemed to be growing out of them, was a pair of immense buffalo horns, tricked out with human hair. However, lack of education did not mean that they were ignorant or stupid; far from it. They understood all about wildlife and the growing of crops. They could weave cloth and tan hides, work in metals, build houses and construct such works as suspension bridges for which a knowledge of mathematics is commonly held to be necessary."

Paths to the remote country in which the Nagas lived invariably ran straight – "one day we would camp in a village at 1,000ft and the next morning go over a mountain 8,000ft high. When it rained the paths became rivers." Unpromising though these initial encounters seemed, Oatts and his companions so impressed the Nagas that they became staunch allies against the Japanese.

Gen Bill Slim subsequently said that "their loyalty even in the most depressing time of the invasion never faltered. Despite floggings, tortures, executions, and the burning of their villages they refused to aid the Japanese in any way or to betray our troops: they guided our columns, collected information, ambushed enemy patrols, carried our supplies and brought in our wounded under the heaviest fire, and then, being the gentlemen they were, often refused all payment. Many a British and Indian soldier owes his life to the naked, head-hunting Nagas".

An officer in the Highland Light Infantry, Oatts had volunteered for service with the Burma Frontier Force in the Chin Hills in 1938, when his regiment had concluded its tour of duty on the North-West Frontier of India. The Chin Hills extend along the Burma-India frontier for 300 miles, stretching from Manipur State to the Arakan. Oatts, who was often surrounded by Japanese in the jungle, had a personal bodyguard which consisted of "a group of 'retired' bandits of extreme villainy but unsurpassable jungle craft".

An indigo planter's son, Lewis Balfour Oatts was born on April 4 1902 and educated at Bedford and Sandhurst. He was commissioned into the Highland Light Infantry in 1922. Much of his early service was spent on the North-West Frontier.

His Chin Hills battalion consisted of numerous warlike peoples who had little in common and often spoke such different dialects that they could barely understand each other.

When the Japanese carved their way through Burma in 1941 they did not at first press into the hills; when they did they met the Chin Levies and got the worst of it. Oatts recalled that one of the Levies regarded throwing hand-grenades as effeminate. He preferred to stalk a

Japanese soldier, let the lever go and then stuff it down his victim's neck; on one occasion he lost an arm but was not put off and regarded the incident as amusing.

The Levies' relationship with their seniors in 17th Division was less than cordial: the Divisional Staff tended to regard them as too unorthodox while the Levies thought the Division was too unenterprising.

One of Oatts's officers sent the GOC six Japanese heads which his men had removed, hoping the General would then show similar enterprise; he was promptly sent back to England for psychiatric treatment. None the less the 14th Army HQ was greatly impressed by the achievements of the Levies in harassing the Japanese and decided that Oatts should form two regular battalions. These then covered the British flank in the advance to the Irrawaddy.

After the war Oatts became administrator at Arbury Hall, Warwickshire (the Gothick showplace of the FitzRoy Newdegates, Viscounts Daventry); then ran the Victoria League in Edinburgh. He was a member of the Royal Company of Archers, the Queen's Body Guard for Scotland.

"Titus" Oatts had the personality and military skills to lead disparate groups successfully in battle; at the same time he was well aware of the bizarre contrasts around him.

Oatts published several books including *Proud Heritage*, a four-volume history of the Highland Light Infantry, which is far more readable than most regimental histories; one of the 14/20th Hussars; another of the 3rd Carabiniers (now part of the Scots Dragoon Guards); and *Jungle in Arms*.

In earlier life Oatts had been an excellent horseman, good polo player, and a keen foxhunter and pig-sticker.

He married, in 1934, Cherry Morris, daughter of a former captain of the Warwickshire County Cricket Club. They had two sons and a daughter.

December 30 1992

# JIMMY WRIGHT

JIMMY WRIGHT, who has died aged 70, was a grievously burned and blinded RAF film cameraman of the Second World War; his example inspired countless other disabled and handicapped servicemen.

For seven years Wright was a patient of Sir Archibald McIndoe, the plastic surgeon, as one of his "Guinea Pigs" at the Queen Victoria Hospital, East Grinstead. Subsequently Wright astonished even that most optimistic and supportive of surgeons by launching a film production company.

Although terribly burned and left with only partial use of his hands, Jimmy Wright was determined to follow the example of his father, Ernest ("Jim") Wright, a Royal Flying Corps fighter pilot in the First World War who had gone on to become a distinguished newsreel war correspondent. In 1944 King George VI decorated both father and son at the same Buckingham Palace investiture with an MBE and DFC respectively.

Jimmy Wright had been commissioned into the RAF as a pilot officer in 1942. He qualified as an air gunner so that he could fly as aircrew, although he was an RAF Film Unit cameraman. While flying with No 223, a Baltimore bomber squadron, he had two lucky escapes before the crash which was to deliver him into McIndoe's hands.

First, his aircraft was hit by enemy fire over mountains in central Italy. He was not wearing a parachute at the time and after struggling into a harness, discovered, as he fell to earth, that he had put it on the wrong way round. He grabbed the rip cord in the nick of time. On the second occasion, he was rescued after an American ship had been hit by an aerial torpedo in the Mediterranean.

Wright was taking off in a Marauder, from the captured Italian naval base at Taranto, when the reconnaissance bomber crashed. The flames disfigured him beyond recognition.

Although he was just alive, an Army warrant officer included Wright's name in a casualty signal in the certainty that within hours he would be dead. As it happened, his father was in the Mediterranean theatre as a war correspondent and flew over to investigate. Jim Wright found his son alive but massively drugged.

Wright Senior's experience of morphia in the 1914–18 War convinced him that such doses would kill his son. He seized a syringe from a nurse and dashed it to the floor. He then arranged for Jimmy Wright to be freighted home – "bandaged from head to foot like a mummy and packed between two aero-engineers in a Liberator", as Edward Bishop put it in his history of *The Guinea Pig Club*.

James Ernest Frederick Wright was born on August 18 1922 and educated at Denham Lodge School and the Regent Street Polytechnic. After a brief spell in a bank he joined Technicolor in 1940 at Harmondsworth as a trainee in the camera department. At one stage he carried equipment for Freddie Young, the celebrated film cameraman.

At the age of 18 Wright was rejected for RAF aircrew because of poor sight, but in 1942 he was admitted through "the back door", as a cameraman wearing an air gunner's brevet. He reported to the RAF Film Unit at Pinewood Studios, where at first he could not understand why "airmen" failed to salute him – until he discovered they were film extras.

Soon he was accompanying bomber operations over France and the Low Countries, before being posted to the Desert Air Force.

On his arrival at the "Sty" (as members of the Guinea Pig Club, McIndoe's aircrew patients, called the Queen Victoria Hospital), Wright recognised the voice of the anaesthetist, Dr Russell Davies, officiating at the first of his many operations. When he was at Technicolor Wright had filmed the wounds of six of Davies's early wartime burns patients.

Now Wright was a Guinea Pig himself, at the outset of a long odyssey of pain, rehabilitation and resettlement which culminated in years of endeavour on behalf of others. In the normal course of events he might not have expected to work again. Yet in 1952 he founded Anglo-Scottish Films at Shepperton Studios.

It proved a testing period for a sightless man. One night he returned home to find that the manservant looking after him had stolen much of his property. But he persevered to produce films for the Central Office of Information and businesses, as well as commercials for cinema and television. In 1961 he set up Film City Productions, which became renowned for its special effects studio. Cinexsa Film Productions followed.

When Granada Television's *Searchlight* current affairs programme needed outside assistance, Wright provided personnel, particularly for overseas locations. He also filmed Bob Hope shows for General Motors.

In 1967 Wright married Jan Jessey, who worked tirelessly alongside him. As a "St Dunstaner" himself Wright did not stint his efforts for the blind. From 1977 he ran the *Spelthorne Talking News*, a local report service for the blind and other handicapped people. In September 1990 he parascended across the Channel from Ramsgate to Dunkirk in aid of the RAF Benevolent Fund's Battle of Britain 50th anniversary appeal. He was accompanied by two fellow members of the Guinea Pig Club, Les Wilkins (who had lost both hands in 1944) and Des O'Connell.

In 1991 Wright produced *Sight by Touch*, a video for the Braille Authority. Wright was appointed OBE in 1980 and received a BAFTA award in 1981. He was on the Court of the Royal School of the Blind, Leatherhead, and the committee of the Julie Andrews Appeal to fight arterial disease.

Irrepressibly cheerful, Jimmy Wright was great company. He was invariably first at breakfast and almost last to bed at the Guinea Pig annual reunions known as "Lost Weekends".

He is survived by his wife and two sons.

February 15 1993

# MONIQUE "AGGIE" AGAZARIAN

MONIQUE "AGGIE" AGAZARIAN, who has died aged 72, flew Spitfire and Hurricane fighters – as well as more than 20 other varieties of RAF and Fleet Air Arm aircraft – during the Second World War.

"Aggie" was one of a small elite of intrepid women pilots to wear the wings and uniform of the Air Transport Auxiliary ferry organisation. One of her contemporaries was Amy Johnson, the pre-war record breaker, who died after baling out over the Thames estuary.

One of the few women taught to fly with the ATA – the majority held peacetime licences – Agazarian was pretty "green" when first confronted with a Spitfire. "I had been on leave," she recalled, "so when they asked me when I came back whether I had done my cockpit checks I thought they would not let me fly if I told the truth. So I said 'yes'.

"You had to be quick taking off in a Spitfire because they 'cooked' if they sat on the ground too long. So I just pointed it in the right direction and went."

Just after take-off, being unaccustomed to the cockpit layout, she caught her gauntlet in the prop control-lever and put it into course pitch. But she managed to recover "and had a glorious time".

"Spitfires really were delightful to fly," she enthused. "You just thought what you wanted to do and it did it. The first time I rolled I was quite nervous. But it turned over so sweetly. You really were part of the machine."

283

The 1st Lord Beaverbrook, then Minister of Aircraft Production, so valued "Aggie" and her fellow pilots that he gave them a pass, stating: "This pilot can authorise his or her own flights."

At the end of the war Agazarian interpreted this as permission for a low-level wing-tip "beat-up" of her mother's Knightsbridge home in a naval Seafire. That final fling typified Agazarian's irrepressible spirit. After resuming her studies on her return to civilian life, she went on to participate in a number of successful civil aviation business ventures.

The daughter of an Armenian-born businessman, Monique Agazarian was born in Surrey on July 17 1920. When she was three her French mother bought a 1914–18 War Sopwith Pup for £5 at a Croydon auction and installed it at the bottom of the family garden.

The much-loved "toy" exerted a lasting influence on the Agazarian children. One brother, Noel, fought with 609 Squadron in the Battle of Britain and was credited with $11\frac{1}{2}$ victories before he was killed in the Middle East in 1941. His Spitfire is displayed at the Imperial War Museum.

Another brother, Jack, was seconded from the RAF to the clandestine Special Operations Executive. Parachuted into France to help the Resistance, he was captured, tortured and executed. A third brother, Levon, flew fighters.

Young Monique was educated at the Convent of the Sacred Heart, Roehampton, before going to a Paris finishing school. Early in the war she helped nurse Sir Archibald McIndoe's "Guinea Pigs" at the Queen Victoria Hospital, East Grinstead. She was also attached to the RAF at Uxbridge.

Determined to fly like her brothers – despite being below the ATA's height requirement of 5ft 5in – she wangled her way through the medical, and learned to fly on Magisters.

When the ATA ferry organisation was stood down at the end of the war she ran a Malcolm Club at RAF Guttersloh in Germany and took a commercial B-licence.

Island Air Services, a passenger charter which also flew flowers from the Scilly Islands, employed her as office manager. Soon she was flying Proctor charters and joyrides from Croydon and the Scillies.

After the company acquired its first Dragon Rapide, she flew the Jersey route too. By 1948 she was managing director of Island Services' London operation. The next year she married Ray Rendall, a former RAF pilot whom she had recruited to fly for the firm. In that period she took IAS into joyriding, operating from Northolt and Heathrow. This proved a popular family treat and inspired some children to become pilots. Flights ranged from 10s to £1.15s for a view of London's dockland.

In 1950, by now chairman of Island Air Services (as the company had become) Agazarian launched weekend gambling jaunts to Deauville, extending the £4 return service to La Baule and Le Touquet. The same year she piloted the IAS Rapide G-ALB Pickles III in the King's Cup air race, but a port engine oil leak forced her to retire on the final leg.

Joyriding flourished at Heathrow until it was curtailed because of the ever-increasing amount of airline traffic. Towards the end of the 1950s she moved to Ramsgate Aerodrome in Kent, but it proved to be too distant from the market.

IAS was wound up and Agazarian briefly joined Air

Links, before taking up residence in Lebanon. In 1973 she returned home and took a part-time job with Air Training Services, the first private company to operate a jet simulator.

When she took the business over in 1976 she worked out of the Piccadilly Hotel with the slogan "Fly Down Piccadilly". Later based at Wycombe Air Park, Booker, Bucks, she established a flight simulator and ground training centre between the Red Baron restaurant and control tower.

She continued to commute to Booker from Knightsbridge in her battered Peugeot ("Ben Hur") until she sold the business last October.

In 1988 she published *Instrument Flying and Background to the Instrument and IMC Ratings*.

Her marriage to Rendall was dissolved in 1973. They had three daughters.

March 7 1993

# CDR WARWICK "BRACES" BRACEGIRDLE

COMMANDER WARWICK "BRACES" BRACEGIRDLE, who has died aged 81, was a Royal Australian Navy gunnery officer with a record second to none; he won a DSC and Bar in the Second World War and a second Bar in the Korean War.

In January 1939 he joined the light cruiser *Amphion* which was renamed *Perth* and turned over to the Australians in June. He served in her in the Mediterranean, and in March 1941 took part in the action when three Italian heavy cruisers were sunk off Cape Matapan.

On the night of April 6 1941 in the harbour of Piraeus, Bracegirdle and another officer were rowing back to *Perth* in a skiff during a heavy German air raid when the ammunition ship *Clan Fraser* was hit and set on fire. There was an ammunition lighter alongside the ship and Bracegirdle and his companion risked their lives to tow the lighter some 50 yards clear before *Clan Fraser* disintegrated in an explosion which nearly killed them.

*Perth* went on to take part in the battle for Crete and in the subsequent evacuation of the army from the island in May when she was badly damaged by air attack. In July *Perth* was in action against the Vichy French in Syria and her shooting resulted in a formidable shore battery being reported "off the map".

Throughout these hectic times Bracegirdle was quite unconcerned for his personal safety and his coolness when directing the ship armament when under fire was a great inspiration to his gun's crews. He was awarded the DSC.

After *Perth* returned to Australia late in 1941, Bracegirdle spent a year at the gunnery school at Flinders naval depot, and then joined the 8-in-gun County Class cruiser HMAS *Shropshire* in December 1942. *Shropshire* sailed for the south-west Pacific, where she operated with the US 7th Fleet, supporting landings by Gen MacArthur's forces in New Britain, New Guinea and the Philippines.

In October 1944 *Shropshire* took part in the largest battle in naval history, the Battle of Leyte Gulf. In the early hours of the 25th, *Shropshire* joined a strong force of US battleships and cruisers lying in wait for Japanese ships off the northern entrance to the Surigao Strait.

Aiming by radar, *Shropshire* contributed 32 8-in broadsides of rapid fire at a range of just under eight nautical miles in a brisk night action during which the Japanese flagship, the battleship *Yamashiro*, was sunk and a heavy cruiser badly damaged.

*Shropshire* went on to give gunfire support to the landings in Lingayen Gulf in January 1945. By then she had fired nearly 2,500 rounds of 8-in shell since December 1943.

In the latter stages, the main danger was not Japanese ships but *kamikaze* suicide aircraft. Bracegirdle trained his gun crews to fire ahead of low-flying aircraft so that shell splashes deterred or even brought the aircraft down.

He also did a crisp trade with American ships, exchanging crates of wardroom whisky for heavier anti-aircraft guns. For all these operations Bracegirdle was awarded a Bar to his DSC and was twice mentioned in despatches.

Warwick Seymour Bracegirdle was born on December 22 1911 into a naval family. His father was Rear-Adml Sir Leighton Bracegirdle, who was to serve as military secretary to the Duke of Gloucester, then Governor-General of Australia.

Young "Braces" was educated at Geelong Grammar School, Melbourne, before joining the Navy as a cadet at the Naval College, Jervis Bay, in 1925. He specialised in gunnery and commanded the winning Devonport field crew at Olympia in 1938.

After the war Bracegirdle passed the staff course at Greenwich, took command of the destroyer HMAS *Bataan* in September 1951 and served in the Korean War, carrying out patrols to blockade the west coast. As a unit commander, Bracegirdle provided effective gunfire to support United Nations operations in defence of friendly islands on the west coast.

For his Korean service he was awarded a second Bar to his DSC and appointed an officer of the American Legion of Merit.

His last two years were spent in London on the staff of the High Commissioner, before retiring in 1957.

"Braces" was the very best type of "Aussie" officer. His sense of humour and his bravery made him enormously popular in every wardroom and much loved by the sailors.

His naval career spawned anecdotes. When one sub-lieutenant (later an admiral), exhausted by watchkeeping in *Shropshire*, was seen to be nodding off at action stations, Braces switched on the loudspeaker full blast and bellowed: "God is watching you Griffiths!"

And when one of *Bataan*'s sailors requested compassionate leave on the grounds that his home town was under flood water 6ft deep, and his wife was only 5ft 3in tall, Braces silently handed him an orange box and stamps to post it.

Bracegirdle was a different man when he left the Navy. Although he worked successfully for Morgan Crucible, Vospers and the Iranian Oil Co, he never had the same zest for civilian life.

But many of those who had served him kept in touch and often came from Australia to visit him. His house in England was a "pommy" outpost for the Royal Australian Navy.

He was married twice, and had two sons and a daughter by his first marriage.

March 23 1993

# DIGBY TATHAM-WARTER

DIGBY TATHAM-WARTER, the former company commander, 2nd Battalion, Parachute Regiment, who has died aged 75, was celebrated for leading a bayonet charge at Arnhem in September 1944, sporting an old bowler hat and a tattered umbrella.

During the long, bitter conflict Tatham-Warter strolled around nonchalantly during the heaviest fire. The padre (Fr Egan) recalled that, while he was trying to make his way to visit some wounded in the cellars and had taken temporary shelter from enemy fire, Tatham-Warter came up to him, and said: "Don't worry about the bullets: I've got an umbrella."

Having escorted the padre under his brolly, Tatham-Warter continued visiting the men who were holding the perimeter defences. "That thing won't do you much good," commented one of his fellow officers, to which Tatham-Warter replied: "But what if it rains?"

By that stage in the battle all hope of being relieved by the arrival of 30 Corps had vanished. The Germans were pounding the beleaguered airborne forces with heavy artillery and Tiger tanks, so that most of the houses were burning and the area was littered with dead and wounded.

But German suggestions that the parachutists should surrender received a rude response. Tatham-Warter's umbrella became a symbol of defiance, as the British, although short of ammunition, food and water, stubbornly held on to the north end of the road bridge.

Arnhem was the furthest ahead of three bridges in

Holland which the Allies needed to seize if they were going to outflank the Siegfried line. Securing the bridge by an airborne operation would enable 30 Corps to cross the Rhine and press on into Germany.

As the first V2 rocket had fallen in Britain earlier that month, speed in winning the land battle in Europe was essential. In the event, however, the parachutists were dropped unnecessarily far from the bridge, and the lightly armed Airborne Division was attacked by two German Panzer divisions whose presence in the area had not been realised: soldiers from one of them reached the bridge before the British parachutists.

Tatham-Warter and his men therefore had to fight their way to the bridge, capture the north end, try to cross it and capture the other side. This they failed to do.

At one point the back of Tatham-Warter's trouserings was whipped out by blast, giving him a vaguely scarecrow-like appearance instead of his normally immaculate turnout. Eventually he was wounded (as was the padre), and consigned to a hospital occupied by the Germans.

Although his wound was not serious Tatham-Warter realised that he had a better chance of escape if he stayed with the stretcher cases. During the night, with his more severely wounded second-in-command (Capt A. M. Frank), he crawled out of the hospital window and reached "a very brave lone Dutch woman" who took them in and hid them. She spoke no English and was very frightened, but fed them and put them in touch with a neighbour who disguised them as house painters and sheltered them in a delivery van, from where they moved to a house.

Tatham-Warter then bicycled around the countryside, which was full of Germans, making contact with other Arnhem escapees (called evaders) and informing them of the rendezvous for an escape over the Rhine.

On one of these trips, he and his companion were overtaken by a German staff car, which skidded off the muddy road into a ditch. "As the officers seemed to be in an excitable state," he recalled, "we thought it wise to help push their car out and back on to the road. They were gracious enough to thank us for our help."

As jobbing painters, Tatham-Warter and Frank aroused no suspicions by their presence in the home of the Wildeboer family (who owned a paint factory), although the area abounded with Gestapo, Dutch SS and collaborators. Even when four Panzer soldiers were billeted on the Wildeboers, they merely nodded and greeted each other on their comings and goings.

Eventually, with the help of the Dutch Resistance, Tatham-Warter assembled an escape party of 150, which included shot-down airmen and even two Russians. Guided by the Dutch, they found their way through the German lines, often passing within a few yards of German sentries and outposts.

Tatham-Warter suspected that the Germans deliberately failed to hear them: 30 Corps had been sending over strong fighting patrols of American parachutists temporarily under their command, and the Germans had no stomach for another bruising encounter.

In spite of Tatham-Warter's stern admonitions, he recalled that his party sounded more like a herd of buffaloes than a secret escape party. Finally, they reached the river bank where they were ferried over by British sappers from 30 Corps and met by Hugh Fraser (then in the SAS) and Airey Neave, who had been organising their escape.

Tatham-Warter was awarded the DSO after the battle.

Allison Digby Tatham-Warter was born on May 26 1917 and educated at Wellington and Sandhurst. He was destined for the Indian Army but while on the statutory year of attachment to an English regiment in India – in this case the Oxford and Bucks Light Infantry – he liked it so much that he decided to stay on. He formally transferred to the regiment in 1938.

He had ample opportunity for pig-sticking: on one occasion he killed three wild boar while hunting alone. The average weight of the boars was 150lb and their height 32in. He also took up polo – which he called "snobs' hockey" – with considerable success.

In 1939 he shot a tiger when on foot. With a few friends he had gone to the edge of the jungle to make arrangements for the reception of a tiger the next evening. As they were doing so, they suddenly noticed that one had arrived prematurely. They shinned up the nearest tree, accompanied by some equally prudent monkeys.

When the monkeys decided it was safe to descend the party followed, only to find that the tiger was once more with them. This time Tatham-Warter, who was nearest, was ready, but it was a close shave.

In 1942 the Oxford and Bucks became glider-borne. This was not exciting enough for Tatham-Warter, however, and in 1944 he joined the Parachute Regiment.

"He was lusting for action at that time," John Frost (later Major-General) recalled of Tatham-Warter, "having so far failed to get in the war. There was much of 'Prince Rupert' about Digby and he was worth a bet with anybody's money."

Tatham-Warter' striking appearance was particularly valuable when the British were fighting against imposs-ible odds at Arnhem. For within the perimeter were soldiers from other detachments, signals, sappers and gunmen, who would not know him by sight as his own men would, but who could not fail to be inspired by his towering figure and unflagging spirit of resistance.

Brigadier (later Gen Sir Gerald) Lathbury recalled that Tatham-Warter took command of 2 Para "when the Colonel was seriously wounded and the second-in-com-mand killed . . . he did a magnificent job, moving around the district freely and was so cool that on one occasion he arrived at the door of a house simultaneously with two German soldiers – and allowed them to stand back to let him go in first."

In 1946 Tatham-Warter emigrated to Kenya where he bought and ran two large estates at Nanyuki. An ardent naturalist, he organised and accompanied high-level safaris and was an originator of the photographic safari. He also captained the Kenya Polo team (his handicap was six), and judged at horse shows (he had won the Saddle at Sandhurst). During the Mau Mau rebellion he raised a force of mounted police which operated with great success.

In later years Tatham-Warter took up carpentry and became highly skilled at inlaid work. Fishing and sailing were his other recreations.

In Richard Attenborough's controversial film about Arnhem, *A Bridge Too Far*, the character based on Tatham-Warter was played by Christopher Good.

In 1991 Dibgy Tatham-Warter published his own recollections, *Dutch Courage and 'Pegasus'*, which described his escape after Arnhem and paid tribute to the Dutch civilians who had helped him. He often revisited them.

He married, in 1949, Jane Boyd; they had three daughters.

March 30 1993

# "MICKY" BUDD

"MICKY" BUDD, one of the most colourful characters of the Submarine Service, who has died aged 79, was chief engine room artificer of the submarine *P.219* (later renamed *Seraph*) and was awarded the DSM for setting a fine example of steady courage during her patrols in 1942–43.

In October 1942 *Seraph* became "the Ship with Two Captains" when, for political reasons, it was necessary to give the impression that she was under American command. She embarked a US Navy captain for a special operation to land Gen Mark Clark in North Africa for his negotiations with French authorities before the Torch landings. To mark the occasion Budd had an inscribed brass plate fixed to the bulkhead of the officers' "heads": "General Mark Clark sat here".

In November *Seraph* again had two captains for a similar clandestine operation to pick up the French general, Giraud, from a point some 20 miles east of Toulon. Budd had a second plate engraved: *"General*

*Giraud, il se crappe ici*". Both plates remained *in situ* until *Seraph* was broken up in 1965.

In April 1943 *Seraph* carried out "Operation Mince-meat" or "The Man Who Never Was". This involved the body of an unknown serviceman, dressed in the uniform of "Major Martin", supposedly an officer on Mountbatten's staff, being dropped overboard at a point from which he could drift ashore on the Spanish coast.

"Major Martin" carried secret documents, designed to delude the enemy into thinking that the Allies' next target was not Sicily but Sardinia and Greece. The papers were duly recovered by the Spaniards and handed over to the Nazis.

Budd recalled that *Seraph*'s sailors were told that the canister containing the body was a weather buoy. They used to sit on it at meal times, only discovering the truth many years after the war.

In May 1944, after a refit in Chatham, *Seraph* was carrying out an exercise dive in the Western Approaches when she suddenly took a bow-down angle and hit the sea bottom at a depth of 500ft – nearly twice her designed safe-diving depth. Hurrying forward to shut off water roaring through an open vent, Budd stumbled over the legs of a sailor "who was on his knees, crying and praying to a photograph of his girlfriend. I kicked him and told him he was a submariner, not a soldier, and to get back on his feet."

In the engine-room, Budd heard an ominous creaking sound and, as he watched, the pressure hull itself split, admitting a fine spray of water. He organised a bucket chain to transfer water from forward to aft while praying *Seraph* would live up to her motto, "I follow on wings".

Using the last of her compressed air and main battery power, *Seraph* dragged herself clear and struggled to the surface. Her hull was covered in mud as far aft as the base of the conning tower, showing how deeply she had been embedded.

Leslie Budd (known all his life as "Micky") was born in December 1913 and joined the Navy as a boy artificer in 1928. After service in surface ships he joined submarines in 1937. In 1940 he served in *Osiris*, which he recalled as "an ancient and cranky O-boat" – although she attacked an Italian convoy off Durazzo in Albania and sank the torpedo boat *Palestro*.

As "outside wrecker" – the traditional name for the artificer who looked after machinery outside the engine room – Budd was in charge of a diving station in the control room. He always remembered the cry from *Osiris*'s captain (a retired officer recalled at the outbreak of war) – "Fuck me! I've hit it!"

In 1948, after promotion to warrant rank, Budd had an uneasy time in an aircraft carrier; an aircraft crashed on the quarter deck where he was drinking a cup of tea. He concluded that aircraft carriers were far more dangerous than submarines.

He was recalled to submarines after *Affray* failed to surface in the English Channel in 1951 – with the loss of everyone on board including an entire submarine engineer officers' training class. Promoted lieutenant in 1955, he retired in 1964.

He did valuable work organising the library and records in the RN submarine museum at Gosport.

Micky Budd was always very proud of being a submariner and had a huge repertoire of submarine stories, which grew taller as the liquid level in his glass sank.

He is survived by a daughter.

March 31 1993

# GEORGE IVES

GEORGE IVES, who has died at Aldergrove, British Columbia, aged 111, was the last surviving soldier of the Boer War.

Determined to surrender to old age only by inches, Ives retained vivid memories of his service in South Africa as a mounted infantryman – notably of chasing enemy commandos. The Boers never tarried for a pitched battle, and were generally content to shoot from the hills, killing more oxen than men. Nevertheless, Ives had a scar from a Boer bullet that had ricocheted off a rock to graze his cheek.

"My job was to get over there and kill Boers," Ives would recall in his soft Gloucestershire accent. "You went to war to kill someone, and they tried to kill you back."

Like most soldiers, he had mixed feelings about his service. He expressed little enthusiasm for the British cause, felt a deep sympathy for the enemy, and remembered uneasily his time guarding their womenfolk in ill-run concentration camps.

Ives was happier to remember the humanity displayed by both sides. On one occasion Christiaan de Wet, the great Boer general, was allowed to enter a British camp during a lull in the fighting to obtain medical supplies for his wounded men. He also remembered the ceaseless quest for beer.

The son of a coachman and a lady's maid, George Frederick Ives was born in France and taken to England to have his birth registered as November 17 1881, to ensure that he would not be called up for French military service. He was brought up largely in France, where his parents worked for the Tidmarsh family. He hoped to become a jockey until he grew too heavy.

Young George was working in his father's grocery shop in Bristol when news of the British defeats at Colenso, Magersfontein and Stormberg arrived in Black Week, December 1899.

In a burst of patriotism, he and thousands of others volunteered to join the Imperial Yeomanry. MPs, barristers, blacksmiths and butchers, few of them with any military experience, poured into half a dozen recruiting centres determined to do their duty.

Ives was one of the 123 who joined the 1st Imperial Yeomanry at Cheltenham. As mounted infantry, they had no sabres and were intended to match the fitness of the Boers' cavalry, but were usually employed in aid of other units. Even so, by their return home only 17 of the original volunteers remained.

Like most of his comrades, he was not inclined to become a settler on the veld after the war, despite government encouragement, but on his return to Britain he found widespread unemployment. Ives sent off for literature about emigration to the Dominions, and decided on his destination by the toss of a florin, with heads for Canada and tails for New Zealand.

It came up heads, and Ives joined a group of 2,000 colonists, including a large number of Boer War veterans, to open up a new wheat belt in the unpopulated Northwest Territories. Under the leadership of two Anglican clergymen, the party muddled its way west to found Lloydminster on what would become the Saskatchewan–Alberta border.

Ives and his father arrived in 1903 and purchased a quarter-section of 160 acres for $10 (£2). Under the preferential rules of purchase they had to break at least 15 acres and build their own shack, made of logs with a sod roof. Their major problem was to find a well.

Ives proved a hard-working and methodical farmer, and at the outbreak of the First World War was surprised to be rejected for service because of a heart murmur.

In 1910 he felt prosperous enough to marry his wife of the next 76 years, Kay Nelson ("I used to call her Cayenne"); they had three sons and three daughters. But his wife disliked the hard life of the prairies, where the washing always froze on the line during the winter. So in 1919 they moved to White Rock, British Columbia, where Ives took a dairy farm until retiring at 60.

This proved merely an excuse to change jobs, and for the next 15 years he worked in a shipyard, building wooden scows, before retiring for the last time.

He and his wife continued to live in their house until 1984, when they moved to an old people's home. Ives proved a genial, if uncompromising, resident.

He pulled his chin up to a parallel bar by the arms until he was well past 100, and remained critical of his children's generation, complaining that youngsters in their eighties and nineties were apt to let themselves go.

After a story about him in the "Peterborough" column of *The Daily Telegraph* in 1992 he said that he would like to attend the Albert Hall service on Remembrance Day. Within a week he found himself brought over by a television producer. Afterwards he greatly enjoyed meeting Queen Elizabeth the Queen Mother, Lady Thatcher and John Major.

Right to the end Ives liked to talk about going down to the Legion for "a couple of pints". He maintained the ethical standards of his youth, and when a writer more than 60 years his junior, who was interviewing him, suggested that they retire to the quiet of his room, he was concerned for her reputation lest it became known she had been to a man's bedroom.

*April 15 1993*

# OLIVER PHILPOT

OLIVER PHILPOT, who has died aged 80, was one of three prisoners of war to escape from Stalag Luft III, in an episode later celebrated by the film *The Wooden Horse*.

The escape from the prison camp at Sagan, Silesia, in 1943 was based on the ruse of placing a hollow wooden vaulting horse some 100ft from the camp wire. At the outset Flt-Lt Eric Williams, whose idea was inspired by the Trojan Horse, and Lt R. M. C. Codner, Royal Artillery, wedged themselves inside the horse, sank a shaft and began to dig a tunnel. Fellow prisoners staged a keep-fit exhibition which duped their German guards for months.

The operation began on July 8 1943, but Flt-Lt Oliver Philpot later joined as third man. Day after day, as PoWs vaulted for two or three hours at a stretch, Philpot toiled at his share of the tunnelling.

Then, at 1pm on October 29, Codner was sealed into the tunnel. After the evening parade, at which the count was falsified, Williams and Philpot were carried out inside the horse. At 5pm they too were sealed in.

Philpot and his comrades waited until it was almost dark and then emerged some 12ins short of the target spot, to find themselves right in the sentry's path. Fortunately the night patrol was late.

Clad in black clothes and face masks, the party made its way into a wood, where it split up: Codner and Williams headed for Stettin, while Philpot plumped for the longer trip to Danzig.

Posing as a Norwegian quisling, Philpot prayed he would not meet any genuine Norwegians as he did not speak the language. His cover story was that he was a margarine executive (his own peacetime occupation) on exchange from Norway to Berlin.

He carried a small suitcase containing shaving gear and wore a black Homburg, an RAF officer's greatcoat and gloves, new shoes, a pair of Fleet Air Arm officer's trousers and a black civilian jacket. He chewed on a pipe, as an excuse for slurring his speech, and for good measure he sported a Hitler moustache.

He bought a rail ticket at Sagan and travelled to Frankfurt-on-Oder. The next morning he caught the slow train to Kustrin, where he joined the Konigsberg Express, went to sleep sitting on his suitcase in a third-class gangway, fell off and exclaimed "Damn!" But his fellow passengers simply laughed.

Challenged by a plain-clothes policeman on the train, Philpot fobbed him off with an identity card which displayed the mug shot of a fellow officer. He changed at Dirschau and boarded a fast train to Danzig.

It was 23 hours since he had broken ground at Sagan. He treated himself to a glass of beer in the station refreshment room, took a tram to recce the docks and returned to an hotel near the station, where he was obliged to share a room.

The next morning Philpot took a ferry trip in the harbour, where he noticed a Swedish ship loading coal. Later that evening he climbed up a mooring cable and wriggled on to the deck.

After lying low for a while he crawled to a door leading to a galley, drank the hot chocolate he found simmering there and stowed away in a coal bunker. Next morning (November 2) the ship put to sea. Having waited until the craft was well clear of Danzig, Philpot revealed himself and was invited by the captain to be a guest for the remainder of the voyage.

The ship docked at midnight on November 3 at Sodertalje, where Philpot spent a night in a police cell. The next day he walked into the British Legation at Stockholm, where repatriation was arranged. Williams and Codner also scored a "home run" by way of Sweden.

The son of a lighting engineer from London, Oliver Lawrence Spurling Philpot was born in Vancouver, British Columbia, on March 6 1913 and educated at Radley and Worcester College, Oxford, where he learned to fly with the University Air Squadron.

In 1934 he joined Unilever as a management trainee and two years later was appointed assistant commercial secretary in the company's Home Margarine Executive.

He reported for full-time service in the RAF in August 1939 and was posted to 42 Squadron as a pilot officer. This Coastal Command unit was equipped with the obsolete Wildebeeste torpedo-bomber.

In June 1940 the squadron converted to Bristol Beauforts and saw action in the Norwegian campaign. On one sortie Philpot pressed home an attack on Christiansand in Norway after his Beaufort had been badly shot up. With his crew dead or dying, he managed to fly back to Leuchars in Scotland, where he made a belly landing.

On December 11 1941 his Beaufort was hit by a German flakship while attacking a freighter at the centre of a merchant convoy. He ditched the Beaufort, which broke in two. Philpot and his crew clambered into a dinghy and were adrift for two nights before being picked up by the enemy.

After the "Wooden Horse" escape he was debriefed by MI9, and did not return to operations. In 1944 he was appointed a senior scientific officer at the Air Ministry.

On demobilisation in 1946 he joined the Maypole Dairy Co; two years later he was appointed chairman of Trufood. In 1950 he became office manager at Unilever House, and the next year moved to T. Walls & Son as general manager. Subsequently he was a director of Arthur Woollacott & Rappings; chairman and managing director of the Spirella Co of Great Britain; managing director of Benesta (later Aluminium) Foils.

In 1962 he joined Union International and from its head office ran eight companies. From 1965 to 1967 he was deputy chairman and chief executive of Fropax Eskimo Food, later Findus. Finally, from 1974 to 1978, Philpot was managing director of Remploy.

In his spare time he gave unstinting service to various charities. He was chairman of the RAF Escaping Society, and served on the National Advisory Council on Employment for Disabled People. He was also overseas administrator for Help the Aged, a member of the general advisory council of the IBA and a manager of the St Bride Foundation Institute.

In 1950 Philpot published *Stolen Journey*. He listed his recreations as "political activity including canvassing, sculling Boat Race course and return (No 452 in Head of the River Race for Scullers, 1986), talking, idling, listening to sermons, reading *Financial Times* and obituaries in *Lancet*".

Philpot was awarded the DFC in 1941 and MC in 1944.

His first marriage, by which he had a son and two daughters, was dissolved in 1951. He married secondly, in 1954, Rosl Widhalm; they had a son and a daughter.

May 6 1993

# BRIG GEOFFREY WESTON

BRIGADIER GEOFFREY WESTON, who has died aged 71, was probably the only Army Brigadier ever to be mentioned in Naval despatches and to win two DSCs.

Weston was also one of those rare men with the strength of character to recover from severe injury and change the course of their lives in midstream. The turning point came in 1949, during the civil war between Chinese nationalists and Communists, when Weston was 1st Lieutenant of the frigate *Amethyst* on the China Station.

In April *Amethyst* steamed up the Yangtse, intending to relieve the British guard ship at Nanking. With hindsight it was perhaps provocative to sail a warship across the front of a Communist army which was just about to cross the Yangtse.

*Amethyst* flew two huge Union Jacks and several white Ensigns, but the Communist gunners on the north bank, who had probably never seen such flags before, mistook *Amethyst* for a nationalist warship and opened fire, mortally wounding the captain and killing several of the crew.

*Amethyst* ran aground. All the guns which could have engaged the Communist batteries were out of action, and the ship was still being hit. Weston, himself badly wounded by shrapnel, took command and maintained morale on board by his shining example of decisive leadership.

When Lt-Cdr John Kerans, an attaché at the Embassy in Nanking, arrived more than two days later, Weston remained in command. He left the ship with the greatest reluctance – on medical advice, for his wounds were grievous – and regretted the decision for the rest of his life.

He recovered sufficiently well at Shanghai to try to rejoin *Amethyst*, with instructions for Kerans which could not be passed in plain language; he had memorised a new code for the ship to use. But negotiations with the Communists for his passage broke down.

Weston was still in Shanghai in July – feeling, as he put it, "like Uriah the Hittite during the siege of Rabbah" – when *Amethyst* made her historic dash down the Yangtse to freedom.

The next month he escaped by junk and merchant ship to Hong Kong, a feat kept secret for fear of offending Chinese political susceptibilities.

For his service in *Amethyst* he was awarded a Bar to his DSC. He was always tight-lipped about his Chinese odyssey, and was not much impressed by the film *Yangtse Incident*, in which he was played by Donald Houston.

Geoffrey Lee Weston was born on August 15 1921, one of nine children of Spencer Percy Weston, a stockjobber who joined the Army, served in both World Wars, rose to brigadier general, won three DSOs, an MC and the French and Belgian Croix de Guerre.

Young Geoffrey went to Seabrook Lodge, Hythe, before joining the Royal Naval College, Dartmouth, in 1935, where his first duty was to line the route for King George V's Silver Jubilee.

In 1943 he served in the sloop *Hastings*, taking part in the Atlantic convoy battles of March and April, and was mentioned in despatches. A year later he was 1st Lieutenant of the destroyer *Catterick* in the invasion of southern France and in operations in the Aegean.

In the winter of 1944–45 *Catterick* was one of the Royal Navy ships which aided the civilian population and maintained order in Greece after the Communist "army of liberation" attempted to seize control of the country. Weston was awarded the DSC.

He was invalided from the Navy in 1950, with chunks of shrapnel still inside him, including "one piece the size of a matchbox" in his liver.

Weston then read law at Cambridge, which he followed with a year as a Fulbright scholar at Kansas University. He was called to the Bar by Lincoln's Inn in 1954, and the next year commissioned as a captain into the Army Legal Services.

He served in Cyprus, Germany, Hong Kong and Northern Ireland. His last appointment before retiring in 1981 was as Brigadier (Legal) at HQ UK Land Forces.

Geoffrey Weston was a true eccentric, who needed the discipline of the Services to pit his idiosyncrasies against. It says much for the Army that it tolerated such a non-conformist for so long. He had a first-class legal brain but was probably a better administrator than advocate, as he tended to become too personally involved in his cases.

Despite his injuries, his frequent strokes and his diabetes (he once said he had every disease except Aids), he played violent games of squash and loved to win, which he sometimes did because his opponent, who knew of his heart condition, feared that the game might be his last.

Weston enjoyed music, chess, Chinese poetry, omelettes (which he made superbly well), arguments and diets, which he was forever starting and abandoning. He wore very good suits which, as he neglected to have them dry-cleaned, bore a permanent layer of cigar ash. A heavy smoker, on one of his many visits to hospital he was amused to learn that the non-smoking heart specialist who had warned him against smoking had died of a heart attack the next day.

He never married.

May 24 1993

# Gp Capt Tom Gleave

GROUP CAPTAIN TOM GLEAVE, who has died aged 84, was a gallant fighter pilot in the Battle of Britain, in which he was grievously burned.

Shot down in flames over Kent at the height of the battle in the summer of 1940, Gleave became one of the first "Guinea Pigs" — burns patients of Sir Archibald

McIndoe, the RAF's celebrated wartime consultant in plastic surgery, at the Queen Victoria Hospital in East Grinstead.

Gleave had arrived there suffering from "standard Hurricane burns", to face, hands, arms and legs. McIndoe ("the Maestro" as Guinea Pigs called him) immediately set about growing him a new nose.

Gleave's seniority, as a regular squadron leader and "elderly" fighter pilot of 32, assured him the office of Chief Guinea Pig for life. For more than half a century he inspired the club's fund-raising and welfare activities, ever mindful of the needs of surviving members as they entered old age.

The years of aftercare were the legacy of the spirit fostered in Ward 3, where McIndoe introduced a regime quite alien to the lie-to-attention, stand-by-your-beds attitude that had prevailed until then. Visitors to Ward 3 often retreated in horror – not because of the appalling nature of the Guinea Pigs' injuries, or the grotesque disfigurement of rhinoplasty patients growing new noses from other parts of their bodies, but at the discovery of beer barrels in the ward, and regular "grogging parties" at weekends.

A German cannon shell had ignited the right fuel-tank of Gleave's Hurricane as he attacked a formation of bombers over Kent; the fire engulfed him rapidly. He felt for the revolver which he wore in the cockpit as a last resort. His clothes were on fire, the skin of his hands and wrists blistering in white bubbles and the flames licking at his legs, but he rejected the option of suicide and struggled to escape, only to be thwarted by his oxygen tube, which refused to disconnect.

Clawing off the helmet to which it was attached, he opened the canopy. Then an explosion ejected him more suddenly and forcefully than he would have wished.

Having landed by parachute near the fighter station at Biggin Hill, Gleave was taken to Orpington Hospital. He came round from an emergency operation to find himself not in but under a bed. There was an air raid, and he could hear the noise of the bombs.

Shortly afterwards his wife arrived. Confronted by her husband bandaged like a mummy with slits for his eyes (the lids were burnt) she asked him: "What on earth have you been doing with yourself?"

"I had a row with a German," replied Gleave. His answer later became the title of his short book about his wartime experience.

Thomas Percy Gleave was born on September 6 1908 and educated at Westminster High School and Liverpool Collegiate School. He joined the Sefton Tanning Company in 1924, and four years later earned a pilot's "A" licence at the Liverpool and Merseyside Flying Club. Later that year he went to Canada, where he worked for a tannery. On his return home in 1930 he was commissioned into the RAF.

Passed out as an "exceptional pilot" in 1931 – and subsequently as an "exceptional fighter pilot" – Gleave was soon a member of the RAF's aerobatic team. In 1933 he determined to enter the record books with a flight to Ceylon, but was obliged to crash-land his Spartan in mountainous Turkish terrain. The next year he qualified as a flying instructor. After several postings as an instructor, he joined Bomber Command on New Year's Day 1939.

When war broke out Gleave agitated for a fighter

squadron, until eventually his wish was granted. He commanded 253, a Hurricane squadron, from June to August 1940, when he handed over to Sqn Ldr H. M. Starr. After Starr was killed on August 31 Gleave resumed command.

Before Gleave was himself shot down his official score was "one confirmed and four probable": postwar investigation raised this to five Me109s on August 30 and a Ju88 on August 31.

Fighter Command's preferred policy during the Battle of Britain was for Spitfires to tackle the escorting 109s, while Hurricanes took on the bombers. For a Hurricane pilot to destroy a 109 was in itself an achievement, but to bag five in one day was astonishing.

The action in which Gleave shot down his 109s would have been sufficient, had confirmation been available, to rate him an official ace and at the least a DFC. Gleave was promoted wing commander while he was lying in bed at the Royal Victoria. Partially repaired by the Maestro, he was restored to non-operational flying in August 1941; a pale patch on his forehead indicated the provenance of his new nose.

Operationally fit by October, he was given brief command of the fighter station at Northolt before taking over Manston, the frontline airfield on the Kent coast. From there, on February 12 1942, he dispatched six Swordfish biplane torpedo-bombers of the Fleet Air Arm's 825 Squadron on their ill-fated attempt to sink the battle-cruisers *Scharnhorst* and *Gneisenau* and the cruiser *Prinz Eugen* as they made their "Channel Dash". All six Swordfish were shot down in the Channel.

Convinced that circumstances had obliged him to send his men on a suicide mission, Gleave stood alone at the end of the runway and saluted each Swordfish as it took off.

Before leaving Manston in September 1942 Gleave pleaded for a long, wide runway of concrete or tarmac to save the crippled and short-of-fuel bombers which, having struggled across the Channel, were unable to reach their bases. Gleave's runway is still maintained for emergency military and civil landings.

Gleave next joined the planning staff of "Operation Round Up" (later "Overlord"), the proposed invasion of Normandy. This entailed a promotion to Group Captain Air Plans, Allied Expeditionary Air Force. For his vital contribution to the invasion Gleave received the CBE and the United States Legion of Merit (later changed for the Bronze Star).

From October 1 1944 until July 15 1945 he was General Eisenhower's Head of Air Plans at Supreme Headquarters Allied Expeditionary Force. After VE Day Gleave returned to the "Sty" for further repairs. He later served as Senior Air Staff Officer, RAF Delegation to France, from 1945 to 1947.

Following further staff appointments at home he underwent more plastic surgery at East Grinstead, and was invalided out of the RAF in 1953. Thereafter Gleave joined the historical section of the Cabinet Office, where he was engaged on official histories of the Second World War. He spent more than 30 years on the task, mainly as a member of the Mediterranean and Middle East team.

He was elected a Fellow of the Royal Historical Society, and was air historian and deputy chairman of the Battle of Britain Fighter Association. He also served the Blond McIndoe Centre for Medical Research and the East Grinstead Trust.

Gleave was twice mentioned in despatches, received the French Legion of Honour and Croix de Guerre, and was awarded the wings of the Polish and French air forces.

He married and had a son (who died in a canoeing accident in Canada) and a daughter.

June 14 1993

# SGT FRED KITE

SERGEANT FRED KITE, who has died aged 72, had the unique distinction of winning the Military Medal three times in the Second World War: all three were immediate awards.

The first occasion was in January 1943 when he was engaged in special reconnaissance duties, three miles west of Tarhuna, in what the citation described as "desperately difficult" conditions: "Sgt Kite excelled himself", as the citation recorded. No hostile anti-tank gun, no field gun or machine-gun opened fire on the regimental front without Sgt Kite reporting accurately the location to the Artillery observation posts.

As the resultant counter-battery fire neutralised the enemy guns Sgt Kite pressed forward with his troop and engaged the hostile gun crews with small arms fire, causing much confusion and considerable casualties. On several occasions he became dangerously isolated. Nothing daunted, he continued his gallant and skilful actions time and time again.

His actions had much to do with the hurried and disorderly withdrawal of the enemy towards last light.

His complete disregard of personal safety, his skilful leadership, and his good humour throughout were a fine example to all who watched him and listened to his wireless reports.

Kite's second MM was won in July 1944 for the actions near the village of Bras, Normandy: "At all times", noted the citation, "he displayed a very high standard of leadership and personal courage, and was an excellent example to the remainder of the squadron." When the squadron was held up by two enemy tanks and two 88mm guns on the high ground at Bras, this NCO, by clever use of the ground, pressed forward under heavy tank fire and knocked out one Mark IV tank, one "Panther", and one of the 88mm guns, and held on to his position under extremely trying circumstances. This allowed the remainder of the squadron to get forward into better positions.

The third MM came soon afterwards. On August 3 1944 at Le Grand Bonfait Kite was commanding one of several tanks on the edge of an orchard, the duty of these tanks being to support a company of infantry. This position was strongly counter-attacked by enemy infantry and at least one Tiger and four Panther tanks. The enclosed nature of the country enabled these tanks to approach within the distance of 400 yards.

All the other tanks in the vicinity of Kite were hit and set on fire but despite this he maintained his position. He assisted in the correction of our own artillery fire, thus preventing the enemy infantry forming up with his tanks for an attempt to advance on our position.

Kite kept his own tank in action and secured at least five hits on enemy tanks at short range before his own tank was hit and he himself was seriously wounded.

The citation stated that "Sgt Kite showed the greatest personal courage and his example of remaining in action against odds that were much against him was an inspiration to all. He undoubtedly helped to a considerable degree to beat off the attack on a feature of great importance."

Montgomery's signature appeared on all three citations, first as GOC 8th Army, then as C-in-C 21 Army Group, and finally as a Field Marshal.

Frederick Kite was born in 1921 and as a young man was a promising hockey and football player; he had a trial for Port Vale before the outbreak of war ended any possibilities of a career as a professional footballer.

He joined the Royal Armoured Corps and was posted to the 3rd Royal Tank Regiment. In May 1940, when the German Panzers had broken through to the coast at Abbeville in the battle for France, 3 RTR were hastily despatched to Calais, on which two Panzer Divisions were converging to take part in the defence of the town.

Sent to reconnoitre the situation at St Omer, they found it unoccupied but in flames. As they moved to occupy it they encountered the full weight of 1st Panzer Division and lost 12 tanks before withdrawing to Calais.

They were then ordered to send a squadron to test the road to Dunkirk and once again encountered 1st Panzer and lost more tanks. The remains of 3 RTR, mustering 21 light and medium tanks, were now confronting the combined strength of two German divisions.

Nevertheless – together with their comrades in the Rifle Brigade, the 60th Rifles, the Queen Victoria Rifles, the 1st Searchlight Regiment and some French troops – they put up such a spirited fight that they delayed the

German advance to Dunkirk and undoubtedly helped to make the evacuation possible.

After escaping from Calais and returning home, Kite was soon sent overseas again, this time to Egypt in November 1940. He took part in Wavell's successful battles against the Italians in the desert, but was then involved in the disastrous ones against the Germans in Greece and Crete.

Kite escaped from Crete with a few other soldiers, in a Greek ship which they sailed themselves. Back in the desert he took part in more battles, including the July battle at Alamein.

After recovering from his wounds he returned to civilian life and became chief wages clerk in a factory.

A cheerful, modest, exceptionally brave man, "Buck" Kite might have had a successful professional career as a gamesplayer if he had not been wounded.

He married, in 1945, Elaine Cooper.

June 16 1993

# SIR EDWARD "WEARY" DUNLOP

SIR EDWARD "WEARY" DUNLOP, the Australian surgeon who has died in Melbourne aged 85, won his country's lasting admiration and affection for his conduct as a wartime prisoner of the Japanese.

Unlike some heroes, whose spectacular exploits are increasingly forgotten, "Weary" Dunlop found his reputation growing with the years, though he was the most unassuming of men. His courage and humanity amid cruel hardship appealed to new generations of Australians. For the lives he saved among fellow prisoners in Java, and later on the Burma–Thailand railway, they saw him as half-hero and half-saint.

It was not only his skills as a surgeon that counted, but his strength in standing between his patients and the Japanese, who tried to drive them out to work on the railway. He became their symbol of hope.

A strapping figure in days of peace – 6ft 4in and 16 stone – Dunlop was savagely beaten by his captors and was twice readied for execution. Tied to a tree to be bayoneted, he heard the officer in charge count backwards from 30. The count stopped at one.

The same night he was again tied to the tree and again inexplicably spared. He concluded that perhaps the officer had come to respect his opinions.

Once, having failed to put lights out when the bugle sounded, he was stood for hours the next day in boiling sun while passing guards struck and kicked him at random. Told that he would be punished if he kept to his criminal ways, he lost his stoicism: "God almighty," he yelled, "don't you think it punishment standing in this sun and being kicked and beaten by a pack of bandy-legged baboons?"

When this was translated the Japanese fell upon him with rifle butts, jeers, boots and sticks, until he was lying in the dust, ribs broken, scalp bleeding. He was then trussed up, leaning backwards with a large log between his thighs and knees.

Four hours later he was asked: "If we were so

forgiving as to release you, would you have hard feelings against the guard?" He replied: "Hard feelings against what guard?"

This was enough to win release. As his circulation slowly returned he stood painfully to attention, bowed and said: "And now if you will excuse me I shall amputate the arm of the Dutchman who has been waiting all day."

"I was determined," he later wrote in his diary, "to show them that Australians were tough." He continued: "I steadied my tremulous hands, injected the brachial plexus and removed the totally paralysed, smashed-up and infected limb with the patient still on his rough stretcher. I patted his pale, sweating head and muttered some reassuring Dutch words to take my leave." He bowed to the Japanese guards and collapsed into bed.

Dunlop believed it was the duty of the strong to look after the weak, and the young after the old.

Ernest Edward Dunlop was born on July 12 1907 at Major Plains, North East Victoria. The younger of two boys, he was brought up on his parents' farm at Sheepwash Creek, near Stewarton, 120 miles north of Melbourne. At seven he was riding a horse five miles to school. Soon he thought nothing of walking barefoot across a frost-covered paddock or milking 20 cows.

Apprenticed at 15 to a country chemist, he qualified as a pharmacist in 1928, winning both the Pharmaceutical Society's gold medals. In 1934, determined to become a surgeon, Dunlop graduated with a first from Melbourne University, where he was given the absurd name of "Weary" (a tortured pun on Dunlop tyres). He was then commissioned as a captain in the Royal Australian Army Medical Corps.

In 1939 he was on the staff of the Postgraduate Medical School at Hammersmith, London, having qualified FRCS after a 10-week course at St Bartholomew's. When the Second World War broke out he was a specialist surgeon at St Mary's Hospital, Paddington.

Dunlop lived in a charmed circle led by Arthur Porritt (later Lord Porritt, Governor-General of New Zealand); he played poker at times with Alexander Fleming, and his friends included Jack Lovelock, the miler.

Dunlop himself was a first-rate athlete, having played rugby for the Barbarians and the British Commonwealth against a Combined Services side.

Enlisting in the Australian Army in London, he served in the Middle East, Greece and Crete before sailing for the Pacific War. By now he was a lieutenant colonel and CO of 2/2 Casualty Clearing Station. He landed in Java in February 1942 and was taken prisoner three weeks later.

Dunlop soon had his first taste of Japanese army ways. Commanding a hospital in Bandoeng, he was given 10 minutes notice to shut it down and move on. He protested that patients were too sick to be moved, and when the Japanese threatened to bayonet the helpless, he stepped in front of the first, a blind soldier with a shattered face, amputated hands and broken leg. After a tense moment he was given one night to break up the hospital.

Dunlop was senior officer of a PoW camp in Bandoeng for three months before being sent on to the Burma–Thailand railway, there to carry out miracles of surgery without medical supplies, in squalor, stench and misery. The men were starved, wracked with dysentery, malaria, beriberi and tropical ulcers.

Needles and masks for anaesthesia were made from bamboo. Thread came from haversacks and parachute cord, a surgical snare from portions of a fork, hypodermic needle and wire. Operations were conducted under hurricane lamps.

A sense of humour and a light use of irony helped Dunlop through. His diary entry for April 10 1944 read: "Deaths: One. An amusing story of a geisha who came per barge for the pleasure of Commander Kukabu! It seems that on the way in she was apprehended by Ometz and was enjoyed by Ometz and three British other ranks for the sum of 15 ticals."

Dunlop kept his diaries in little notebooks and on scraps of paper, carefully hidden, and did not publish them until 1986.

Having spent the first year hating the Japanese beyond measure, he came to see them as a collection of good and bad, prisoners themselves of a ruthless and terrible system. After the war he worked for closer ties with Asian countries, including Japan. "Surely," he wrote, "some increased understanding should emerge from a tragic conflict in which, when all is said and done, Japanese losses vastly exceeded our own."

After the war Dunlop returned to surgery in Melbourne and a distinguished career. During the Vietnam War he took a surgical team to South Vietnam to work among civilians.

He was appointed a Companion of the Order of Australia in 1987, having been appointed OBE in 1947, CMG in 1965 and knighted in 1969.

He married, in 1945, Helen Ferguson, who died in 1990; they had two sons.

July 5 1993

# ELEANOR STRUGNELL

ELEANOR STRUGNELL, the missionary who has died aged 106 at Concepcion, Chile, was the oldest member of the South American Missionary Society, known throughout South America as "Granny Struggles".

An eccentric and redoubtable character, Strugnell devoted her life to the poor and downtrodden of South America. Her nickname was derived partly from her name, partly from her indefatigability and partly from a line in her favourite hymn: "Jesus knows of all our struggles."

The Rt Rev Douglas Milmine, former Bishop of Paraguay, said of her: "Her eccentricities exasperated some, but endeared her to many. She was a missionary of the old school, unassuming and willing to do anything."

Eleanor Strugnell was born into a poor family in Oxfordshire on January 31 1887. At birth she was so weak and tiny that her parents laid her in an empty shoebox beside a wood stove to keep her warm until death released her. But young Eleanor went on to attend a local school and to qualify as a teacher.

In 1920 she was accepted by the South American Missionary Society and sent to teach in an orphanage in Argentina. Within a few years she moved to Chile, where she learned the language of the Mapuche, one of the most tenacious of the Indian tribes, among whom she lived in humble style.

In term-time she taught at local mission schools and in the summer months rode to the more remote villages, vigorously haranguing the natives about hygiene and the Scriptures.

In 1941 she married Canon William "Daddy" Wilson, a retired medical missionary much older than herself, whom she inspired to return to missionary work. Together they travelled the country in a converted bullock cart loaded with medical supplies, Bibles, and a battery-powered magic lantern with which she showed both health education and Christian material.

After her husband's death she reverted to travelling by horse, struggling through mud and fording fierce rivers.

In her eighties "Granny Struggles" began teaching English conversation at Tamuco University, while still visiting the villages in her spare time. At the age of 90 she finally accepted that her riding days were over, but persuaded her students to let her ride pillion on their motor-cycles. She continued to be active until finally disabled by a stroke.

In her latter days, though virtually speechless, she still sought to convert the susceptible to Christianity by asking them to read aloud appropriate Biblical passages.

After reaching the age of 100 "Granny Struggles" finally lost all power of speech. On receiving her congratulatory telegram from the Queen and Queen Elizabeth the Queen Mother, though, she found the power to exclaim: "La-la-la!"

August 30 1993

# JOAN HUGHES

JOAN HUGHES, who has died aged 74, was one of the first women pilots to fly four-engined bombers in the Second World War.

Small and fragile, she astonished Bomber Command operational squadrons by her ability to handle the Stirling and other "heavies". She overcame the anxieties of the Air Ministry and went on to become an Air Transport Auxiliary (ATA) ferry pilot.

Early in the war, though, Hughes was involved in an almost disastrous accident. In 1941, soon after ATA women pilots had been granted permission to fly Hurricane fighters, she ferried a Canadian-built Hurricane from Prestwick, Scotland, to RAF Finningley, Yorkshire. After take-off she found that she could not move the selector lever which raised the retractable undercarriage. Preferring not to report the problem over the radio, lest she renew doubts about her size and strength, Hughes decided to simply kick the lever. It moved and the wheels retracted.

But as she approached Finningley she discovered that she had damaged the lever and could not lower the undercarriage. Eventually she was obliged to make a belly landing on grass.

Hughes was unharmed, and the accident committee accepted her argument that the aircraft had malfunctioned. Soon afterwards she was flying the Spitfire, a faster plane.

Later in her life, Hughes's reputation for flying just about anything made her a natural stunt pilot for films.

In *Those Magnificent Men in Their Flying Machines* (1965) she piloted a replica of the diminutive 1909 Demoiselle. In *The Blue Max* (1966) she flew a replica of the 1917 German Pfalz.

In 1968 a feature film was made of the *Thunderbirds* television series, and for the flying sequences Hughes was chosen to stand in as Lady Penelope. During the filming, she was prosecuted for flying a Tiger Moth under a motorway bridge near High Wycombe.

She had been given permission to land on the motorway, taxi under the bridge, and take off again. In the event the weather was turbulent, and Hughes decided it would be safer to fly straight through. She was cleared of all charges at Buckinghamshire Quarter Sessions.

Joan Lily Amelia Hughes was born in 1918. From the age of 15 she took a 40-minute flying lesson every week. At 17 she obtained a private pilot's licence and became a familiar figure in flying clubs, always willing to lend a hand and to learn from experienced aviators.

The test pilot Alex Henshaw recalls the great support Hughes gave him when he was preparing a specially modified Percival Mew Gull (G-AEXF) for a flight to Cape Town and back in 1938. He completed the flight in a record time of four days, 10 hours and 20 minutes, including 27 hours and 19 minutes spent on the ground in Cape Town.

Until war broke out, Hughes was a Civil Air Guard flying instructor. On January 1 1940 she was among the first eight women pilots to sign a contract with the ATA. When the ATA expanded the next year, Hughes conducted entry tests and gave instruction to new recruits.

After the war Hughes instructed at the West London Flying Club from 1947 to 1961 and afterwards at the

British Airways Flying Club. She was much in demand to teach captains of Concorde and other airliners to become light aircraft instructors. She gave 1,200 hours of flying lessons in all.

Hughes was appointed MBE in 1945.

She was unmarried.

August 30 1993

# SADIE TALBOT

SADIE TALBOT, who has died aged 105, was the first woman to be awarded the Military Medal.

A dentist's daughter, she was born Sara Bonnell on June 4 1888 and educated at Bedales. After leaving school she lived at home and, as she recalled, "looked after the servants, that kind of thing".

She did, however, learn to drive, and at the outbreak of the First World War, when she was 26, joined the First Aid Nursing Yeomanry (FANY) as an ambulance driver. The FANYs had been founded in 1907 as an all-women mounted volunteer Corps and trained as "the connecting link between the fighting units and the hospitals".

Members had to qualify in first aid, horsemanship, veterinary work, signalling and camp cookery. Such requirements guaranteed a versatile intake, but though the FANYs were ready in 1914, the War Office remained sceptical.

"My good lady," female volunteers for France would be told, "go home and sit still. No petticoats here!"

The FANYs were not discouraged: many applied to the Belgian and French armies; Sadie Bonnell joined the

Canadian Army Service Corps. The endless streams of soldiers wounded in the bloodbath of the trenches were carried or led to the advanced dressing stations, then on to the field hospitals or Channel ports. Transported over poor roads and jolting railways, many died in agony *en route*.

Bonnell won her Military Medal in 1917, when she came under heavy fire while collecting the wounded from a dressing station near the Front – the shells narrowly missing a poison gas dump nearby. The citation read as follows: "For gallantry and conspicuous devotion to duty, when an ammunition dump had been set on fire by enemy bombs and the only available ambulance for the removal of wounded had been destroyed ... [Bonnell] arrived with three ambulances and, despite the danger arising from various explosions, succeeded in removing all the wounded. [Her] conduct throughout was splendid."

Her Military Medal was presented in the field by Gen Sir Herbert Plumer, Commander of the 2nd Army. Bonnell herself always made light of her valour. "It wasn't courage," she declared. "I was there to do something useful. There was a job we had to get done."

Sadie Bonnell was a tall (5ft 11in) and energetic woman. She loved fast motor cars and between the wars drove a six-cylinder AC with a red fish mascot on the bonnet.

She married first, in 1919, Major Herbert Marriott, whom she had met in France, and who died of influenza in 1921, having been gassed in the war.

She married secondly, in 1948, Charles Talbot, who died in 1967.

September 13 1993

# BRIG DAME MARGOT TURNER

BRIGADIER DAME MARGOT TURNER, who has died aged 83, survived two shipwrecks and three-and-a-half years as a Japanese prisoner of war to become the leader of the Queen Alexandra's Royal Army Nursing Corps.

The ship on which Turner was evacuated from Singapore in February 1942 was sunk by Japanese bombers and its passengers machine-gunned in the Java Sea. Turner and a few others managed to swim to the small island of Pompong, where the surviving nurses tended to the wounded, tearing strips off their dresses to make bandages.

A small cargo ship rescued some of the castaways, including Turner, but within hours it too was bombed and wrecked by the Japanese. She later described the horrors that ensued: "The cries and screams of the wounded, the helpless and the dying were quite terrible; and the fact it was in the middle of the night made it all so much worse. Dead bodies and debris from the ship were floating everywhere."

She and another nurse managed to pull eight women and six children on to a raft. Over the next four days Turner watched them all die. The deaths of the children were the most harrowing: "On the second day the children went mad. We had a terrible time with them — and lost them all. I examined each of them with great care before committing their small bodies to the sea. The

327

last one was a very small baby, and it was difficult to know when it was dead."

Turner ate seaweed and drank rainwater collected in the lid of her powder compact. By the time she was picked up by a Japanese battleship she was too weak to stand or eat and had been burnt black by the sun.

She was interned on the island of Banka, off Sumatra, where rations consisted of two bowls of rice a day, and sometimes a little dried octopus. In April she was moved to Palembang in Sumatra, where local Dutch people brought the prisoners green vegetables and pork. Life in the camp was gentle: the internees played bridge and mah-jong, and organised classes in Malay, French and Dutch. Turner nursed, cooked, and shifted sacks of wood and rice.

But the Japanese would assert their authority by insisting on a "Tenko", or count of prisoners, at a moment's notice. "We had to drop everything we were doing and stand out in the roadway, probably at the hottest part of the day, and wait to be counted. I found it very irksome and humiliating having to bow to the Japanese soldiers but I soon learnt my lesson at one of these 'Tenkos' when I failed to do so and a Jap hit me in the face and knocked out one of my front teeth."

In October Turner was sent to nurse Chinese and Malays at a native hospital, where she worked in the operating theatre and tended to outpatients with tropical ulcers. But the next April, without explanation, she and three other nurses were thrown into the Palembang jail. Their fellow prisoners were Malay and Chinese thieves and murderers who, on the whole, treated them kindly. Turner saw many prisoners beaten and tortured by the Japanese guards; several died.

On their release in September the women were returned to the camp, which had moved to a cramped stretch of swampy ground. Six hundred people slept in 10 vermin-infested huts, with 27 inches of space allotted to each woman. They carried out all the camp's manual labour, chopping firewood and fetching water in the heat of the day from the bottom of a steep hill.

Some of the women set up a choir and "orchestra", in which they would hum the parts of the violin, viola, cello and double bass. It was banned in April 1944, when the camp was put under military control. The new commanders also stepped up the number of "Tenkos", and many women, already half-starved, died when forced to take on hard labour.

In October the prisoners were moved back to Banka. Their new camp was freshly built and spotlessly clean, but there was even more work and less food than before. There was also disease — scores of women were struck down with malaria, beri-beri, dysentery and "Banka fever". Turner helped dig graves for the many dead.

After a hellish four-day journey in April 1945, Turner arrived at her final camp, a deserted Sumatran rubber plantation. On August 26 the commandant announced that the war was over, and the Japanese issued the women with lipstick. Male PoWs from neighbouring camps soon joined them, taking over the manual labour and hunting pig and deer in the jungle. Towards the end of September they were all flown to Singapore, from where Turner sailed at last for Liverpool.

Margot Turner was born in Finchley, London, on May 10 1910, and educated at Finchley County School. She trained for four years as a nurse at St Bartholomew's Hospital and in 1937 joined the Queen Alexandra's

Imperial Military Nursing Service (she said she was drawn to the QAs' red capes). Within a year she was posted to Bareilly hospital, near Delhi. The six QAs were kept busy, especially during the outbreaks of malaria in the hot season, but in many ways their lives were idyllic.

They were lent ponies and motor cars by the British officers stationed at Bareilly, and taken to dances, films and picnics. Turner rode every morning, and played golf and tennis.

When war broke out she made repeated applications for active service until in February 1941 she was told to report at Bombay for posting to an unknown destination. Turner was dismayed to find that the ship on which she sailed from Bombay in March was bound even further from the battlefields – to Malaya. She was put in charge of the operating theatre in a military hospital at Tanjong Malin, near Kuala Lumpur.

But she was soon in the thick of war. In December 1941 the Japanese bombed Malaya and invaded from the north. The wounded began to flood in to the Tanjong Malin hospital and, as the Japanese advanced, the staff and patients were ordered to move to Singapore. The town's railway station had been razed by bombs before the staff could get away, but they eventually reached their destination.

The island was under heavy bombing, and Turner helped to operate on the injured at the Changi hospital throughout the day and far into the night, regardless of air raids. In February all the QAs were evacuated from Singapore. There were continuous air raids on the docks as Turner boarded the *Kuala*, and several people were killed on the quayside. It was to be three-and-a-half years before she again set sail from Singapore harbour, and finally made her way home.

On her return to Britain in October 1945 Turner was eager to return to work. After 18 months serving in England, she was posted to Malta and then Benghazi in 1947, Cyprus in 1948, Egypt and then Eritrea in 1949. When she went home in 1950 she was promoted major.

In 1953 she led the QA contingent in the Coronation ceremony. She was posted to Hamburg in 1954 and to Bermuda in 1955. Two years later she became commandant of the Preliminary Training School at Aldershot and two years after that Matron at Millbank. She was sent to Hong Kong in 1961, and to Cyprus in 1962; later that year she went back to England.

In 1964 she was made Matron-in-Chief and director of Army Nursing Services, the highest position in the Queen Alexandra's Royal Army Nursing Corps (as the QAIMNS had been renamed).

Soon after her retirement in 1968 Turner was appointed Colonel Commandant of the Corps. She was appointed MBE in 1946 and DBE in 1965. In 1956 she was awarded the RRC.

Turner was a resilient, strong and simple woman. "I don't think about myself very much," she said, "I think about what I have to do." A committed Christian, she harboured no bitterness towards the Japanese. *The Will to Live*, Sir John Smyth's account of her life, was published in 1969.

October 2 1993

# MAJ-GEN MICKY
# WHISTLER

MAJOR-GENERAL MICKY WHISTLER, who has died aged 83, had a career of remarkable variety in which his cheerful disrespect for pompous and hidebound senior officers brought numerous reprimands, but did much to improve the efficiency and morale of his men.

Micky Whistler's career abounded with unusual incidents. On one occasion his adjutant's Italian wife appeared in his office, produced a stiletto and threatened to stab him if he did not let her husband go to Cyprus.

A clergyman's son, Alwyne Michael Webster Whistler was born on December 30 1909, educated at Gresham's and Woolwich, and commissioned into the Royal Corps of Signals in 1929. He recalled that, on exercises with the 4th Guards Brigade (commanded by Viscount Gort), they would pause at 11am for Madeira and cakes, supplied by a van from Fortnum and Mason's which followed them everywhere.

Of his subsequent life in the Signals mess at Aldershot he remembered: "My horses proved one of the most popular things, especially trying to get them into the mess and jumping them over the sofas. On one occasion we drove a small Citroën into the mess, but could not get it out without taking the door posts with it."

In 1932 Whistler was posted to India, where he served at Rawalpindi, Karachi, Jabalpur and Peshawar, and became Master of the Nerbadda Vale Hunt. When the Indian Cavalry were being mechanised, Whistler had the task of showing them how to employ their radios.

In 1939 he was adjutant of the Signals training battalion, which he was ordered to increase from 900 to 9,000. In 1944, when he was in the Arakan in Burma, he was abruptly recalled to take the course at the Staff College at Camberley.

On his arrival he found that there was a debate about whether he should be a student or an instructor. During the six-month course he received no pay, because the Indian Army could not pay someone at the Staff College in England, and the British Paymaster could not pay someone in the Indian Army.

Back in Burma Whistler acquired an L5 Light Aircraft, which he used for visiting remote detachments in the jungle. He also worked closely with Force 136 (SOE), during which time he met a 72-year-old named Tulloch, too old to belong to any regiment. A former white hunter from Africa, with a long white beard, he had already done 11 parachute jumps.

Earlier in the war Tulloch had spent 10 days in Berlin. Whistler asked him how he had managed to do so without speaking a word of German: "I was a Spanish onion seller," he replied, "and they don't speak much Spanish."

During his service with 19th Indian Division and XII Army, Whistler was twice mentioned in despatches. At the end of the war he was posted to BAOR, where he found himself public relations officer to 68 British and 30 American correspondents (he was the sixth holder of the appointment in two years).

Whistler went on to serve as DAAQMG in a mixed

unit. For his first inspection of the women's wing the inmates had polished the mats on the underside, so that he fell on his back. He rose to his feet and inspected every part of the barracks with extreme thoroughness.

The chief WRAC officer was annoyed by this and persuaded the GOC to publish an order, saying that inspecting officers should not look in her women's drawers. Whistler sent her a copy with the words underlined in red, adding: "You could have expressed it better." But the WRACs gave him a superb farewell when he left, several limbs being broken in mess games.

After attending the Joint Services Staff College, Whistler commanded 3 Division Royal Signals. Further staff appointments took him to the Far East and BAOR, and he then became successively Signal Officer-in-Chief, War Office; chairman, British Joint Communications Board, Ministry of Defence; and Chief of the Defence Staff (Signals).

Whistler was honorary Colonel of Princess Louise's Kensington Regiment, Colonel Commandant, Royal Corps of Signals, and honorary Colonel, 32nd (Scotland) Signal Regiment. His all-round ability – he was an MFH, a pilot and a useful polo player – eventually won him the Princess Mary Medal, one of the Royal Signals' highest awards.

Whistler was appointed CBE in 1959 and CB in 1963.

He married, in 1936, Margaret Louise Michelette Welch. As she had royal connections and a royal godparent, a wedding in London would have been expensive, and neither of them wanted this. To avoid this, Whistler sent himself a telegram recalling himself to Poona, where the wedding took place on a more modest scale. His wife died in 1987. They had a son and two daughters.

October 7 1993

# PETER KEMP

PETER KEMP, the soldier, author and war reporter, who has died aged 78, was probably the last surviving Englishman to have fought for the Nationalists in the Spanish Civil War; and as an officer with Special Operations Executive during the Second World War he also served with distinction in Albania, Poland and South-East Africa.

As a soldier and, afterwards, a war reporter, Kemp was the epitome of a knight-errant, continuing to be drawn to the sound of gunfire for most of his life. He was once described in a confidential Foreign Office brief as "personable, erratic and of romantic right-wing views".

He was badly wounded in 1938, shortly before the Battle of the Ebro, when his jaw was shattered by a mortar shell. He was not expected to live, and had to undergo operations without any anaesthetic, apart from a bottle of brandy.

Kemp also possessed rare depth of feeling. In his autobiography, *The Thorns of Memory* (1990), he described two incidents which were to stay with him all his life.

Not long before he was wounded in Spain, while serving with the Spanish Foreign Legion, he was ordered to shoot an Irish deserter from the International Brigades, knowing that if he refused he would himself be shot.

The second incident occurred at the end of the Second World War, in Thailand. Lt Klotz, a French officer Kemp was escorting to a boat, was shot in the back by an Annamese while two American officers looked on.

It was Kemp's passionate opposition to Communism that took him to Spain on the Nationalist side, although he had no love for the Fascist Falange. Later, he fought alongside Communist partisans against the Axis forces in Albania, where he had to make contact with Enver Hoxha, who imposed Stalinist rule on his country for 40 years.

When news of Hoxha's death in 1985 reached Nicaragua, where Kemp was visiting the Contras as a journalist, he was observed by a colleague to raise his glass of beer and exclaim: "Stoke well the furnaces of Hell!"

Kemp also came up against Communism in Poland in 1945, when the Red Army was advancing through the country, and spent three very uncomfortable weeks as a prisoner of the NKVD (predecessor of the KGB). He continued to observe the rise and spread of Communism after the war, and to do whatever he could to counter it.

During his many adventures Kemp showed remarkable bravery and resilience; he was also the most considerate and gentle of men, with a self-deprecating modesty and a humorous twinkle in his eye. His wide circle of friends included many of a younger generation, who were stimulated as much by his engaging company as by stories of his wartime experiences.

A son of the Raj, Peter Mant MacIntyre Kemp was born on August 19 1915 in Bombay, where his father, Sir Norman Kemp, became Chief Justice. He was edu-

cated at Wellington and Trinity College, Cambridge
(where a college magazine attributed to him "a deplorable
tendency to simper").

On coming down he read for the Bar but in November 1936 decided to postpone his final examinations (in
the event he never took them) in order to go to Spain to
fight in the Civil War which had started that summer.
He set off for the Iberian peninsula, armed with an
enormous 1918 .44 Service revolver, a prismatic compass,
an Army & Navy Stores medicine chest and Hugo's
*Spanish in Three Months without a Master*.

Initially Kemp joined the Carlist *requetés*, whose
traditionalist, monarchist beliefs accorded with his own,
and spent some time fighting on the outskirts of Madrid,
where the enemy was often no more than a few yards away.

After the Jarama battle, and while serving in the
Basque country, he longed to join a better trained and
equipped force. A chance meeting in Burgos with Gen
Millan Astray, the one-armed and one-eyed founder of
the Spanish Foreign Legion, led to his joining the 14th
Bandera of that élite corps. He was one of very few
foreign officers in the Legion in command of a platoon.

At Berlanga de Duero and Teruel, Kemp took part
in the campaign during the appalling winter of 1937–38,
and then in the breaking of the Republican front south
of the river Ebro in Aragon. He was wounded several
times, at least once when facing a British battalion of the
International Brigades; he learnt afterwards that he
would have been shot if captured. His final injury, from
the mortar explosion near Lerida, put him out of action
for the rest of the Civil War.

When Kemp returned to Spain in 1939, to seek

discharge from its Foreign Legion, he was cordially received by Franco who thanked him for his contribution and personally authorised his release.

Back in Britain shortly before the outbreak of the Second World War, he came across Douglas Dodds-Parker (later a Conservative Foreign Office minister) who introduced him to MI(R), the forerunner of SOE. Kemp was commissioned in January 1940, and trained as a cavalry officer at Weedon in Northamptonshire.

In the spring MI(R) called Kemp to the War Office and he joined SOE's first training school at Lochailort in Scotland. After an aborted mission in Gibraltar – he arrived to find that dirty tricks in Spain had been disallowed – he was inveigled into joining the submarine *Clyde* on the promise of an opportunity to board and seize a U-boat lurking in the Canaries.

But the scheme was thwarted by a British destroyer which scored an own goal by depth-charging *Clyde* and nearly sinking her. Kemp sailed home to "several useful courses" – industrial sabotage, parachuting and under-cover work.

Then, in 1942, Kemp joined the Small-Scale Raiding Force, undertaking hair-raising night raids against German signal stations on the Casquets, a rocky islet in the Channel Islands, and on the Brittany coast.

The next year Kemp dropped by parachute into Albania to join the British military mission, which was raising resistance to the occupying forces. His ambition to get to Kosovo, then part of northern Albania, was delayed by the mission's leaders, "Billy" McLean (*qv*) and David Smiley, because they so enjoyed Kemp's company.

Altogether Kemp spent 10 eventful months in

Albania, covering its length from the Greek frontier to Montenegro and once visiting the capital, Tirana. For this he had to obtain permission from Hoxha, who was concerned at how conspicuous Kemp appeared.

He furnished him with a suit belonging to a short, portly friend. "You may not look much like an Albanian," Hoxha said, "but at least you won't be mistaken for a British officer."

Unable to speak the language, Kemp nearly fell into German hands, but managed to see the Tirana airfield and note the incidence of enemy aircraft. Twice surrounded by enemy forces, he first shot his way out and the next time managed to escape disguised, despite his height, as a woman. Struck down by malaria, he assailed his fellow guerrillas with delirious passages of Boswell and addressed them as though he were Dr Johnson himself.

When he travelled to Kosovo, by mule and on foot, Kemp was in constant danger of being betrayed to the Germans by Kosovars, who feared that an Allied victory would return them to Yugoslav rule under the hated Serbs.

Kemp would often don an Italian overcoat over his uniform, and a Bulgar fez of black lambswool. On one occasion he was reported dead after he and a German had fired simultaneously and both had fallen.

Kemp later told the story against himself, recalling that his friend and compatriot Alan Hare had said of him: "I alone knew it couldn't be true: you would never have been wide-awake enough to fire at the same time as a German."

Having been ordered by SOE in Cairo to abandon his Kosovo contacts because they might be working against

Tito's partisans, Kemp made his escape from Albania in mid-winter, over the mountains to Montenegro, harried not only by German patrols but also by other unfriendly factions.

After a spell of leave in 1944, Kemp parachuted into Poland at the end of the year, finding himself opposed by Germans, Cossacks and the advancing Soviet army. After his release from prison by the NKVD, he spent two months in Moscow waiting for an exit visa.

Next Kemp became a member of Force 136, SOE's organisation in South-East Asia, and parachuted into Siam. On the Siam—Laos border in 1945, Kemp ran arms to the French and helped to rescue them from the Japanese and Annamese (Vietminh).

He was less than impressed by his first contact with American troops, who appeared to support the Vietminh against the French. Kemp's time in the Far East ended rather more agreeably when he was sent to liberate Bali.

Kemp was awarded a DSO in 1945 and retired from the Army. Tuberculosis halted his activities for a time; he took a job with a life assurance company, which he kept until his retirement in 1980, enjoying the irony that his own life was almost uninsurable.

When Soviet tanks invaded Hungary in 1956, Kemp made his way there, as a correspondent for the *Tablet*, "to do what I could to help". He was able to help three Hungarian students out of Budapest and over the border to Austria.

Many journalistic assignments followed during the next 35 years, to Indochina, Central and South America, Rhodesia and the Congo. He also returned to Kosovo and Albania, as a correspondent for *The Sunday Telegraph* and the *Spectator*. In one of his last articles, in 1990,

Kemp warned of the almost inevitable bloodbath between Serbs and Albanians in Kosovo.

When almost 60, Kemp was still risking his neck, flying low-level night operations with the Royal Laotian Air Force in a converted Dakota armed with Gatling guns.

In 1979, having passed his 64th birthday, Kemp went to Rhodesia for the *Spectator*, expressing the hope that he would be able to do a parachute drop with the Selous Scouts. But his apparent disregard for his personal safety was combined with a natural concern for personal comfort. Several friends recall him worrying, before he embarked on a hazardous trip, whether he should take with him one pullover or two.

Apart from his autobiography, Kemp wrote three books about his wartime experiences: *Mine Were of Trouble*, *No Colours or Crest* and *Alms for Oblivion*. He consoled himself that perhaps his "own small role in the struggle against the two most dangerous evils of this century, fascism and Communism" had contributed to the dawn of freedom in Eastern Europe; and he also found comfort in quoting from Horace's 29th Ode: "Not Heaven itself upon the past has power."

He was twice married and twice divorced.

November 3 1993

# NELL ALLGROVE

NELL ALLGROVE, who has died aged 83, endured extraordinary privations as an Australian nurse captured by the Japanese during the Second World War.

Born Ellen Mavis Hannah at Claremont, Perth, in 1910, she began her career as a pharmacist before switching to nursing. She trained at the Royal Alexandra Hospital, Adelaide.

At the end of 1939 she joined the Royal Australian Army Nursing Corps and was sent to serve in Malaya. She was with the 2/4th Australian Casualty Clearing Station when the Japanese invaded Singapore in December 1941.

The hospitals, although swamped with casualties, were mostly destroyed and Mavis Hannah, with 64 other Australian nurses, was ordered to leave on February 12 1942. They joined the crowds seeking a place on the *Vyner Brooke*, which had seen better days as the property of the Rajah of Sarawak.

The ship, a dirty old tub, was obliged to run the gauntlet of Japanese spotter-planes along a route known as Bomb Alley. The nurses were hardly fortunate to gain a passage: the *Vyner Brooke* was bombed and sunk on St Valentine's Day.

Many passengers drowned, including 12 of the Australian nurses. Sister Hannah could not swim, but for two days and nights she clung to the side of a raft. When she finally landed on Banka Island she was immediately taken prisoner by the Japanese.

She spent the next three years in camps in Sumatra, where mere survival — on a diet of two ounces of rice a day — required a formidable will. "If you couldn't laugh at the Japs," she recalled, "you'd had it." Although she earned many blows through her refusal to humble herself, she managed to find ways of getting her own back.

When ordered to carry water for the officers' baths,

she said: "We never omitted to make our protest in it first, in a way that comes naturally."

When the Japanese "tried to make geisha girls of us" the Australians covered their uniforms with oil and dirt. A Japanese officer who had the temerity to tell Mavis Hannah that he loved her was promptly felled for his pains. Rather than lose face, he kept quiet about the episode.

Mavis Hannah was the only one of the eight sisters of 2/4 Casualty Clearing Station to leave the camp alive. Four were machine-gunned, two died of disease, one was drowned. Of the original 65, just 24 survived. Mavis Hannah weighed 4st 6lb when she was liberated.

In 1946 she married Joseph William Allgrove, a planter whose wife had died while he was a PoW on the Burma railway, and became known as Nell Allgrove.

In 1953 the Allgroves left the East and set up house at Dedham in Essex. Nell Allgrove campaigned tirelessly to gain adequate pensions from the Australian government for nurses who had been interned.

She also raised funds for MENCAP and LEPRA and was active in the Colchester branch of Queen Alexandra's Royal Army Nursing Corps Association. But she never forgot or forgave the past. Recently, after attending the Remembrance Day ceremonies at the Cenotaph, she unceremoniously turned some Japanese tourists out of a public house.

Earlier this year Nell Allgrove returned to Banka Island for the unveiling of a memorial to the nurses who had perished. But this time she was in a wheelchair, for the blows which the camp guards had inflicted had caused her spine to deteriorate.

Joseph Allgrove died in 1984; they had two sons and a daughter.

November 10 1993

# GEN SIR PHILIP CHRISTISON, BT

GENERAL SIR PHILIP CHRISTISON, 4th and last Bt, who has died aged 100, had a career reminiscent of one of John Buchan's heroes.

In his youth Christison was a first-class athlete and rugby footballer. He also played several musical instruments, was fluent in Gaelic and an expert in ornithology. He distinguished himself in both World Wars. In Burma – where he was known to colonial troops as "the Smiling General" – he was one of the three Corps commanders who triumphed under Gen Slim.

Said to have served in more regiments than any other officer in the British Army, Christison ended his military career as GOC Scottish Command and Governor of Edinburgh Castle.

The second son of Surg-Gen Sir Alexander Christison, 2nd Bt, Alexander Frank Philip Christison was born on November 17 1893. His father became the first doctor to give chloroform in an eastern theatre of war when he treated Ensign Wolseley, who recovered to become a Field Marshal and to acquire the nickname "Our Only General" for the number of his campaigns.

Wolseley's policy for obtaining advancement was to try to get himself killed at every opportunity, and had

Christison *père* not been present on the first occasion, his career would have ended abruptly.

Young Philip was educated at Edinburgh Academy and University College, Oxford (of which he was later an honorary fellow). He was a first-class shot and played rugby for the University.

In 1914 he was commissioned into the Queen's Own Cameron Highlanders and the next year won an immediate MC at Loos. The battle cost some 60,000 casualties, most of them in the first 24 hours, and the steadiness and tenacity of the Scottish regiments became legendary.

Amid the carnage Christison found himself in the company of 80 Camerons who had lost their officers and were dispirited. His efforts to encourage them failed until he was inspired to break into song. His rendition of *The March of the Cameron Men* in Gaelic revived their fighting spirit and they returned again to the fray.

Though shot in the groin during hand-to-hand combat, Christison returned to command a company at the Somme. At Arras he won a Bar to his MC.

After the war Christison returned to Melrose as Adjutant of the 4th Bn King's Own Scottish Borderers, and in 1924 he went to Paris as assistant manager of the British Olympic team.

In 1937 he was commanding the Duke of Wellington's Regiment, and from 1938 to 1940 the Quetta Brigade. From 1940 to 1941 he was Commandant of the Staff College, Quetta. He became a major general in 1941 and a lieutenant general in 1942.

Two years later he was commanding 15th Indian Corps in operations on the Arakan front, where the rear of 7th Indian Division was encircled by 6,000 Japanese but fought back to win a decisive victory. The manifold hazards of the battle did not deter Christison from repeated visits to the front, and he was venerated by his Indian troops for his cheerful imperturbability. His links with them were strengthened by his grasp of Urdu, which he used on formal parades – he had also acquired a broad knowledge of Indian traditions.

Christison had several narrow escapes. Once, as he was taking a picnic lunch under a tree, a Japanese 75mm shell landed close by, blowing away his sandwich and glass.

He was appointed CB in 1943, and the next year knighted in the field by Earl Wavell, Viceroy of India, representing King George VI. In 1945 he was awarded the DSO, and inherited the baronetcy from his half-brother, Sir Robert Alexander Christison, 3rd Bt, a former Vice-Consul at Lima.

In the summer of 1945 Christison was embroiled in an embarrassing situation when Sir Oliver Leese – the Commander of Allied Land Forces, South East Asia (ALFSEA) – decided to remove Slim from command of XIVth Army and to put Christison in his place.

Leese said that Slim was exhausted and, moreover, that Christison had more experience of the kind of amphibious operations anticipated. Though Slim was astonished he did not complain, but Mountbatten expressed doubts and Alanbrooke, the CIGS, was furious.

In the resulting compromise Christison took command of the XIVth Army while Slim was on leave, and Slim was appointed to command ALFSEA in place of Leese. Since Slim remained on leave, Christison deputised for him in that post also.

On Slim's return, Christison returned to command 15 Corps, which he led into Rangoon in May. On

September 3 1945 he took the surrender of the Japanese 7th Area Army and South Sea Fleet at Singapore, representing Adml Lord Louis Mountbatten.

From 1945 to 1946 Christison was Allied Commander, Netherlands East Indies, where the situation remained volatile. The Japanese were rearmed to help the British repel the Indonesians led by Soekarno, and Christison earned the respect of his former enemies.

In 1946 he became GOC Northern Command, and from 1947 to 1949 he was GOC Scottish Command and Governor of Edinburgh Castle, as well as ADC General to King George VI. He was appointed GBE in 1948.

Christison retired in 1949 and bought a fruit farm at Melrose, which he farmed for the next 42 years. He was Deputy Lieutenant of Roxburghshire in 1956.

In retirement he was Colonel of the Duke of Wellington's Regiment and of the 10th Gurkhas, and honorary Colonel of 414 Coast Regiment, RA. He was also president of the Scottish Unionist Party, of the Army Cadet Force, Scotland, and the Earl Haig Fund. He was vice-president of the Burma Star Society, and in latter years spoke out against the dissolution of Highland regiments.

Christison's musical talent was much admired, though his fondness for the bagpipes was not to everyone's taste; he was chairman and president of the Clarsach Society from 1947. He published *Birds of Northern Baluchistan* and was co-author of *Birds of Arakan*.

In 1991 Christison, who had worn the Cameron tartan throughout the First World War, made a generous donation towards the commissioning of a painting depicting the last occasion on which a kilt was worn in action – thought to be in 1940, shortly before the withdrawal of the 1st Cameron Highlanders to Dunkirk. During the First World War the conduct of the kilted Highland regiments had caused their respectful enemies to christen them "The Ladies from Hell".

"The kilt put the fear of death into the Germans," Christison recalled. "Of course, undergarments were not allowed in those days."

Christison married first, in 1916, Betty Mitchell, daughter of the Bishop of Aberdeen and Orkney; they had two daughters and a son, who was killed in Burma in 1942.

After the death of his first wife in 1974, he married Vida Wallace Smith, who died in 1992. There is no heir to the baronetcy.

December 23 1993

# INDEX

349

# Index

Edited by HUGH MASSINGBERD

**The Daily Telegraph**
# BOOK OF OBITUARIES

*A Celebration of Eccentric Lives*

PAN BOOKS  £6.99

'A blissfully – one might almost say
divinely – witty collection'
CRAIG BROWN

'Recent history made hilarious'
MARY KILLEN

'A sure-fire success . . . the hit of the season'
JEFFREY BERNARD

'Pure Joy'
JOHN GROSS

0 330 34979 1